Also by M.G. CRISCI

Papa Cado

Call Sign, White Lily

Save the Last Dance

Avarice

Indiscretion

rise and fall of

Mary Jackson Peale

by **M.G. Crisci**

ORCA PUBLISHING COMPANY
Carlsbad, CA 92011

Designed by Good World Media
Edited by Robin Friedheim
Cover Art: "Venetian Mystery" by M.G. Crisci

Manufactured in the United States of America

Library of Congress Control No.
2009907911

ISBN 97809663360-5-4

Life should not be a journey to the grave
With the intention of arriving safely
in an attractive and well preserved body.
But rather to skid in sideways,
chocolate in one hand, martini in the other,
Body thoroughly used up, totally worn out
and screaming
Woo Hoo what a ride.

ACT 1

~ ~ ~

Born and raised in the seaside community of Brighton, England, Mary Jones was the only daughter of a third generation local fisherman named Reilly and his childhood sweetheart, Chloe, the daughter of an innkeeper, who tended to their modest home.

Neither parent was educated in the classical sense—Chloe attended but two years of high school; Reilly took to the seas at the age of 14. Yet each developed a passion for more intellectual pursuits, she, romantic poetry—particularly the verses of Lake poets Longfellow, Wordsworth and Yeats, and he, Italian opera—particularly *La Bohme* (it made him cry) and *The Barber of Seville* (it made him laugh).

When Mary was just three, Chloe took to reading her favorite passages in soft, soothing tones till she fell asleep. When Mary was a little older, Chloe would take a break from her mundane, daily tasks and walk hand in hand with her daughter to the Brighton Cliffs. There, overlooking the thundering waves, Chloe would read Wordsworth aloud with the cool mist blowing in their faces.

"Mary, feel the grandeur of nature ," she would urge.

> *I wandered lonely as a cloud*
> *That floats on high o'er Vales and Hills,*
> *When at once I saw a crowd*
> *A host of dancing daffodils;*
> *Along the Lake, beneath the trees,*
> *Ten thousand dancing in the breeze.*

Reilly had familial rituals also. On days of calm seas and blue skies, Mary would board the family's sole source of income, a modest red, green and white boat named *Gazzo di Fortuna* (the fishing boat of good fortune). Once the nets were in place, Reilly would serenade his daughter. While self-taught, Reilly's voice was strong and proud, his timing surprisingly professional.

Many years later, Mary would recall one particular day. She was about six. While at sea, the salty breezes suddenly turned bone-chilling blustery. Reilly saw his tiny daughter silently shiver and shudder. He wrapped her in a blanket and held her close. His strong frame was warm and comforting to the little child. He noticed how cold Mary's hands were. He turned on his tape recorder and began to sing *Che Gelida Manina* (How Cold Your Hand is). "Father, what do the words mean?" asked Mary when Reilly had finished his duet with Pavarotti. "The song is about a poor young poet by the name of Rodolfo who meets a beautiful young lady, Mimi, who has been without heat. He notices how cold her hand is and suggests she stay with him, and that he will share what little he has although he is no millionaire."

"Why do they sing in Italian?"

"Because Italians invented opera," said Reilly. "Why did they invent opera?' asked Mary innocently.

"That's for them to know and you to find out. When you get older, maybe you'll travel to Italy."

~

The cheery, outgoing Mary soon developed rituals of her own. She reveled in telling tall tales with a delightfully dramatic flair.

"Mum, I saw Edgar again this morning!" said the eight-year-old. Edgar was a 60-foot-long sea horse with sparkling white teeth that lived in the water, a mile down the road from the family's modest cottage—a product of her vivid imagination.

"And what was he doing?"

"He was chasing some fish into the cove so daddy could catch them in his nets."

"Was Edgar successful?"

"Absolutely, positively," said the child, rolling her eyes and waving her hands expressively. "I counted a hundred fish, perhaps more. Daddy's going to be very happy."

This particular day, Reilly arrived home two hours earlier than usual. "Chloe, darling, had me one hell of a day. The bass practically jumped into the boat. If I put any more fish in the hole, *Fortuna* might have sunk. Sold the entire lot to old man Johnson in a heartbeat. How about we celebrate? Take Mary down to the docks for an ice cream after dinner."

Mary smiled at Chloe, nodding a mature, "I told you so."

~

Two weeks later, Reilly day again had been bountiful. He had sold his significant catch to a buyer a few towns away. There he was treated to a cup of hot cider by the buyer's daughter, an attractive thirty-something woman with long, sun-bleached blond hair, blue eyes and a very shapely figure tucked under work overalls. One kindness led to another, the cider morphed into a sexual encounter that Reilly determined was better sex than he had experienced in recent years with Chloe.

It also didn't help matters that Chloe had also let herself go physically. The fair-haired young bride with apple cheeks and fiery red curly hair was replaced by a plump, rounded pumpkin with a wrinkled wrapper caused by excess exposure to the sun.

Reilly decided it was time to leave for greener pastures. The way he saw it, leaving Chloe with their modest house was payment enough for the fifteen years. So, after fifteen years of marriage, Reilly simply never came home. At first, Chloe thought his boat had sunk and he drowned. But after a week of searching, the townsfolk and the harbor patrol concluded he had just left. Reilly left no note, no forwarding address, no explanation, and most importantly, no money.

When reality set in, Chloe stoically declared, "Mary, we'll just get on with our lives. May the buggar rot in hell!" Chloe never spoke of Reilly again. Nor did Mary. It was as though Reilly never existed. A disillusioned Mary developed her own defense mechanism. She never translated another libretto or listened to another opera...until Gianni. And she began to question what she called "the normal order of society."

~

Life—post Reilly—was particularly hard, in the beginning.

Chloe had a school-age daughter, no savings, and no particular employment skills. Dressed in her Sunday best, she begged and pleaded for the job opening she had found in the local paper. "But, you have absolutely no theatre experience," countered the skeptical assistant manager.

"I know, I know, but I love Pinter, Beckett," responded Chloe with a certain fire in her eyes.

The man paused. He had a hunch. Two days later, an excited Chloe began her—and her daughter's—lifelong love affair with the theatre. She was named part-time gal Friday at the Theatre Royale on New Road in the center of Brighton, generally considered by London critics a regional theatre "of the first rank."

After overhearing a few disingenuous comments from the actors about the theatre's hiring a "weathered woman," Chloe went on a personal restoration frenzy. In a matter of weeks, she lost twenty pounds, restored the original luster to her red hair and generously applied the latest wrinkle-removing moisturizers. The final touch was a low-cut, dark-rose dress that highlighted her generous bosom. The same actors who had labeled her an old lady were now actively trying to seduce her.

When she had finished her chores, Chloe would watch rehearsals, memorize lines and mimic the lead actress's performances from a distant corner of the theatre lobby near the ladies' room. One day, unbeknownst to Chloe, while the cast took a break from rehearsing a revival of the popular play *Old Times*—a dark, intense comic drama set around a love triangle—the play's youthful director, Martin Thurgood, accidentally stumbled into one of Chloe's imaginary rehearsals. *After the way you've humiliated me, how can you say our time is here and now*, said Chloe in a particularly bitter interpretation of the heroine Anna.

"While your interpretation of Anna is interesting, your delivery seems a touch too melodramatic," volunteered Thurgood unannounced.

Chloe was startled and embarrassed. "I'm sorry. I hope I didn't disturb you."

"There's nothing to be sorry about. You were quite good."

"Really!" said Chloe appearing like a wide eyed teenager.

"Would you like to read for a part?"

"Really!"

"You might be a perfect understudy for the part of Anna."

"Really!"

"Fact is we haven't found the right person yet, and we are a week away from opening night. God forbid if my lead,

Nora Pennington, becomes incapacitated. You already seem to know the part, so how about you read right now?"

"Really!"

"Is your vocabulary restricted to the word *really*?" smiled Thurgood.

"I'm sorry. My name is Chloe."

"Good. Very good, that's a start. Do you know any multi-syllabic words?"

"Actually, I'm quite well versed. You've just taken my breath away. I never imagined…in my wildest dreams." One hour later, after a brilliant reading, Thurgood offered Chloe the job of understudy…at three times the salary she was making as a girl Friday.

Two hours later, Chloe and Thurgood were in his flat making love. It was the most sharing, tender sex that Chloe had experienced in almost fifteen years. "I had almost forgotten how much I liked sex," laughed Chloe. "My marriage was like an unforgiving sandstorm in the desert. No matter where I hid, the conditions never improved."

"Well, we certainly don't want you to wilt in the sun again," smiled Thurgood as he returned for round two and three and …

Somewhere between the sex and conversational chatter, Chloe also managed to obtain Thurgood's appointment of Mary as his new gal Friday. Thanks to Thurgood, Chloe became a regular fixture in the numerous regional theatres within a 300-kilomtere radius of Brighton. Despite the fact that she was beautiful, spontaneous and well critiqued, Chloe knew she wasn't destined for the London stage. But the theatre did provide Mary and Chloe a comfortable lifestyle. Fortunately for Chloe, the theatre was about far more than the money. Performing live was about personal fulfillment.

The Thurgood affair ended rather abruptly when he received an offer to direct a revival of Noel Coward's comedy of manners, *Design For Living*, at the prestigious Theatre Royal, Drury Lane in London's West End. As far as Chloe was concerned that was "two strikes and you're out" for the male species!

Mary wouldn't be far behind regarding her mother's assessment of men.

2

~~~

AT 14, MARY COULDN'T be described as sexy or seductive in the conventional sense. But her long, curly red hair, dark-green eyes and ever-present smile exuded an understated elegance and self-confidence that attracted the opposite sex like bees to honey. She also had a penchant for tastefully displaying her physical assets through sheer pastel-colored blouses that tended to drive the local boys into a frenzy when she passed.

Of all the boys in school, she was most attracted to a handsome upperclassman with black wavy hair and a cute bum, named Robert (AKA Bobbie) O'Toole. One late spring evening while she and a group of her girlfriends were meandering through the amusement park not far from the water's edge, Bobbie and a few of his friends met the girls at the ring-toss tent where for 50 pence one was given five plastic rings to toss at a line of open soda pop bottles. If a ring remained on the bottle neck, the winner got to pick a stuffed animal from the shelf.

Bobbie had seen Mary before but never in this light.
"Mary, how about I try to win you an animal?"
"Why?"
"Because I'd like a prize in return." The way he looked into her eyes gave her goose bumps.
"What kind of prize?" she laughed, knowing full well.
"Come on...you know...it has to happen sometime."
All eyes were on Mary. She paused to heighten his anticipation. She nodded yes. She was ready to lose her virginity. But it wouldn't come cheap! "The deal is you've got to get two rings and two stuffed animals."
"That's not fair. That's hard."
"Life's not fair," she laughed. "Besides, think about your prize. That should be motivation enough." That was that. Mary had made her final offer.
"Okay, okay," agreed the already aroused young man. After four tosses, he had one bottle neck.
Mary smiled sensuously as she slowly dragged her finger across her mouth. "Real men don't choke."
The entire group laughed, all except the determined Bobbie. He tossed his fifth and final ring: it rattled around the bottle for what seemed like an eternity and then came to rest on the neck. Everybody cheered, including Mary. Bobbie took Mary over to the shelf. She picked a stuffed lion and a stuffed lamb. Bobbie then took Mary's hand and started walking. "Where are we going?"
"You got your prize, I want mine." A smiling Mary turned and waved goodbye to her friends.
Minutes later, Bobbie found a quiet setting surrounded by bushes in the North Laine area, a section of town populated by audaciously clothed prostitutes, spaced-out punks, Goths and lunatics who couldn't care less what their neighbors were doing. As soon as they settled on a patch of grass, Bobbie clumsily went to work, attempting to unbutton Mary's blouse and raise her skirt.

"I imagined we'd get to know each other a bit," said Mary, thinking of preliminary foreplay. This was her first time, and she imagined bells, whistles and romance.

Bobbie was of a different mindset. "Let's just do it. I'm ready." He continued to unbutton her blouse. A button snapped off. "Jesus, Bobbie, take it easy." Moments later he penetrated Mary. After what seemed to Mary to be just a few awkward, uneven, and somewhat painful thrusts, Bobbie moaned and rolled onto the grass. "Mary that was great!"

Mary didn't know exactly how to respond. The man of her dreams was a sexual dud. A selfish lug, who possessed none of the tenderness and sensitivity she had imagined. She hadn't even become aroused, and he was spent. It was an evening Mary would not soon forget.

3

~ ~ ~

ACADEMICALLY, MARY WAS extremely bright. She was awarded a scholarship at the nearby University of Sussex, where she enrolled in the Bachelor of Arts program, majoring in Drama and Cultural Studies, and making the dean's list 11 of 12 semesters prior to graduation. During university, consciously or subconsciously, Mary morphed into a cultural snob, limiting her immediate circle of friends—male and female—to those with an artistic or intellectual leaning.

While proud of her daughter's scholarship and academic achievements, Chloe was concerned about Mary's ability to support herself with such an esoteric degree and that limited circle of friends particularly if, like her Mum, the proverbial "white knight" didn't make an appearance.

As time permitted, Mary watched Mum's theatre rehearsals and attended her plays. Chloe affectionately declared her daughter "a theatre rat." Mary, like her Mum, became obsessed with the rhythms and circumstances of theatre creation and production. By her final year rolled at Sussex, she had held insightful interpretative conversations—some of her professors called them raging debates—with virtually every producer and director of Mum's shows.

As she was wont to do on afternoons after class, Mary paid an unannounced visit to Chloe's rehearsal, only to find she had arrived after the fact. Upon entering her Mum's dressing room she heard what sounded like a series of soft erotic moans from behind the dressing screen to the right of the mirrored makeup table. Mum was making passionate love with her co-star, a substantially endowed woman named Annabelle Lee Sartre (no relation to Jean Paul). She watched quietly for the better part of a half hour, becoming quite aroused in the process.

"Chloe," smiled the dark haired, blue eyed Annabelle Lee, "I think we have an audience." The embarrassed, stark naked Chloe looked at Mary and rushed behind the dressing screen, searching for her clothes.

"Motherrrr," chuckled Mary, "if you're looking for your panties and bra, they're on the chaise lounge over there."

"Oh Mary, I'm so sorry…" mumbled Chloe feeling embarrassed that her daughter saw her having sex with another woman.

"Sorry about what? It looked like you were having a smashing good time. I'm only sorry your friend noticed me. I was wondering what you were going to do for an encore."

"Mary, that's a dreadful thing to say," said Chloe.

"Why?" interrupted Chloe's partner devilishly. "I find that a rather intriguing question! By the way, I'm Annabelle Lee. You have one proud Mum. She's told me a lot of wonderful things about you. How about we verbally spar over a spot of tea on Main Street?" suggested Annabelle Lee.

Twenty minutes later the girls were eating croissants and jam and washing them down with freshly brewed Kenyan Orange Pekoe tea. Annabelle Lee was not the least bit inhibited. She decided the gender issue should be addressed directly.

"I hope you don't mind, your mother and I having it on. We're both trying to find our way."

"What does that mean?" questioned Mary.

"My husband decided to leave me about the same time Reilly left your Mum. He parting comments made me feel like an obsolete air-raid shelter." Even Chloe had to smile.

"Right now your Mum and I trying to determine if our feelings are based upon a spiteful rebound or genuine caring. We're also dealing with the antiquated belief that Lesbian relationships remain one of society's aberrant behaviors."

"Mum, how do you feel?"

"I think I love Annabelle Lee."

"You think?"

"No, I don't think. I do. Very much, in fact," said Chloe reaching her hand out to Annabelle Lee.

"At some point, we'd like to get married," said Annabelle Lee.

Mary was surprised by their depth of commitment. Exchanging affections with another woman was one thing, the desire to become a same-sex marital partner appeared a more complex matter.

Annabelle Lee sensed Mary's hesitancy. "Don't be arbitrary or shamelessly judgmental," she suggested.

"Maybe I should have a go myself," suggested Mary sarcastically.

"Maybe you should," responded a dead serious Annabelle Lee.

~

Shortly thereafter, Mary decided to make love to an attractive fellow drama-school classmate and known lesbian, Phoebe Trincas. Mary invited Phoebe out for a drink.

"I'd be delighted," smiled Phoebe devilishly. "I was starting to think you didn't notice me."

Phoebe suggested a gay bar called Macho Maureen's on Queenstown Lane, which was renowned for its uninhibited patrons and their outrageous behavior. Mary's initial response was a coy "never in a million years." Phoebe's gentle prodding and singular tenacity promised "an experience Mary would not soon forget."

Maureen's was more attractive and sophisticated than Mary had expected. A large, mirrored walnut burl bar dominated the center of the room, surrounded by small booths with tall opaque dividers covered with erotic drawings. Each booth had a small table and two to four red-velvet lounge chairs, depending upon the size of the booth. The bar was tended by two tall, well-groomed, female bartenders who filled orders for a collection of topless waitresses. To keep the clutter to a minimum and add a certain *joie de vive*, there were no stools at the bar, and the background music featured smoky jazz such as Billie Holliday's seductive version of *At the End of An Affair* and Bobby Hackett's steamy trumpet playing *After She's Gone*. At the far end of the bar was a small dimly-lit stage.

By the time the ladies had consumed two Kettle One martinis, Phoebe began a sensuous exploration of Mary under the table. She placed her right hand on Mary's thigh and began a gentle, circular massage. A sense of pure pleasure covered Mary's face.

"Your thong is a mite wet, love," whispered Phoebe softly. Phoebe slithered down the lounge bench and embraced Mary, tenderly nibbling on her ear to enhance her arousal.

"Oh god!" moaned Mary. "What are you doing?"

"Nothing you haven't requested," smiled Phoebe.

They engaged in some sophisticated and tender foreplay until Mary was titillated beyond reproach. Phoebe was everything Bobbie O'Toole was not, thought Mary—experienced, sharing and thoughtful. Phoebe continued to gently explore as Mary had a surge of orgasms.

"I think it's time to go," whispered Phoebe.

"Go where?" asked Mary.

"My place." Twenty minutes later the girls were frolicking in Phoebe's bed, where they made love till 2 a.m. Mary absolutely adored the evening's reverie. The experience convinced her that tender, sensitive lovemaking with a woman had significant advantages. There was no posturing. No macho insecurities. No faking.

~

Mary was supremely confident the performing arts were her calling. But after appearing in numerous school and local theatrical productions she concluded—like her Mum before he—she was not destined to become a great actress. Despite knowing her lines, she lacked the timing, the flair that great actresses possess. Unlike her Mum, she was not willing to settle for a life of bit parts and second rate productions. She still wanted to be associated and with theatre's *crème de la crème*.

After much soul-searching and professional consultations with people she respected, Mary concluded her destiny was to become THE great theatrical agent who identified and nurtured diamonds in the rough. Admittedly, she had no idea where to start.

~ ~ ~

ELIZABETH MANLY CLIFFORD WAS a graduate student in the School of Behavioral Psychology at Oxford. She was tall, athletically fit and extremely attractive with dark brown eyes, high cheek bones, thick brown eyelashes and silky, curly brown hair. People said she looked like the theatre and film diva Olivia de Havilland.

Elizabeth's father, Sir James, was a fourth-generation descendant of Sir Wimbley Townsend, generally considered a prime mover in maintaining historic castles in the North West Region of Cumbria, far from London and the beaches of Brighton. Like the rest of the Townsends, he had spent his youth living far beyond his means.

Elizabeth's Mum, Lady Anne Clifford, her father, her brother William and sister Margaret were born and raised in Skipton Castle at the edge of the Lake District National Park, one of the most beautiful natural areas of the United Kingdom. Unlike Sir Wimbley, her father, Lord Clifford, left a substantial estate.

Lady Clifford's philanthropy was legend. She had used her enormous resources to restore historic churches and castles to their former glory, and then she donated them to the Episcopal Church. Lady Anne's Way, a 100-mile walk through places associated with Lady Anne Clifford, was listed in the historical register. It started at her birthplace, Skipton, passed through Wharferdale and Wensleydale, and finished at Brougham Castle near Penrith in Cumbria, where she died at the age of 83.

Fortunately for Sir James, the enormity of the Clifford estate allowed him to spend most of his time raising his profile in the proper social circles by indiscriminately squandering the family's trust funds as a major patron of the theatre. As a pseudo-intellectual, he was most proud of two achievements. He was elected chairman of the board (and the main financial contributor) to the reconstruction of The Royal Shakespeare Theatre in Stratford-on-Avon and pro bono managing partner for the Noel Coward Theatre renovation in St. Martin's Lane in London's West End, where his position and five million pounds—not necessarily in that order—awarded him four front-and-center box seats in perpetuity.

When asked why, of all the theatres in London's West End he selected the Noel Coward Theatre for endowment, he replied wryly, "I like his quotes." (For example, when Coward was asked who was his favorite critic, he replied with just the proper hint of irony, "I have always been fond of drama critics...I think it is so frightfully clever of them to go night after night to the theatre and know so little about it.")

Despite the Clifford family's significant wealth, its superficial tranquility and noted philanthropic leanings, Elizabeth's life was anything but tranquil. To begin with, she was the third of three children. "An unplanned and unwanted circumstance," as her father described his youngest in his dark, private moments (i.e., after two glasses of vintage port).

Then there was the matter of Elizabeth's "pedestrian aspirations," as Lady Clifford depicted them. While the rest of the family respected their ancestral heritage and privileged place in society, Elizabeth yearned to be her uninhibited, iconoclastic self. Her classification as the "family contrarian" offended her deeply because she believed, much like her great-great-grandmother, Lady Diane, her inheritance was a gift, destined to be returned to society.

It was her custom, during school breaks and holidays, to search for her own identity by visiting every nook and cranny of England rather than subject herself to the meddlesome jabs of her father, whom she had come to detest. She was confident her geographic and philosophical explorations would one day provide insights into her own *raison d' être.* The more she traveled, the more academically fascinated she became with the "whys" of alternative lifestyles and their place in contemporary English society, although she herself remained staunchly heterosexual. It would be an understatement to say she raised a few eyebrows when she decided to title her graduate thesis "Societal Consequences of Misunderstanding the Lesbian Lifestyle."

Given her growing interest in the lesbian thought process, it was only natural that she would spend some time in friendly Brighton, where she assumed the burgeoning gay community would be easier to observe and research than similar communities in the more populous, more impersonal London.

~

It was a glorious sunny morning. Elizabeth, who arrived after dark, had slept soundly in the picturesque New Seine Hotel in Kemp Town, an 18th Century Georgian structure owned and operated by a warm, friendly gay couple, John Sweitzer and Gaffney Brown.

"I'm dreaming of a warm, flaky croissant, homemade marmalade and a steaming hot latte," said the ravenous Elizabeth as she stood at the front desk.

"That description, darling," said Gaffney pointing with his finger, "sounds precisely like the Café Sainté down the block on the right side of the street. They have the most divine fresh homemade baked goods."

Moments later Elizabeth was standing in front of a large window stocked with freshly baked cakes and pies, fruit and cheese Danish and buttery croissants. The place was a study in contrasts—exuberant groups chatting and debating robustly sat side by side with pensive individuals working quietly at dedicated internet-connected work stations. All had one thing in common... nobody appeared to be over 25. "I'd like two of those fabulous looking croissants. Do you have any marmalade?"

"Dearie," said the crusty lady with generously pierced ears behind the counter, "First time at Sainté's, eh?"

"How did you know?"

"Can't get your Mary Poppins outfit round here," teased the lady.

"I understand," smiled Elizabeth, looking at her rather dowdy long skirt and high-collared lace blouse in the large mirror behind the counter as she scanned the casual, outrageously colorful and tattered attire of the other patrons.

"Fresh jams and marmalades are on the counter by the window, dearie."

Tray in hand, Elizabeth looked around the room for a free table. There were none. She spotted an empty seat at the table where Mary was reading, sipping her latte. "Would you mind if I take that seat?" Mary looked at Elizabeth's croissants and smiled, "No problem, but where's your friend going to sit?"

"What friend?"

"I was just looking at your tray and assumed."

"You should never assume," smiled Elizabeth. "This little piggy plans to eat both croissants."

The girls took an instant liking to each other. "Hi, I'm Mary," she said extending her hand.

"And I'm Elizabeth," responded Elizabeth warmly, looking at the book Mary was reading. "Do you like Pinter?"

"Frankly, *The Caretaker* is a bit more menacing and intellectually violent than I originally imagined," said Mary.

"Yes and no," responded Elizabeth. "Viscerally, I don't care for old Davies." If I were Aston or Mick (the two protagonist brothers), why would I invite a homeless man with unfulfilled dreams to come live in my already cramped flat? Life was already difficult enough."

"That's interesting. It sounds like you're studying Pinter. Are you a literature major or something?"

"No. I'm actually working on my masters in psychology at Oxford."

"You're certainly a long way from home. What are you doing in Brighton?"

"How do you know I'm not from Brighton?"

"First of all, you don't sound like us. And then we…(Mary paused because she didn't want to insult the stranger)."

"I know, I know," smiled Elizabeth. "Nobody around here dresses like me."

"You said it, not I."

"So is Pinter part of your thesis?"

"Not exactly." Elizabeth, having known Mary for all of five minutes, was not about to volunteer the title of her thesis…just yet! "Actually not, I just happened to have seen a number of his plays."

"Do you have a favorite?"

"Probably *The Homecoming*. Teddy's father Max, reminds me of my nagging, aggressive Father, although Father is quite a bit more educated than Max."

"Well, responded Mary, "At least you've got one."

"Oh sorry," said Elizabeth, assuming Mary's Father passed.

"No it was nothing like that."

"Like what?"

"You assumed he died."

"True."

"Well, dearie, don't assume," glared Mary. "The buggar left one day in the middle of the night when I was fourteen, and we've never heard from him again."

Elizabeth, concerned the conversation was becoming too personal, changed the subject. "And, what do you do?"

"I'm a senior at Sussex and will one day be known as one of the legitimate theatre's most influential agents," said Mary matter of factly.

"I'm impressed by your modest goal and clarity of purpose," chuckled Elizabeth shyly.

"You mean, my dreams, yet to be fulfilled, to paraphrase Pinter," laughed Mary.

Elizabeth smiled. Mary did likewise. Both sensed a budding chemistry. Mary intuitively felt Elizabeth was someone with whom she could have a meaningful relationship. Elizabeth, who was a heterosexual at that point, was not exactly sure what she was feeling.

"When you're not doing research," said Mary, "where do you actually live?"

"I'm from Cumbria in the Lake District."

"Well, you are certainly a long way from home....I know, I asked you this before, but why are you visiting Brighton?"

"You won't laugh, will you?" asked Elizabeth self consciously. "My thesis is about 'The Societal Consequences of Misunderstanding Lesbian Behavior.' It's my understanding that this area is heavily populated by the alternative lifestyle."

"The alternative lifestyle! Elizabeth, you make being a lesbian sound dreadful. Have you been grappling with your identity for a long time?"

"Goodness me," said Elizabeth with a hint of horror. "I'm not a lesbian. I'm just here to study lesbian behavior patterns."

"Why would you pick such a thesis if you weren't involved?"

"Perhaps just to upset my Father. He's been quite vocal. I'm the family's unnecessary third child."

Mary just stared at Elizabeth for what seemed like an eternity but in reality was only 30 seconds. "Suppose I told you I was a lesbian."

"I wouldn't have imagined…"

"Well," interrupted Mary, "I'm not really. That was just a test."

Elizabeth smiled. She appeared quite relieved.

"I'm actually bisexual. I like men and women, just depends on how I feel at the time. There are pros and cons to each. Mum's bisexual also. We frequently compare notes."

"Is this another test?" asked Elizabeth.

"No. I really am bi-sexual. Frankly, it's a great feeling."

Mary's matter-of-fact disclosures aroused Elizabeth's curiosity. "Do you really believe a woman can get that aroused by another woman?"

Mary opened the buttons on her blouse just enough so that Elizabeth could see her generous, rounded breasts. "Since you're here to do research, maybe I can be one of your case studies?"

"Whatever do you mean?" said Elizabeth pseudo innocently.

"I'm going to prove my hypothesis," said Mary quietly, "but you must promise not to scream or yell or make a scene."

"Promise. Now what?" asked an intrigued Elizabeth.

"Now, nothing! Just drink your latte."

Suddenly Elizabeth could feel Mary's warm hand probing beneath the table, slowing pushing her skirt up. Elizabeth held true to her word. She just sat and smiled as Mary continued her exploration, sliding her hand into Elizabeth's now moist panties.

"What did I tell you? It feels good doesn't it?" whispered Mary provocatively. Elizabeth silently licked her lips until they were moist. "HMMM …MMMM."

"Just relax. I'm going to make you climax."

"No, you aren't," said Elizabeth, playfully daring her to try.

A few gentle but firm thrusts later, Mary's hand was wet with the juices of passion. She gently removed it from Elizabeth's panties. "My, my, look what Mummy found under the table!"

They both laughed. They had consummated what would become a long, intense and fulfilling relationship. "How long are you planning to stay in Brighton?" questioned Mary.

"I'm booked for the week at New Seine."

"I know Johnny and Gaffney pretty well," smiled Mary affectionately. Why not cancel the reservation? You can stay with Mum and me. We have plenty of room, and I suspect you'll get a real education for your thesis."

The generally cautious Elizabeth surprised herself by looking into Mary's light blue eyes and responded immediately and affirmatively. "But I insist on paying you. I don't want your Mum to think I'm a freeloader."

"I plan on you paying, just not with currency," smiled Mary, devilishly.

~~~

"MUM, THIS IS MY NEW FRIEND, Elizabeth," said Mary in the front room of their spacious two-bedroom flat with views up and down the beach. "She's from Cumbria, I've invited her to stay the week before she returns to Oxford."

"Any friend of Mary's is always welcome," said Chloe, warmly looking at the wholesome Elizabeth. "Where are you from?"

"I know, I know," smiled Elizabeth. "Promise I'll buy something more Brighton as soon as I get settled."

Chloe laughed.

"Elizabeth's going to share my room, okay with you Mum?"

Mum smiled knowingly. "Fine with me. What about you, Elizabeth?"

Elizabeth eyed Mary affectionately. "Yes. Absolutely."

For the remainder of Elizabeth's stay in Brighton, the girls developed a daily routine. Breakfast at Café Sainté—flaky buttery croissants and mocha lattes, clothes shopping at the secondhand boutique Rose Marie, which was littered with threadbare, pleated linen skirts, denim jeans weathered and worn at the knee and buttocks, small tongs to cover vital spots and see through blouses.

Tummies full and shopping bags in hand, the girls strolled the wide pebble beaches, imbibed the fresh salt air and shared their most intimate thoughts. Finally, they would find a deserted spot on the beach, out of general view.

~

"Oh, god! Oh god! More, more. Again, again," pleaded Mary breathlessly, as her quivering lips tasted the salty ocean breezes on the isolated Brighton Beach hilltop. Elizabeth obliged by spreading Mary's wings farther, plunging her tongue more deeply and more actively.

After almost two hours of exquisitely sensuous lovemaking, Elizabeth paused, took a deep breath and slithered up Mary's fully-clothed body—less a pair of silk panties. There, her moist warm lips shared her recent repast with her willing partner. "I love you," she murmured.

"And, I you," responded Mary as she rose and stared solemnly at the white caps continuously crashing against the rocky shoreline.

"Hey, why so glum?"

"Will you come and visit me?"

"Of course. You need only ask, and I'll be there." The emotionally spent ladies embraced one more time then fell fast asleep side by side, their heads shaded in wide-brim, yellow straw hats and their eyes closed to the bright summer sun.

~

"How about on the next school break, you'll come spend time at our home in the Lake Country?" asked Elizabeth on that final evening. "Mother and Father will find you challenging."

"That sounds ghastly."

"Not really. They're just a mite conventional."

"What's a mite?"

"They're straight as an arrow."

"I guess that means we'll be introducing old Mum and Dad to the 21st Century."

"Quite so," snickered Elizabeth mischievously.

~

"I hate sappy goodbyes," said Elizabeth packing her bag. "But I wish a memory."

"We have lots of memories," smiled Mary.

"I mean something tangible."

"Our memories are pretty tangible to me. Did you have something specific in mind?"

"As a matter of fact, I did," said Elizabeth. "Remember the arcade down by the pier?"

"Remember. I know every plank, every nail. I walked home from secondary school on that pier five times a week."

"Then *think*," urged Elizabeth.

Mary paused for a moment. "Ahhh, that silly picture booth machine."

"Precisely," said Elizabeth.

A few minutes later, the girls walked arm in arm into the booth at the arcade. "You know that old Rod Stewart standard, *Every Picture Tells a Story*? We get four shots, so they tell a story."

"You are such a romantic loon," smiled Mary.

"The pictures go pretty quick, so we've got to be prepared," directed Elizabeth. "Pose one is sad. That's a metaphor for two lonely people. Pose two is happiness because we've met. Pose three is a look of love because that's where we are, and pose four are tears of separation."

"How long have you been planning this photo shoot?" laughed Mary.

"Concentrate. I'm about to invest two pounds."

"No problem. Sad, happy, love, tears." Four flashes of light and two minutes later, the girls were standing at the print chute awaiting the finished product. "Well," said Mary looking over Elizabeth's shoulder, "are we satisfied?"

"They're perfect," said Elizabeth ripping the film strip in half. "I get sad and happy, you get love and tears." The girls placed their respective pictures in their wallets and then tenderly embraced.

Mary never asked why Elizabeth divided the pictures in that fashion.

~~~

THREE MONTHS LATER, MARY traveled across England to the Clifford family homestead in the historic, unspoiled town of Ullswater in the heart of the Lake District. It was quite dark by the time the spartan Kendal and Windermere railway train reached the last stop at Barrow-in-Furness. After traveling 12 hours—ten on conventional train from Brighton and two on the K&W—Mary was exhausted.

"How far is Ullswater from the train station?"

The conductor smiled. "You must be Elizabeth's friend?"

"How did you know that?"

"Around here everybody seems to know everybody's business."

How quaint, thought Mary privately.

"The Cliffords are just a short taxi ride across the lake."

"Taxi?" stared Mary blankly.

Minutes later, she was ushered aboard a rickety old steamer boat. As the steamer chugged across the choppy waters, Mary started to become nauseous; the "driver" in a soiled crumpled shirt smiled. "Hang on, young lady, we're almost there. This lake has a mind of its own."

A radiant Elizabeth stood under a small pole light as the water taxi neared the dock. The girls waved excitedly. Mary's stomach settled instantly. The taxi driver placed her bag on the dock as Elizabeth came running. They embraced warmly. "I've missed you so much," said Mary.

"And, I you," responded Elizabeth noticing Mary's pale green complexion. "My dear, what happened? Are you all right? You look frightfully ill."

"I had no idea England was so big!"

"I guess I should have warned you. It is a bit of a trip, isn't it? I think you'll find the Lake District fascinating. But that's for the morning. It's supposed to be glorious. Mother and Father have held dinner. I bet you're famished."

"Well, let's put it this way. A crumpet a day rarely satisfies the hungry soul."

"My goodness, that's all you've eaten?"

"Correction. That was all there was to eat. The train had some kind of electrical problem, which meant we had cold tea and yesterday's soggy crumpets. The staff was very apologetic, and everything was complimentary, so I guess matters could have been worse."

They both laughed.

Minutes later, they were motoring down a wet dirt road in a fully-equipped Range Rover, muddy water splashing everywhere.

"My god, did you have a monsoon up here?"

"Do you know much about the Cumbrian climate? Well, we are not only the northern most county in England, we are its wettest. This part of Cumbria gets about ten times the average rainfall in London because of all the surrounding hills. You get used to it, and when the sun shines, it's quite lush and beautiful. We'll do the lake tomorrow on Father's steamer. You'll see."

Mary thought quietly, *Wonderful, another painful steamer ride on the lake.* "No worries," said Elizabeth. "Father's steamer is an elegant, sturdy vessel." Elizabeth had read her mind.

~

Mary was speechless as they drove up the massive driveway and over the bridge.

The family's long-time chauffeur, Edward Tatersal, opened Elizabeth's door with a scowl on his face, "Miss Elizabeth, you know Sir James does not want you driving by yourself in the dark. Particularly when rain's about. Do you wish me to become gainfully unemployed?"

"I wasn't alone, Edward. I was with my friend Mary."

"My dear, you are incorrigible," smiled Edward.

"Would you please help her out and put the car away. And tell William to fetch Mary's bags."

"Father, Mother," said Elizabeth loudly as the two women entered the massive three-story entry hall. "I'd like you to meet my dear, dear friend, Mary Jones."

Elizabeth's parents seemed friendly but quite proper, thought Mary as she smiled and shook hands. Sir James was handsome and tall—some six foot three inches—with thick wavy brown hair, mustache, steel-gray eyes and a posture stiff as a board. Lady Clifford's facial features, though delicate and feminine, were overshadowed by her pasty white complexion and long dark hair shaped into an exaggerated beehive on top of her head. She too had the posture of a wooden plank.

"Why don't you refresh? It's quite the journey from Brighton," smiled Sir James as he scanned Mary to determine her lineage, breeding, posture, attire.

"We'll await you and your friend's presence in the parlor for a cocktail before dinner," said Lady Clifford. "William, take the young lady's bags to the Brougham suite."

"Yes, my lady, right away." The portly, balding William with double chin and pot belly reminded Mary of Alfred Hitchcock as he waddled up the stairs.

Dinner was spectacular. Foie gras with white truffles, followed by medallions of local venison accompanied by fresh carrots and beets from the garden.

"Elizabeth tells us you've just graduated from Sussex. What are you planning to do?"

"Partially because of my Mum, I've been around the theatre all my life. I've tried acting and directing. I'm dreadful at both, but my teachers tell me I have an aptitude for analyzing and improving scripts. So I've decided I'd like to become a theatrical agent in London, maybe one day own my own agency."

"Tough, cut-throat business," said Sir James. "And terribly subjective. I mean, how can you characterize a play as a hit or flop before it's staged?"

Mary didn't want to debate. After all, she had just met Sir James. "You have a point, sir," said Mary respectfully.

"Do you know what our family does with some of its wealth?"

"James, that's a boastful question to ask our guest."

"Lady Clifford, it's okay…sir, I have no idea."

"We are substantial patrons of the London theatre. Our goal is to provide funds for aspiring playwrights to evolve and perfect their craft. We may be able to at least provide you with a few relevant connections to jump start your search."

"That's terribly generous of you, Sir James. I'd be most appreciative."

"My dear, if you were a man, I'd suggest a glass of Sandeman's and a Macanudo in my den."

"Do we have a backup plan?" smiled Mary.

"Do you have a suggestion?" said Sir James, returning the smile.

"How about a brief tour of the castle before we retire? I've never stayed in a castle before."

"My dear," said Lady Clifford still unaware of Mary's name. "Are you sure you're not too tired?"

About an hour later, Mary had visited every public room but one. "That was fascinating; I had no idea your home had so much history."

"That's what five hundred years will do."

"Sir James, I hope you don't mind, but I'm terribly curious."

"About what my dear?"

"We've walked by this room a number of times, but you've never so much as referenced it. I'm starting to imagine a dungeon of horrors where unpleasant guests are stored."

"My dear, we do have a vivid imagination....It's merely my collection of artifacts from Papua New Guinea. Lady Clifford absolutely abhors the stuff and the fact that it was produced by man eating cannibals. Personally, I find it fascinating that a rudimentary culture could produce such macabre and crude yet functional and fanciful artifacts." Moments later guest and guide were standing in the middle of a large room divided into five sections, each with a strange sounding name— Bougainville, East Sepik, Southern Highlands, Milne Bay and Madang. Every wall was covered with brown cloth pegboards adorned with shields, spears, giant wood hooks, fertility carvings, medicine man masks and carved vertical posts. "The sections of the room represent the five most populated administrative districts in Papua New Guinea where most of the artifacts were actually made using only sticks and stones more than a hundred plus years ago."

"What is this unusual-looking object?" questioned Mary, pointing to a six-foot-high flat piece of wood covered with crude figures and birds and colored with natural pigments.

"Interesting choice," said Sir James. "That is actually a house sign that was customarily placed outside a family tent. The figures represent the family's history, how many relatives and children live there, etc. The elaborate colors and details suggest a large family with a significant net worth.... by New Guinean standards."

"Fascinating," said Mary bored to tears.

"From time to time, the London museums borrow some of these pieces for a special exhibit. But it's still a relatively unknown form of artistic expression that probably won't be recognized until Elizabeth's children have children and they're all grown up." James looked at his watch. "My dear, I'm so sorry. It's almost midnight, and I've been jabbering about a bunch of cannibals."

~

Mary was escorted to her room by Sir James.

"Delightful to finally meet one of Elizabeth's friends."

Mary quickly scanned the area. She concluded the only path to Elizabeth's door was directly past Sir James and Lady Clifford's bedroom suite. Mary chose the conservative course. After all, it was the first night; the couple had not developed any specific plans to deal with the obstacle, and she was exhausted from the trip, the dinner, the tour and the conversation.

Elizabeth, for her part, thought about sneaking down the hall, but she wasn't quite ready to test her Father's hearing capacity. She figured Mary was going to be there for a week, and there would be less challenging opportunities for privacy.

7

~ ~ ~

THE MORNING WAS PRECISELY as Elizabeth had predicted, a glorious, sunny day. Ullswater Lake, clearly visible from the large oval terrace at the rear of the castle, was calm and shimmery, and the view of the surrounding green-blue mountains was breathtaking. "My god," said Mary as her eyes completed a 360 ° panorama, "this is the most beautiful place I have ever seen."

"Not only does every generation of the Clifford family agree, there were some quite notable poets who felt the same way. Wordsworth lived right up the road, while Shelly, my personal favorite, lived on that ridge to your right. Yeats, by contrast, preferred the flatlands at the western corner of the Lake."

Sir James paused and sighed deeply as a beautiful yellow-and-brown butterfly fluttered by. "Those were men of sensitivity. Stanzas with soul. Emotions rarely found among today's so-called contemporary poets," said Sir James contemptuously.

"Father, I was thinking. You know how much I like to go out and about on the steamer."

"Yes, my dear, you are no doubt this family's little tomboy," said Sir James with a twinkle in his eye, not realizing he had just been set up.

"Why don't I take Mary out on the lake and show her our magnificent landscape first hand. The water is still. I'm sure they'll be no problem. We can keep in touch via the radio if that will make you feel more comfortable."

"William, tell the Captain to ready the boat. And please have Rebecca make a nice picnic lunch so the girls don't starve out on the water."

"Thank you, Father," smiled Elizabeth, as she kissed him on the cheek.

"Mother and I need to visit our solicitors in London today. Assuming our driver does not encounter any usual traffic delays, we should be back before nightfall."

~

Elizabeth carefully steered the 50-foot steamer away from the dock and down the middle of the lake until they were out of view of the Castle.

Elizabeth slid her dress off while she was steering to highlight her extremely sheer two piece mini-bikini. Mary walked over and initiated a prolonged French kiss. "God, my pants have been wet ever since you suggested the boat ride. I would have died had your Father decided to come along."

"There are only two people who will *cum* aboard this ship today," laughed Elizabeth.

"When we get to that cove, I'm going to drop anchor."

The rest of the day was devoted to intense lovemaking in the captain's suite, followed by lunch, followed by more lovemaking, followed by cocktails, followed by more lovemaking. Somewhere in the middle of their intensely erotic day, Elizabeth played tour guide.

"I'm exhausted," said Mary. "Don't you ever have enough?"

"I don't have the frequency of opportunity that you do."

"For goodness sake, Elizabeth, I'm not a nymphomaniac; I'm just a perfectly normal, healthy bisexual."

"That makes me insanely jealous…That you're having sex with a man while I'm saving myself for you. It's like you're cheating and I'm not."

"Sex is sex, love is love. They are quite different matters," said Mary.

"Can you separate the two?" asked Elizabeth.

"Absolutely." (Although as Mary was to learn some time later, it was not as easy as it seemed.)

They puttered around the lake as Elizabeth provided some interesting tour guide commentary. "As you know the most famous Romantic Movement poet was William Wordsworth. He lived his whole life within twenty miles of here. He schooled at Hawkshead, domiciled in Grasmere as an adult and eventually passed of old age at Royal Mount. Perhaps far more important than the geography, was the fact that he celebrated nature in these very hills and valleys which remain virtually unchanged. Nature to him was a great restorative and spiritual guide in life."

"I can see and feel why," said Mary observing the landscape.

"There's something particularly special not far from here. You game?" Elizabeth anchored the boat in the low crystal-clear cove and the girls waded to the shore. Once on land Elizabeth took Mary's hand and led her through a field about a half mile inland. There in front of them stood an endless array of wild, bright yellow daffodils as far as the eye could see. "Well," announced Elizabeth.

"It's about the most beautiful thing I've ever seen."

"Have you ever read Wordsworth's poem 'I Wandered Lonely as a Cloud'?" asked Elizabeth.

"Wordsworth wrote that poem right here. As a child, I would come here and recite the words privately to myself."

"Would you do that for me now?" pleaded Mary.

As the words rolled off Elizabeth's tongue, the sun playfully peeked from behind a single white cloud, creating shades of sunshine over her flawless complexion.

The girls returned to the castle dock just before dark, figuring they would beat Mother and Father home. Since her parents were away all day, Elizabeth never attempted to call shore. Consequently, she never realized William had turned the ship's two-way satellite telephone onto monitoring mode for safety reasons.

~

"I've decided my niche," announced Mary confidently. "Mary Jones shall become the 'princess of discovery.'"

"And, your kingdom, My Lady?" teased Elizabeth.

"London's dearth of talented young playwrights primed for that big break in the West End."

"And, how does the Belle of Brighton plan to infiltrate that incestuous club?"

"Persistence… And my engaging theatrical persona."

"And what might that be? (Pause) Let me guess. You're going to don a top hat and smoke a big cigar like Churchill?"

"Mary Jones is going to be *une femme trés colorée*—a playfully outrageous, fun-loving and insightful agent who delivers, first time, every time."

"I don't know," volunteered Elizabeth. "We are talking London, not Manhattan."

"It's my persona. You don't have a vote," said Mary getting defensive.

"But I love you the way you are."

"Elizabeth, pleaaase. It's just a facade. It's not real. I'll always be me. People fundamentally don't change. They are who they are."

"I don't necessarily agree. People can become who they think they are."

"This debate is getting a little esoteric," said an increasing disinterested Mary whose mind was made up.

"What about me? Do I fit into your master plan?"

"Fit. You're the love of my life. My forever partner. After you finish at Oxford, I want you to join me in London."

"Father will have a stroke. He won't allow it."

"Elizabeth, you're twenty-two, a legal adult. He can't stop you."

"He'll shut down my trust income."

"We won't need it. Besides, unless I'm mistaken, once you turn twenty-one you have the right to control your trust disbursements. His bark is without legal bite. Check that with your solicitor."

"Who just happens to be Father's best friend."

"Then get somebody else."

"This conversation is boring me," said Elizabeth beginning to disrobe. "Let's go back down stairs and do something more stimulating."

Conversation ended.

~~~

LADY CLIFFORD CHANGED the couple's plans in London. Their old friends, Nigel and Lucy Wentworth, from Dover, were on holiday in the city. "James, I've decided we should stay in town this evening to celebrate Lucy and Nigel's 30th anniversary." Lady Clifford called the Grosvenor Hotel, their home away from home.

"Lady Clifford," said the desk clerk, "I'm so sorry, My Lady."

"Are the Cliffords not considered privileged guests?"

"Yes, certainly, My Lady."

"Then settle the accommodations, or do I need to talk to the manager about your behavior?"

"No, My Lady."

~

Sir James decided to check on the girls via remote satellite between meetings. He was stunned by their intimacy. He was beside himself. He was angry, disappointed, embarrassed, determined to sternly reprimand Elizabeth.

"I think we should go home. Now," said Sir James, not ready to reveal the cause of his urgency.

"James, I'm sure Elizabeth and Mary are fine. God knows you've had your ear glued to that satellite telly. Just let William know we've changed plans. He's perfectly capable of informing the girls. We're going to be late for dinner. Shan't be rude and keep the Wentworths waiting."

Sir James was atypically reserved at dinner. His mind was preoccupied with the potential family scandal that he had a daughter who was a filthy, perverted lesbian, and what that could do to his reputation as one of England's preeminent Christian philanthropists?

~

After the sunset love fest, Elizabeth skillfully guided the steamer back to the Castle docks. There they were greeted by William. "My dear, I was starting to worry when you didn't answer my call. Sir James rang to say he and your Mum are staying in London for the evening. Their meeting ran over."

"Oh, how disappointing," feigned Elizabeth as the ladies smiled at each other.

"I believe he tried to contact you aboard the ship."

The ladies were so preoccupied with envisioning their evening tryst, neither heard William, nor realized the implications of his statement.

"Dinner is almost ready; perhaps the two of you would like to freshen up after a day on that salty river."

William started to place Mary's carry bag in her assigned room. Elizabeth interrupted.

"William, can you keep a secret?"

"Certainly, Madame."

"I mean a really big secret?"

"As they say at Scotland Yard, mum's the word," smiled William zipping his lip with his right hand.

"Please put Mary's bag in the master suite. She and I will be sleeping there tonight."

William's eyebrows rose. "Yes, I understand."

After dinner, the ladies retired to the suite for another round. During the session, Mary, who had removed some whipped cream from the kitchen after dinner, placed it carefully on Elizabeth's breasts and slowly licked it all off. Elizabeth, moist with anticipation, stared and laughed at the room's strangely hand-painted ceiling awash with angels and other Biblical figures. "I've never had sex in Church before." She'd also never left her bikini thong in Church, which was an unfortunate by product of the night's intense activity.

~

"So Father, Mother, how was London?" asked Elizabeth at lunch the following day as the foursome sat on the sunny veranda overlooking the lake.

"About the same. Rainy, damp, overcast and wonderful," said Sir James.

"When do you return to Oxford?"

"Monday next."

"Father, why so glum. Going to miss your little girl?" teased a completely unaware Elizabeth.

Sir James stared at Elizabeth. "Suppose I told you the satellite telly on the steamer was accidentally left on. What would you have to say for yourself?"

Elizabeth and Mary froze. Their eyes were filled with terror. "Whatever do you mean?" said Elizabeth, trying to maintain her composure.

"I believe you know what I mean, young lady."

"Sir, do you always spy on your children?" glared Mary.

"Only when I feel it's absolutely necessary," responded Sir James crossly. "What are you two bantering about?" inquired Lady Clifford, completely in the dark.

"We have a bit of a scandal, my dear. Turns out your daughter is a lesbian. She's in love with this tramp. They plan to live in London off the family trust."

"That's preposterous," said Lady Clifford.

"Dear, don't tell me. I heard them on the satellite phone having a go."

Oh, my God."

"There's more. Look at this," said Sir James pulling Elizabeth's thong from his pocket.

"Oh my God," said Elizabeth.

"I found these in our bed last night. It seems as though these two tramps know no bounds."

"Father, let me explain. We truly love each other, and…"

"And nothing! I want this tramp off the grounds immediately. We'll decide how to deal with you later!"

"I quite agree," chimed Lady Clifford. "This instant won't be soon enough."

Minutes later, her bag hastily packed, Mary was being driven to the steamer station by William for the long trip back to Brighton. Neither said a word.

Little did Mary realize she had seen Elizabeth for the last time.

~ ~ ~

"I WILL HANDLE THIS IN MY OWN WAY," said Sir James. Lady Clifford nodded her approval and retired to their boudoir while Elizabeth and Sir James retired to the parlor.

"I trust you're ashamed of yourself?" asked Sir James calmly from his winged back leather chair by the roaring fireplace.

"No, I love her."

"Women loving each other is aberrant, decadent. Not intended by God."

"I don't agree."

"Have you no concern for the family's reputation?"

"I'm concerned about having my own life."

"What if I said your behavior is grounds for removal from our family trust?"

"I believe it's grandfather's trust and that once I turn twenty-one I will receive legal control of those assets allocated to me."

From Sir James's point of view, each answer was more brazen than the last. Finally, at wits' end, he arose from the chair, picked up a massive fireplace iron and slammed it on the hearth. "God damn it, you are a shameless vixen, damned to hell. This family will not be party to your perverted affair."

"Father," retorted Elizabeth as she stood fearlessly face to face. "You cannot frighten me with your bloody bellowing. You could care less about my happiness. It's all about your God Almighty reputation."

"How dare you speak to me like that," said Sir James as he swung the giant andiron in anger over his head. Elizabeth, thinking he was trying to hit her, ducked and slipped to the floor. On the way down, her head struck a pointed edge of the fireplace, blood gushing instantly. She whispered for help and put her hand out. Sir James just stood and watched silently until the life bled out of her. Then he calmly checked her pulse to make certain she was dead as she lay in a pool of blood.

"William, you're needed here right now. We've had a dreadful accident."

A horrified William cried, "Should we call the hospital, the police?"

"No. She was not a Clifford. Satan dropped her diseased soul on our doorstep. We did our best. I want to forget."

Sir James then ordered William to clean up the blood stains, put the rags into a large plastic bag and haul them down to the steamer so that he and William could dispose of them somewhere out in Lake Ullswater. When William returned from the dock, Sir James had him perform exactly the same chore with Elizabeth's remains. He then wiped the remaining blood off the floor and placed the rags into the bag. The two men then carried her body to the steamer and drove out to the deepest part of the lake. There they dumped both bags overboard and waited to make sure they sank.

"You knew, didn't you?" said Sir James to William.

"Not initially."

"And why didn't you say something?"

"Would you have believed me?"

~

That evening Sir James slept in one of the guest suites. At the breakfast table, Lady Clifford asked "What happened last evening?"

"It was quite argumentative, my dear."

"In what way?"

"She refused to declare the error of her ways. She said she preferred not to live under our roof. She packed her bags and insisted William drive her to the ferry landing, where she planned to wait for the morning steamer so she could go live with that lesbian tramp."

Sir James's story seemed incredible. Lady Clifford decided to casually seek validation from the one person she had come to trust more than any other in the world. "That so, William?"

"Yes, My Lady, that's so."

Lady Clifford shook her head. "That brazen hussy! Where did we go wrong?"

"My sentiments exactly," concurred Sir James. "And, for the record my dear, we did nothing wrong."

~

William carried the weight of the world upon his shoulders for the next two weeks. He knew he had been an accessory after the fact. The right side of his brain told him to report the matter to the police. It was the proper thing to do. The left side reminded him he was now 64 years old. Could he really endure the rigors of prison confinement?

Sir James cared not a hoot about William's inner turmoil. But he did care enormously about the fact that William was starting to have nightmares about the matter and increasingly talking in gibberish. It was just a matter of time before William broke down.

10

~~~

A WEEK HAD GONE BY SINCE Mary ungracefully exited Skipton Castle. There was not a single word of communication from Elizabeth. She was worried. Mary had felt the rage in Sir James's eyes firsthand. She was convinced he was capable of anything. Finally, she got the nerve up to ring the castle. William answered the phone.

"She doesn't live here anymore," said William matter of factly.

"What do you mean, she doesn't live there anymore?"

"Just what I said, no more, no less." William then placed the phone on the receiver.

"Who was that?" asked Lady Clifford.

"Just a wrong number, Madame."

A frantic Mary then called the police station in Grassmere, the closest town to Lake Ullswater. "Sir, I want to file a missing person's report. My friend is missing."

"And, who might that be, young lady?"

"Elizabeth Clifford from Skipton Castle. Oh, dear God, I fear that something terrible has happened to her."

"Easy, Madame, easy. There's nothing to worry about. The lass had a spat with her Father and decided it best to leave home and move to London. She'll be back. You know how those things go. Sir James stopped by to tell us all about it and to keep a look out for her.

~

Two weeks later, William was in the local market buying the weekly provisions.

"Have we heard from the young lady yet?" said the shop-keeper.

"No. All I can say is Elizabeth and Sir James had quite the row. I presume she's living somewhere in Brighton."

"Brighton?" responded the shopkeeper quizzically. "I was talking to Inspector Sean O'Reilly of the Grassmere Police outside Church Sunday past. He thought Elizabeth moved to London. So why Brighton? That's more than fifty miles from London Centre."

"Goodness," said William backtracking. "Did I say Brighton? I meant London. You know the older we get, the more senile we become. But then you're too young to know about that."

When William arrived home, he felt obligated to tell Sir James what had transpired.

"No worries," said Sir James lightheartedly, "those things happen. Just be more careful in the future. Particularly, since at some point the police will probably return on a follow-up call."

Sir James was now convinced that William would be a terrible liability in future interrogations. The next day, Sir James decided to go fishing on his steamer. "William, it's such a beautiful day, and I know you like fishing. Why don't you join me?"

"Oh, sir, I couldn't. I have numerous chores to complete. Some other time perhaps."

"Damn the chores, William," bellowed Sir James, "The boss is ordering you to take an extra paid holiday. Offers like that don't arrive every day."

"Very good, sir." William changed into casual clothes and the two men puttered off to the middle of the still lake. There they baited their hooks and waited for the feisty rainbow trout to bite.

"Funny thing about fishing," said Sir James, "You wait and wait for the right moment. When it comes, you've got to be ready because it might not come again. Know what I mean?"

William laughed. "I do, sir, I do."

"Same thing with a good woman, eh, William?"

"That's true, sir. True."

"I never asked you before, but did you ever marry?"

"Oh, I met my love a long time ago. Three days before the wedding, she was hit by a car in Battersea, a few blocks from her home. Died instantly. Never found another like my Margaret. Here I am getting old by myself."

"Surely, you have other family?"

"All since passed, including my brother and sister."

"Well you've always got us," smiled Sir James, thinking the perfect situation for what he was about to undertake. "I'm going to get me a stout, can I get you one?"

"Let me, sir."

"No, today William, you're my guest."

"Sporting of you, sir. Don't mind if I do."

Sir James went below, got two Guinness Stouts and a gray steel hatchet, which he placed in a white towel. When he returned, he handed William one of the stouts.

As William reached for the stout, Sir James took one mighty swing at William's head, splitting his skull and splattering blood all over his clothes and the boat's deck. William gasped once or twice, eyes bulged, his body shuddered and he expelled his last breath. Sir James picked up the limp body and tossed it overboard. Then he moved the boat a half mile or so downstream to deeper waters, cleaned the blood around the deck and placed the blood-stained rags, his blood-stained outer garments and some lead weights in a burlap bag (similar to the one used for Elizabeth), tied it securely and dumped it overboard.

His story to the police? He invited William for a day of fishing. The man drank too much, tottered to the front deck of the steamer, lost his footing and slammed his head into the ship's sharp steel anchor brace, falling portside into the lake before Sir James even realized what had happened.

Some ten days later, after dredging the lake in the appointed spot, William's body was found with his skull split, precisely as Sir James had described. The case was marked closed. The burlap bag never surfaced.

11

~ ~ ~

"OFFICER," PROTESTED MARY, literally screaming into the telephone at Ullswater's entire detective bureau of one—the burly, red-nosed Inspector O'Reilly.

"You know, people can be unpredictable."

"Elizabeth's absolutely my best friend. She simply wouldn't move to London without contacting me."

"Perhaps. Perhaps not. Young ladies have a mind of their own these days. Have you checked the London Directory?"

"I have. There is no listing for an Elizabeth Clifford, an E. Clifford or even a Liz Clifford."

"Maybe she switched to a mobile phone?"

"She detests mobile phones."

"Takes all types. My daughter's about Miss Clifford's age and she practically lives on the darn contraption," chuckled O'Reilly. "Text messages here, pictures there, voice mails everywhere. When was the last time you actually spoke to her?"

"About a month ago."

The "about a month" response caused O'Reilly to wonder how well Mary really knew Elizabeth.

"And how long did you say you've been best friends?"

"Three months."

"Have you talked to Sir James?"

"No, I haven't."

"Doesn't that seem like a logical next step?"

"I can't. I can't call Sir James."

"And why is that?"

"Elizabeth told me my recent visit caused quite a row."

"A row about what?"

Mary hesitated. "It's a rather personal matter."

"Young lady, if we decide to investigate further, we will talk to Sir James. Do you understand what I'm saying?"

Mary paused. "We told him we were very much in love. He said he'd have none of it."

"Are you trying to tell me Elizabeth Clifford is a lesby?"

"Yes."

"Can you prove that statement?"

"Elizabeth can."

"Well, for the moment, we don't know where Elizabeth is, do we? I've known the Cliffords personally for the better part of twenty years. They are a model family—community-minded and generous to a fault. I assure you, there's never been a hint, even a rumor of lesbies in the family. For goodness sakes, Sir Clifford is a church deacon."

"My intuition tells me something is terribly wrong," pleaded Mary.

"So does mine, my dear. I understand lesbies are quite the backstabbers. We didn't have a lovers' quarrel, did we?" laughed the officer with a significant degree of sarcasm in his voice.

"What a terrible thing to say!" responded an offended Mary.

Officer O'Reilly abruptly hung up.

Mary sat frustrated and speechless. She began to cry. Chloe heard her sobbing from the living room across the hall. "Dear, dear, what's the matter?"

"Elizabeth seems to have disappeared off the face of the earth."

"Oh, she'll reappear," said Chloe confidently, trying to lighten the atmosphere. "She's probably just hiding from that warm, wonderful creature you described as her father."

"Well, that's possible. He certainly is every bit the bully."

"Mary, speaking from experience, men like Sir James always seem to have a bag on. But if you remain steadfast and stand your ground, they melt like snowflakes in the sun."

"How do you know so much about 'these sort of men'?"

"I used to attract them like flies."

"But I thought you and Annabelle Lee were…"

"We are, my dear. I converted exclusively to the sensitive, more passionate sex some time ago, thanks to your father."

"I guess I'm not quite there yet," said Mary.

"Excuse me," paused Chloe. "I thought you and Elizabeth were an item."

"We are, but I still enjoy the occasional go with the opposite sex."

"How does Elizabeth feel about that sort of thing?"

"She's okay with the occasional romp, so long as it doesn't become addictive."

"I don't believe I've ever heard promiscuous behavior described in such a high brow manner. Moving on. Annabelle Lee is coming for dinner. Apparently she has some very good news she wants to discuss."

"Do we know what it is?" smiled Mary.

"Actually, no."

"Mum, mind if I go freshen up and relax a bit before dinner. Today has been a day."

"I understand, dear. I'll give you a shout when Annabelle Lee arrives"

Mary took a hot shower infused with lavender and chamomile oils. A certain urgency filled Mary's being as her mind and she decided it was time to confront the bully of Ullswater on the telephone. After all, what damage—physical or emotional—could he possibly inflict from 1,200 miles away?

"Clifford residence, may I help you?" said the male voice Mary assumed was William.

"William, this is Mary Jones. You know, Elizabeth's friend. I was wondering if I could talk to Sir James?"

"Young lady, this is he speaking. What business do you have calling here? I thought I was rather clear with Elizabeth when you were here."

"Sir James, I know you don't condone our relationship. But I truly love your daughter, and I'm worried about her. Nobody seems to have heard from her, and she hasn't called me."

"My dear, if I knew where she was, and I don't, you would be the last person on earth I would tell. You've brought Satan's very soul into our good home!" bellowed Sir James. "You blasphemous, perverted hussy. 'Love my daughter!' How disgusting! That's not God's order. Never, and I mean never, call here again." Then Sir James slammed the phone in Mary's ear.

12

~~~

"MARY DEAR," BECKONED CHLOE. "Annabelle Lee is here."

After a brief chat, the threesome sat down to dinner.

"Child," interrupted Annabelle Lee, coming directly to the point, "what in the world happened to your face? Your mascara is running down your cheeks. You look like that dreadful Gene Simmons rock fellow. Have you been crying?"

"Yes."

"Why?"

"Elizabeth hasn't called or emailed in almost a month?"

"Why don't you just call her?"

"I did. A computer voice said her landline was not in service at this time. And her emails were never opened. Finally, I gathered the courage to call Sir James, who curtly dismissed me—unwilling or unable to give me any information."

"What about the local police?"

"As far was they're concerned Sir James and his family walk on water. He had his own interpretation of the facts—

Elizabeth and I had a lover's spat. In deference to me, she moved to London, leaving no forwarding details."

"Terribly rational," said Annabelle Lee.

"That's what I said. My intuition tells me there is more."

"Child, I don't know what to suggest, short of going to London yourself and searching her out."

"I'm not sure I'd even know where to start," responded Mary.

"How about as a theatrical agent's assistant?" smiled Annabelle Lee.

"I don't understand...."

"Well, I know how much you want to become a theatrical agent, so I called an old friend, Julian Belfrage, about opening a few doors."

"You mean THE Julian Belfrage!" screeched Mary in delight.

"Of course, THE Julian Belfrage. I told him all about you. How smart and committed you were, and how terribly knowledgeable you were about the subtleties of theatre."

"Oh my God, Julian Belfrage!" said Mary suddenly transformed into a giggly, wiggly, gawky 22-year-old.

"He'd like to meet you when you get to London."

"Oh, my God. Brilliant, brilliant, brilliant!"

"When she gets to London?" said a surprised Chloe.

"How else do you expect your daughter to break into the business? She sure as hell can't do it from Brighton. Chloe, I thought that was understood before I made the call."

"Mum, you knew and didn't say anything?"

"I wasn't about to steal Annabelle Lee's thunder." Then she turned to Annabelle Lee. You're right," said Chloe backpeddling. "Whatever was I thinking? It's time for my little girl to spread her wings and live her dreams."

Mary was overwhelmed by the moment. A small-town girl at heart, who rather liked the concepts of order and control, was about to enter the bustling mass of humanity and circuitous metropolitan labyrinth known as London.

"What if I'm not ready?" said Mary.

"Dearie, I've watched you mix it up with those directors and playwrights at the Theatre Royale. Trust me, you're ready."

"But what about accommodations? Where shall I live? How do I find a flat? What do I...."

"Relax Mary, it's not like you're going to outer regions of Tibet. London is now quite civilized. They have newspapers in English, the people speak the same language as we do and they even have television in homes," teased Annabelle Lee sarcastically.

"I sound like a complete plank, don't I?"

"Beyond complete," said Annabelle Lee.

Mary then turned and looked at her mother. "Mum, I hope you don't mind."

"Darling, just remember me when you become rich and famous. I'll want a ruby red Maserati."

"By the way, Annabelle Lee, how do you know Julian Belfrage?" wondered Mary.

"I used to be Mrs. Belfrage."

"What a ripper! That's totally awesome," exclaimed Mary.

"I'm not sure that's exactly the way I'd describe our marriage."

"How would you describe it?" asked Chloe with a mixture of surprise and inquisitiveness.

"He was a handsome bloke with fabulous connections. I was a young theatrical diva who wanted desperately to be the next Glenda Jackson. He seemed to know everybody who was anybody in London. I figured he was my road map, my compass to success. For the first two years, he treated me like a princess. Then he got bored. He'd say, 'Annabelle Lee, you know I love you. But being with the same person all the time lacks a certain *joie de vivre*.'"

"So he cheated?"

"Souvent, souvent."

"Why didn't you just leave?" asked Mary.

"First of all, it wasn't like a secret. Somehow we eliminated the naive charade that he was meant to be forever faithful. Plus, I was living the good life. There wasn't anything he wouldn't provide—except fidelity."

"So, why did you finally break up?"

(Pause.) "That last night, I had been out to the theatre with a group of lady friends. Noel Coward's *Private Lives* at the Lyceum on Regent Street, as I recall. One of them had a dreadful headache, so we all went home early. I walked into the bedroom, and there was Julian having sex with a handsome young stud. They looked like two horses humping in a barn."

"How perfectly dreadful!"

"When Julian saw me, he just laughed and kept humping the young man. He dared me to join them."

"And, you did…" paused Chloe.

"I packed my bags and left. Shamefully depressed about my own inadequacies in bed."

"And you want my daughter to call on such a man for a favor," said Chloe.

"That was personal. Mary's needs are professional. Julian is a master at separating the two. Trust me, he'll be charming. He'll test you to see how knowledgeable you are. If you pass muster, he'll take you on or usher you off to a friend in need. The way Julian looks at things, you'll owe him a favor, and his friend will owe him a favor."

"What kind of favor?"

"Just assume it will be something wicked, like stealing trade secrets. The trick is to get what you need from him before he tries to call in the favor. Then get the hell out of there."

"You're telling me to use him and then discard him?"

"Like a pile of repulsive refuse."

"That would make me no better than him."

"Not really. If you beat him to the punch, you'll be better than him. You'll also have the consolation of watching Julian seethe. He abhors losing. At anything."

"Frankly, I'm not sure I want to play…"

"My dear," interrupted Annabelle Lee. "Ultimately, the choice is yours. Play by the rules of the West End Theatre Game or become big fish in the Fringe Theatre World. London is no different than Broadway. There are the Haves and the Have-Nots."

13

~ ~ ~

BELFRAGE HAD BUILT A THEATRICAL empire in and around the West End. The Strand to the south, Oxford Street to the north, Regent Street to the West and Kingsway to the East. Forty of London's largest and most prestigious theatres were within walking distance of his penthouse offices at 80 Glasshouse Street, a magnificent modern steel- and-glass skyscraper towering over the historical neighborhood.

He spent his days with playwrights and directors whose properties had already been reviewed and edited by his staff and deemed commercially viable. Rejects never reached Belfrage's desk. In the evening, he wined, dined, entertained and did what he had to do to get major investor groups to invest in his productions. During the past decade, Belfrage had an average of three successful productions a year running simultaneously, employing top-flight stage talent such as Maggie Smith, Ben Richards, Simon Russell Beale, Roger Allam, Judi Dench and Kathleen Turner.

His preferred method of entertaining was to invite guests to his breathtaking 20,000-square-foot, four-bedroom flat at One Hyde Park in the heart of Knightsbridge, which at £85,000,000 (over £4,000 per square foot) was rumored to be one of Europe's most expensive apartments.

If he were tending to a mixed party (men and women), the evening would begin with a private luxury-goods shopping tour at Harrods' Department Store. Whatever an investor selected, Belfrage would have his staff handle all the details of purchase and shipping, including the intricate export maze known as VAT (value added taxes).

When his guests were exclusively male, which was the case about 90 percent of the time, Belfrage would serve more than vintage port and Cuban cigars for dessert. He usually had a stable of the most glamorous and adventurous hookers booked for the evening. Every imaginable fantasy and fetish was accommodated in his bedroom suites. Guests were then discretely chauffeured home in the wee hours of the morning to avoid any public-relations scandals.

There were always lingering questions about Belfrage's larger-than-life persona in the daily tabloids. After all, how could an East Ender from the working-class side of London legitimately accumulate the wealth necessary to live that kind of Knightsbridge lifestyle? A lifestyle normally reserved for those of inherited wealth and "situational" Middle Eastern billionaires like Hamad bin Jassem bin Jaber Al-Thani, the Foreign Minister of Qatar, and Princess Diana's beau, Dodi Fayed.

The *Daily Sun* expended numerous front pages, attempting to skewer Belfrage, who took delight in the fact that he, a reputable and successful theatre mogul, was the public grist of hollow, nebulous witch hunts. In the end, the running feud gave both parties what they needed. The *Sun's* sensational headlines drew readers, which allowed them to raise their advertising rates, while Belfrage got millions in free publicity, which kept his brand in full view of prospective investors.

~

Having studied the publicly available information on Belfrage, Mary targeted the outskirts of central London as a logical place to locate a flat and, like Belfrage, be within a stone's throw of the theatre district.

Knowing she wasn't planning to spend much time in her hotel room that first week, she opted for a modest flat in Camden Town. From there, it was three stops on the tube to the station at Hyde Park Corner, her neighborhood of preference, where she scoured the areas of Belgravia Square, Egerton Gardens, Cadogan Square and Hans Place with her *London Times* in hand. Since the adverts did not list prices, she concentrated on those realty agencies with the largest number of listings and rang them first.

"Frost, Green and Archer, may I help you?" said the very pleasant and terribly proper voice on the other end of the telly.

"I'm new in town. Relocating from Brighton, and was looking for a rental flat in Central London. Since I'll be working in the theatre, I was thinking Knightsbridge."

"Very good choice, Madame, and a specialty of Frost, Green and Archer." The receptionist assumed Mary to be an "A" list prospect, someone who knew her area of interest and was willing to pay the outrageous going rates. "At the moment, all our principals are at showings. The market is extremely active, and flats are being scooped up rather quickly. Would you mind terribly if I put you into Mr. Frost's voice mail? He specializes in rentals."

"That would be lovely," said Mary. "Thank you."

As it turned out, Mary and Mr. Frost exchanged numerous voice mails but never connected. While it wasn't the way Frost typically operated, he wanted to get the ball rolling with his new prospect, so he made appointments by phone to show Mary two one-bedroom flats on Wilton Crescent and Montrose Place, both within walking distance of Belgravia Square.

The first—and only—meeting of agent and prospect was a study in misunderstandings.

Frost arrived in a trademark Edward Sexton (Prince Charles's tailor) single-breasted, pointed- lapel custom-made suit, a heavily starched blue pin-striped shirt with a white collar and French cuffs, and maroon club tie subtly dotted with foxes and hounds. The obligatory starched white handkerchief sat neatly in his outer breast pocket.

Mary arrived in what could best be termed scruffy casual—jeans with tattered edges, high heel boots, a sensually revealing midriff blouse and casually flowing curly red hair. In her mind, she had knocked the entire ensemble out of London's trendy *Today's Woman* magazine. Unfortunately, it wasn't Knightsbridge fashion, and it certainly wasn't Frost's cup of tea. He knew instinctively time invested in Mary was going to be a horrific waste. But he had made a commitment to both the renter and landlord, so with the classic British stiff upper lip, the appointments were kept.

Both flats were equally spectacular. Turn-of-the-century, stone townhouses painted white with gracious, furnished lobbies. Ten-foot-high ceilings, massive sunlight-flooded windows and generously proportioned living rooms with formal dining alcoves, an eat-in kitchen, and oversized master suite and guest baths.

"These flats are larger than Mum's flat in Brighton," said Mary innocently.

"Really," said Frost, rolling his eyes. "Do we have a preference?"

"I could live in either. Guess it's just a matter of the differences in the weeklies."

"The weeklies?" wondered Frost. "Whatever do you mean, Ms. Jones?"

She thought he was having her on. So she returned the spoof. "The weekly tariff, Mr. Bond. Mr. James Bond."

Frost was lost. He had little patience for silly games. He wanted to deliver the bad news quickly and professionally.

"Ms. Jones, the rent for these flats are exactly the same. £108,000 per annum."

"You mean as in £9.000 per month?"

"Not as in, rather, precisely for."

"Let me think about it," said a stunned Mary.

"You do that, Miss Jones. If you don't mind, I must run to my next appointment. We'll be in touch."

"I understand," said Mary as Frost quickly disappeared around the corner.

~

"Christ, Mum, why didn't you or Annabelle Lee say something?" said Mary on the telephone later that evening.

"For goodness sake, it never even occurred to me you were going to look in Knightsbridge. I thought everybody knew it's beyond outrageously expensive."

"I certainly know that now. £9,000 for a one bedroom flat. So where should I look?"

"I would suggest the East End. It's a real sleeper of London. Used to be a very working class area loaded with docks where ships unloaded their wares for the rest of the city and pubs that were a bit grimy."

"Sounds perfectly dreadful for a single girl from the seashore!"

"Mary, that was in the early 1900's. It's being gentrified. Last time I was down near Tobacco Dock, they had built a huge shopping village and the townhouses that wind around the Thames on Wappoing Street, Garnet and Monce have all been restored and modernized. The Tube even has a station right at Wapping, so you can get to Central London in a matter of minutes. My recollection is that coffee shops and bookshops were popping up all over the place, and lots of young artists and actors were moving in. I read somewhere it is London's hotbed of contemporary art."

"Sounds cool. I guess I should check it out."

"I would. By the way, I just read something about the British Library opening an East End branch on Cable Street.

The first event is called The Josephine Hart Poetry Hour. I think they are reading Auden. I know how much you like his poetry."

The more Mum talked, the more the East End sounded like Mary's kind of place.

The next morning, she bought a copy of the local daily newspaper, *The East Ender*, and began to scour the real estate adverts. The first thing she noticed was that there were a number of listings in her price range. Secondly, as in the West End, there seemed to be a few agencies that owned most of the listings.

She liked the sound of the name Bill Bling, so she called the Bill Bling Agency. Bling himself answered the phone. Mary explained her situation. "So, Mum thought at this stage of my life, the East End might be a good fit."

"Why did she say that?"

"Well, apparently she's been there. She knew about the gentrification, the art scene, etc."

"Why don't you stop by the office; we'll call your Mum, I'll tell her what we've got. Maybe she can help us narrow things down a bit. I'll even throw in a cup of coffee."

The next morning, Mary took the tube from her hotel to Wappoing Station. Bling's tiny second floor office was a block away in what was once an old tannery factory cleverly converted into commercial space during the early 1980's. "Not exactly Oxford Street, eh?" said the athletically built, handsome, dark-haired young man.

Mary looked around the modest office stacked with theatre memorabilia, antique neighborhood photographs, multiple-listing books, flat flyers posted on the walls and a single out-of-date laptop computer tottering on the edge of a dusty, cluttered desk. "I was looking for Bill Bling."

The man smiled. "Let me find out if he's here. Who shall I say is calling?"

"Mary Jones. I called yesterday about a flat on Campbell Road."

The man spun his old swivel mahogany office chair around the empty office. Then looked Mary in the eye with a huge grin. "Hi, I'm Bill Bling. I understand you're looking for me?"

Mary started to chuckle. "Only if you're a realtor."

"Madame."

"The name is Mary."

"Mary, then. I am who you seek. I am a realtor by trade during the day, an actor by profession at night, and, as my Mum explains it, I am a fourth-generation Bling. You may have misunderstood my enunciation on the phone yesterday, which is entirely possible," said the man, "because my friends tell me I'm indecipherable even when I'm sober, which is not too often."

Mary was having a good roll. "You find me humorous, Madame. I mean Mary."

"The Bling thing is hilarious."

"Great, great, great grandfather owned the name long before some couture icon decided to rename us jewelry.'

"So you come from a line of Bling, Bling, Bling and Blings," giggled Mary.

"Mary, let's get serious. I'm a busy man," teased Bling. "You mentioned the flat on Campbell Road. Personally, having now met you, I think that location might be a little too noisy for you. How about we have a go around the neighborhood, and I show you a few properties along the way?"

"I want to warn you in advance. I'm on a budget. I can only spend about £125 a week until I start my new job."

"No problem. I may have just the flat for you." Bling's walking tour began with the open-air markets on Burdett Road and Petticoat Lane near Middlesex Street, continued past Sir John Franklin Pub at St. Leonard's Road and East India Dock Road. It ended at the recently renovated 100,000-square-foot Truman Brewery off Hanbury Street, where the smell of freshly-made Indian curries, kebobs and skewers of marinated lamb sat side by side with Chinese specialties like marinated dog and West African alligator gumbo.

"My goodness, I had no idea how international the East Side was."

"Neither does most of London."

"Why is that?"

"Well, it does have a sordid history. Back in the 1800's this was a secondary dock area for goods earmarked for Central London. It was a pretty tough place. There were rather violent battles over working conditions. Most ordinary folks were afraid to walk the dimly lit streets after dark. It wasn't even considered part of London proper until the 20th Century. By then, the unions had gained a foothold, people began earning a fair wage and the Johnnies cleared the area bringing law and order. Once things settled down, the streets around the docks started to get transformed into reasonable accommodations. That process of upgrade continues to this day."

"I see lots of interesting little handmade craft shops down the side streets. In that respect, it reminds me a bit of home."

"Where's home?"

"Brighton."

"I've only been down to that seaside once or twice. It was quite beautiful, although the abundance of tarts, young men on the dole, and druggies was a bit unnerving"

"That's a terribly harsh analysis," responded Mary indignantly.

Realizing he didn't want to ruin a beautiful friendship before it began, Bling deftly changed the subject.

"What brings you to London?"

"I'm planning on becoming a theatrical agent."

Ahhh, thought Bling, *the clue I'd been looking for. She's an artsy type.* "Let's take a walk around Herald Street, Bethnal Green and Vyner; it's become quite the gathering place for the contemporary art scene. Galleries and home of the young artists they represent fill the streets. Personally, I can feel the energy." They stopped in front of the Herald ST Gallery. "ST

66

happens to be one of my personal favorites. The directors, Nicky Verber and Ash Lange, have discovered some of the city's edgier artists."

Mary looked in the window at the show in progress. The poster read, "Dan Colen's 'Birdshit Paintings.'"

"Bill, to tell you the truth, I'm not sure I understand the artist's concept. The show looks like a bunch of bird shit on a bunch of canvas that Colen stretched, hung and exorbitantly priced."

"That's it," smiled Bling.

"That's what?" wondered Mary.

"I know Dan personally. I leased him a flat on Belvedere Road. Your interpretation is the message he is trying to deliver."

Mary was confused. "I think I'll stick to making my name in the theatre. It has form, meaning, and content with beginnings, middles and ends, although not necessarily in that order.

"That's why you'll love living in the East End," said Bling suddenly remembering he was in the real-estate business.

"The area has attracted some very gifted young writers, actors and directors who could not afford the prices of Central London. They took over some of the old music hall theatres like the Half Moon, the Orleans and the Blue Elephant, and produced updated versions of classics like *Murder In The Cathedral*. Most recently, the area has become a hotbed of experimental works, the new fringe theatre, if you will."

"The new fringe theatre. What's that?" asked Mary.

"It's like America's Off-Broadway. Contemporary material, inexpensively produced with the hope of critical acclaim and a move to the West End, where the big money resides."

"I assume the productions are uneven."

"That's why it's called fringe. The works are not yet ready for mainstream commercial audiences willing to pay big ticket prices. But much of the material is quite good, the actors quite polished and the productions surprising inventive and arresting. Many moons ago, Tom Stoppard began his rise to fame on the East End."

"I had no idea."

"I would think the East End Fringe Theatre would be an ideal starting place for a young, aggressive theatrical agent looking to build a client list."

Mary was impressed by Bling's analysis. "I would think the competition for clients is intense."

"Actually not. The conventional agents are looking for the polished, stage-ready property. You know 'diamonds in the rough' need not apply. Nobody seems to have figured out that the young bucks—despite all their bravado—recognize their work needs retooling for mainstream commercialization and are quite open to professional criticism.

"Do you know any diamonds in the rough?"

"Absolutely."

"So what do I have to do to get a referral?"

"Rent this next apartment I'm about to show you. It's the best piece of inventory in the docks area. And, it would be a sublet from writer-director David Marks."

"Who's David Marks?"

"A true diamond in the rough you will want to know. A future superstar...with the right agent advising and working with him.

"Where's he off to?"

"One of David's recent plays, *Hell and Other Funny Places,* had a delightful run on the East Side. It was picked up by the Theatre Royal on Drury Lane, and opened two weeks ago to sell-out crowds. Between advances and buy-outs, David's got a few quid in his pocket for the first time, so he decided to move to Covent Garden. David writes, directs and lives reality. He's never laughed in his life. His middle initial is 'I.' It stands for intensity."

"Are we white lying just a little bit?"

Bling's mobile phone rang. "Understand. No problem. About ten minutes is fine..." That was David. He's just getting out of the shower. He wants to show you the apartment right now. You can decide for yourself."

Minutes later, they were at the end of an inactive dock tucked in a harbor alcove and filled with first-floor retail establishments. The sun was glistening off the calm waters. "David's apartment is the corner flat," said Bling, pointing to two large picture windows that occupied the corner of the building. As you're about to see, the flat has uninterrupted views of the river 24 hours a day."

The door opened at the top of a tiny staircase. There stood a skinny, long-haired, thirty-something male in torn jeans, torn sneakers and a dirty tee shirt. "I assume you're Mary," scowled the man, "I'm David. Might as well come in and take a look around. That's what you're here for."

Bling nodded at Mary as if to say, was I right or was I right? "Mary, you'll find the apartment is particularly spacious and filled with light. There is even something rare in London—ample closets. To add to the feeling of spaciousness David had done a nice job of using white glossy paint and strategically placing mirrors to magnify the view. And, the kitchen has all modern appliances."

"The kitchen's wonderful. David, do you like to cook?"

"No."

"Have you thought about leaving the mirrors and what you'd want for them?"

"You can have them."

"I'll take it," said Mary.

"Don't you want to think about it?" questioned a surprised Marks.

"What's there to think about? I like the place. The price is fair. I can move right in."

"Mary," said Bill, "How about we celebrate over a sandwich and a pint at St. Katherine's Dock. My treat."

"The food's not very good. Too greasy," mumbled Marks.

"And, you would suggest...." asked Mary not expecting a response.

"The food court at the Truman Brewery."

"That place is gigantic. I wouldn't know where to start. I couldn't even decipher some of the food on the menus. They were quite exotic."

"Suit yourself. The food is great and cheap. If you want I can show you the best places to nibble."

Bling laughed. "David rarely comes up for air, much less invites people to lunch. He must be very fond of you my dear."

"I'm not buying, I'm just showing," responded Marks in clipped fashion.

"Just out of curiosity," rebutted Mary," does expending all that energy, delivering monosyllabic responses ever build your appetite?" She thought her sarcasm terribly humorous.

Neither Marks nor Bling caught Mary's send-up.

She pantomimed raising her hands to her mouth to simulate eating, then pointed two fingers at the men and began walking toward the door. They stared blankly.

She mimicked Mark's primitive conversational structure.

"Enough banter. Are you hungry? Let's go to the Truman. Have some lunch. You select, I buy."

Marks finally smiled a shy smile. "Am I that bad?"

"Worse," smiled Mary.

"I'm starved. Let's eat. You're going to love the Paraguayan *pollo conquistador*."

"Whatever," smiled Mary.

By the time lunch ended, Marks was speaking in multi-syllabic sentences, smiling at Mary's wry sense of humor and giving her two front-row tickets for *Plummet & Friends*. He also suggested they meet again for lunch, sans Bill Bling, and even offered to buy.

14

~~~

WITH THE FLAT ISSUE SETTLED, Mary's focus was now Belfrage.

"We should talk about Julian before your first contact. He's a bit quirky," said Annabelle Lee on the telephone.

"Translation?"

"To begin with, getting that first meeting requires a suck-up to whoever guards the gate. You must make him or her feel like you're enormously beholden for permitting the king to step down from his throne and meet you."

"You must be kidding."

"Remember, this is the theatre business. That means a platter of show with just a smidgen of substance. Once you get through the gatekeeper and meet the king, your noteworthy persona has got to smack him right in the face. Subtlety is not a Belfrage strong point."

"How does Julian define 'noteworthy persona'?"

"Something unique that draws attention to you. He's convinced unless you get the attention of playwrights, directors and investors, you have nothing. Think television adverts. Unless somebody sees and remembers the advert, it doesn't matter what you're selling."

"Translation?"

"He has to believe there is something about you that can make him or one of his associates money. Remember, there are only two currencies in the theatre business: hard cash and favors owed."

"Any ideas? Elizabeth hated my initial thoughts."

"That's up to you honey. Just keep your mind open, and stay flexible. Look at the careers of some of his friends...Elton John, Elvis Costello, and Boy George."

"So, you're suggesting I become a rocker?" teased Mary.

"Be serious! I'm merely suggesting that you devise a persona that's relevant to the theatrical community."

Mary was in need of inspiration. She turned to two old friends, her mirror and a few sticks of cannabis sativa. One evening, after getting totally stoned, divine insight arrived. She would position herself as the wholesome, ruthless cultural diva, who could smell an important young playwright or a commercially viable property 10 kilometers away.

Position clear in her mind, Mary needed the appropriate wardrobe. First stop was the Sunday morning markets on Middlesex Street. There she found two outrageous outfits, replete with short skirts, colorful wigs, fishnet stockings and form-fitting private parts designed to turn heads equally in London's Chelsea, Battersea and the West End. After a few rehearsals in front of her mirror, Mary developed a sensuous swagger that accentuated her well-proportioned figure and shapely legs. To complete the package, she decided on an exaggerated intonation, not unlike the old movie icon, Bette Davis. "Daaarling this, daaarling that," became her salutation of choice.

She figured once she had Belfrage, and prospective clients for that matter, in her sights, her theatrical knowledge, creative sensibilities and engaging personality would seal the deal.

~

Ready to road-test the sum total of her first week's activities in London, she invited Marks to dinner.

"I've been working on my persona. Tomorrow I'm going to crash Julian's office."

"I'm not sure I understood what you just said. But it sounded like there was a free dinner in there somewhere, so the answer is yes."

"Where shall we meet?"

"You're the East Ender."

"There's a great little Indian restaurant, Tommy Bok Toy's, on the India Street Wharf."

"You're having me on."

"No, truly," said Marks, "the India Street Wharf is not far from the old tanneries. As I understand it, sailors from India used to dock their merchant ships on the East End to unload dyes and silks that were used by the tanneries to make bolts of high end fabrics."

Mary laughed. "I meant an Indian restaurant named Tommy Bok Toy's."

"Haven't got a clue," laughed Marks.

Marks arrived first. He selected a quiet corner table and ordered a pint of Kingfisher Ale. The glass was three-quarters empty when a woman arrived who looked vaguely like the Mary he had met recently. Marks couldn't believe his eyes. Mary walked over, smiled, gave him a kiss on the cheek and sat down. "So, daaarling…so, what do you think?"

"About what?" asked Marks not sure how to respond.

"My Belfrage persona."

"I must be a little daft, what did you just say?"

"I want to stand out when I see Julian tomorrow…you know, so I'd get the job."

"As what? A hooker. You must be crazy thinking Julian Belfrage will react positively to that ghastly outfit. Who is advising you?"

"That's your opinion."

"And, that phony exaggerated accent. It makes me barf."

The gauntlet was thrown. Mary decided to rise to the challenge. After all, she had the inside track from Annabelle Lee on what moved the man.

"Tell you what. Let's make a little wager. If I get the job, you buy me dinner for the week."

"And, if I win?"

Impossiüble," responded Mary with an exaggerated French accent.

"Let's just suppose."

"Then you pick the prize."

"I get to shag you for an evening."

Mary was taken aback.

"Mary, there's more to the world than becoming a goddamn theatrical agent."

She paused to reflect on Mark's comment. He was right, but she wasn't ready to get off the moving parade anytime soon.

"So...do we have a deal?" pressed Marks extending his hand across the table.

Mary smiled. "David, I think there is something I need to tell you.'

"Let me guess," teased David. "You're a transvestite."

Mary took a deep breath. She wished she didn't have to but...No, but I am a lesbian."

"You're kidding." David genuinely found Mary attractive for all the right and wrong reasons.

"Are you telling me, you're absolutely and positively committed to that persuasion forever and ever, regardless of opportunities, circumstances, curiosities and interests?"

Mary smiled. "I'm not sure I could say yes to such an all-encompassing query. I've never thought about it in such terms."

David reached his hand across the table. "Then let's just agree, 'Deal,' and cross that bridge when we come to it."

Mary made a funny facial expression as she turned up her nose. She was thinking. David did have a terribly quick wit. And, there was no doubt he had a certain gritty attractiveness. She figured. What the hell. Who knows? Never is a long, long time. And, it had been almost seven years since Bobbie O'Toole.

~

The company name, Belfrage and Associates, was meant to be as sedate and stylish as his choice of office location, design, furniture and accompanying accoutrements. Belfrage planned every last detail, and every detail had a purpose. The walls were a mixture of polished English walnut and smoked glass to capture the magnificent 27th and 28th floor views of Central London. The furniture was understated Italian, mostly dark cream, burnt burgundy and camel-colored. Museum-quality antiques appeared randomly placed (although they were not). Despite the opulence and grandeur, the place was meant to feel comfortable and inviting.

The office had three goals: make investors feel their money was with an unquestioned winner, telegraph that Belfrage was a man of exquisite taste to snobby "A" List directors, and convince playwrights that Belfrage representation was tantamount to membership in a very exclusive club.

"Daaarling, you must be Sarah Fender. Such a pleasure. I'm Mary Jones, we spoke on the phone. I believe I have a ten o'clock with Julian?" said Mary confidently to the sophisticated, long-haired receptionist, who doubled as Belfrage's personal assistant and gatekeeper.

The slender, attractive black-haired Sarah, a girl from middle-class background who had grown into a polished sophisticate in her three years as Belfrage's personal assistant, winced at the sight of what she concluded was a tasteless, vulgar transient. The dress, the wig, the fishnet stocking, etc. She decided to protect her boss from this lowlife until she had a chance to prepare him properly. "Goodness, I'm so, so sorry. A bit of an emergency has arisen, could we reschedule? Mr. Belfrage has been called out of town. He'll return in a fortnight."

"Oh dear," said Mary, noticing Belfrage, from pictures she had seen, sitting behind the desk in his office, door slightly ajar. Best Mary could tell he was merely reading some documents.

"Why don't I just say bon voyage," said Mary, as she confidently strutted into Belfrage's office.

"Julian, dear, Mary Jones. You know, Annabelle Lee's niece," said Mary confidently reaching over to shake Belfrage's hand. "According to your delightful assistant Sarah, I gather you'll be unable to keep our appointment. Some business emergency?" Mary dared him to ask her to leave. Sarah stood silently in the doorway. Belfrage looked at his calendar, scanned Mary and nodded to Sarah. "I think we can squeeze you in before I have to go."

Face saved, Sarah closed the door.

"So Annabelle Lee tells me you want to be a theatrical agent? Why in God's name? With your arts background, I would think your preference would be academia."

Mary sat down and crossed her legs, black panties purposely in full view. She spoke directly, economically and forcefully, with no airs or accents. "Sir, I get a rush from the excitement of live theatre. I also think my DNA is programmed to identify commercial successes, I have great rapport with directors and playwrights and, like you, I enjoy the good life that money and power can offer."

Belfrage was impressed by Mary's clarity of response, but found her physical appearance off- putting. "My dear," said Belfrage leaning back in his chair. "It's only June."

"I beg your pardon," said a confused Mary.

"I was just wondering why you're dressed in your Halloween costume so early?"

Mary sank in her chair. Either she'd misunderstood Annabelle Lee, or things had changed. She was about to find out. It was the latter.

"I can almost guess what the hell this is all about, Annabelle Lee," volunteered Belfrage. "That's one of the reasons we're no longer married. When I met Annabelle Lee, I was a struggling agent. I needed a persona. She called it a 'shtick' after some damn Jewish-American phrase I never quite understood. In the early days, she was helpful. She was as outrageous as I was. Once I started to represent big-time clients, it was time to become proper English. Today, Belfrage and Associates reeks of breeding, aristocracy, implied wealth, infinite good taste. That's where the big money rests."

"I'm sorry."

"No need to be sorry. I sat you down and asked you a tough question right out of the box. Your answer was superb and articulate. More importantly, it was honest and passionate. There aren't many young people who have that kind of effect on old Julian."

"Thank you."

"So what do you want?"

"To be a smashing good theatrical agent."

"I know that. I meant how much money do you need?"

"Enough to cover the rent, food, transportation and some lifestyle essentials."

"Such as?"

"Well, I like to dine out with friends, have the occasional pint, and attend the theatre."

"You'll get all the tickets you ever need here, plus before long—if you're any good that is—you'll be joining me and our clients at dinner all over town. I'll pay you £500 a week plus some."

Mary felt she was worth more than that and began to negotiate. She didn't understand the "plus some." "Julian, this is London."

"Mary, dear, this isn't a negotiation. That's THE offer. Period. You either take it or you don't. Do you know how many kids in London would kill to work for Belfrage and Associates?"

"When do I start?" smiled Mary stretching her hand out.

"As soon as you access the 'plus some' account."

"I don't want to sound stupid," chuckled Mary, "but what is a 'plus some' account?

"It means go out and buy a real wardrobe on my account. I never want to see you in this office again dressed like that. If I had a back door, I'd insist you take it."

Sarah will make the arrangements. You can use my account at Harrods. At least, I know they'll take care of you properly."

"What's the catch?" said a cautious Mary assuming she had met Belfrage all of a half hour and he was already hitting on her. It was not the way she wished to enter her chosen profession.

"The catch? What the hell are you talking about?"

Mary stopped dead in her tracks.

"You just better be as good as Annabelle says….no, *better.* This company has an image in the creative community that took ten years to build. Understand?"

"Perfectly." Mary again paused. "What's my budget?"

"I thought we understood each other," smiled Belfrage. 'Plus some.' I expect you to report for work day after tomorrow."

"Done."

Mary went straight to Harrods and had the time of her life. She bought two Armani work suits, an Estrada dress, two Dolce and Gabanna collecziones plus accoutrements that included six pair of Jimmy Choo shoes, four Versace blouses and several Prada handbags. She spent £21,376… plus some.

~

"May I make one more suggestion," said the Harrods salesperson.

"Sure," said Mary.

"The hair must go," said the lady pointing to Mary's red curly hair.

"But that's me," protested Mary.

"Was you, about £20,000 ago."

Two hours later, a long, straight black-haired Mary departed Harrods beauty salon.

15

~~~

"DAVID, WHAT ARE WE DOING TONIGHT to celebrate?" crowed Mary on the telephone to her new best friend.

"You got the job?"

"Done deal."

"When do you start?"

"Thursday."

"I'm impressed. Guess I was wrong."

Mary bit her tongue. She wanted to tell him he actually won, in person.

"A celebratory toast at St. Elizabeth's pub around six? I'm buying."

"Done," said Mary.

She purposely arrived 15 minutes late in order to see David's expression as she walked across the floor in her new Armani outfit and shoulder-length shiny black hair. Every pair of male eyes in the place was focused on her. She stopped and stood quietly in front of him.

"My god, is that you?" he asked incredulously.

Her eyes gleamed with pride. She turned seductively.

"You look utterly ravishing."

"Thank you."

"So tell me, to what do we owe this metamorphosis?"

"Let's just say, Belfrage barfed when he saw my original persona."

"Hallelujah, wisdom survives! Good guys can still finish first. Exquisite taste has not been relegated to the trash heap. And the new expensive clothes? That is a genuine Armani, is it not?"

"He gave me a 'plus some' account."

"What the hell is that?"

"He sent me to Harrods on his account. Told me to buy whatever I needed and to show up for work ready to properly represent Belfrage and Associates."

"And the agreed accommodation?"

"Whatever are you talking about?"

"No wealthy middle-aged man spends that kind of money on a beautiful young woman without strings attached."

"Trust me, he's a really nice guy."

David wasn't convinced, but there were more important matters. "Does that mean I won the bet?"

"Yes, it means you won the bet."

"Does it mean there may still be hope for a man in your life?"

"I'm not sure about that," said Mary, referring to long-term commitments.

David appeared frustrated. Mary realized he misunderstood. "I'm not ready for any long-term commitment at the moment. It's career first."

"Smashing. Truly smashing," said a suddenly transformed David. "How about after dinner we pick up a few of your things, and we show you my new apartment in Chelsea?"

"I don't think so," responded Mary.

"I'm totally confused," said an again frustrated David.

Mary raised a tiny red silk Prada bag and smiled deliciously. "I believe I already have everything I'll need."

~

Marks made them pepper-and-brie omelets and French roast coffee as they watched the sun rise. "That was delicious," said Mary, scrapping her plate empty. I had no idea you were such a great cook."

"And, I had no idea you were god's gift to men." smiled Marks.

"Thank you," smiled Mary, who had enjoyed herself immensely. David was everything Bobbie had not been. Her heretofore firm convictions with respect to her sexual orientation had been shaken. But it was not a conversation for that moment.

"How about a return engagement?" pressed David.

"Sorry, love. Rain-check. Mary's gotta get a few hours sleep before her first full day at the office."

David called a cab. He didn't want her wandering into the tube in the wee hours of the morning. It was still not the best of neighborhoods. No point in tempting fate.

Once the cab arrived, Mary gave David a tender kiss goodbye and headed home.

An exhausted Marks pulled the sheets over his head to shield the morning light and went back to sleep.

~

"Far as I can go, Madame," said the cabbie with a turban. "Everything is dead end streets. No outlets."

"I thought you knew where to go."

"Old neighborhood. Street changes not yet in book. New to London."

"Great," said a frustrated Mary. "Just freakin' great." She had a vague idea she wasn't far from her apartment, so she tossed a five-pound bill on the front seat and headed west. As she wandered the empty streets, she paused to watch the glorious yellow and purple sunrise make its way over the glistening Thames, and to reflect on her good fortune of the last few days and her newfound friendships in Bling, Marks and Belfrage.

Suddenly, out of nowhere, a rotund, bearded figure sneaked up behind her and pulled the Prada bag from her shoulder. She looked for help. There was none to be had. Mary became indignant and angry. She started to scream and chase the huffing and puffing man down a dark, dead-end street. "I have you right where I want you, you bastard," she screamed as she took off her long, thick Dolce & Gabanna belt with a huge metal buckle at the end. She swung it as hard as she could; the chubby man tried to duck. The buckle slashed his cheek. Blood began to squirt down his white cotton shirt.

"Crazy bitch! Here take back," said the terrified robber named Mujib, in some combination of English and Arabic. The fear in the man's eyes further enflamed Mary's rage. She slashed the man again, this time opening a deep wound in his chin. Mujib lay whining and wallowing in a pool of his own blood. Mary picked up her bag and kicked him in the groin.

Mujib's two buddies, less than a block away, heard the commotion and came running. Mary now found herself trapped. Mujib stood behind her with her belt buckle in his hand while the other two burly, bearded Arabs blocked the front.

"Crazy lady, beat shit out of Mujib. Now your turn!"

Mary tried to scream. One of the men held his hand over her mouth while the other tied her hands behind her back. The more she tried to resist the more they punched her in the face. Blood was streaming from her mouth and nose. As Ghulam prepared to rape Mary, she vigorously shook her head from side to side, struggling to free herself.

A nearby policeman had just come on duty and followed the strange sounds of pain and whimpering which lead him to Mary and her three friends.

"Stop, you bastards," screamed the policeman as he blew his whistle for assistance. The three men dropped her torn bag and dashed down the alleyway. Within minutes, Mary was placed in ambulance, administered oxygen, some intravenous fluids and rushed to the emergency room at nearby Mile Hospital where she received 26 stitches, a heavy dose of painkillers and some Valium to relax her.

"Officers," said the doctor on duty, "I would suggest you let the young lady rest. You can take her statement when she's regained some of her strength."

~

At 3 p.m. the detectives returned.

Taking her statement was more like an inquisition with certain presumed behavior.

"Madame, what were you doing walking the streets in that neighborhood so early in the morning."

"I had just spent the evening at a friend's house," said Mary.

"And, your friend let you wander the streets? By any chance did you and your friend take any drugs?"

"No. It wasn't like that."

"Like what? You do know prostitution is against the law."

An indignant Mary sat up in bed. "Are you people daff? I got my arse kicked by three men who robbed me then tried to sexually assault me and you're accusing me of prostitution! What about the three men? Apprehend the bastards. Isn't that your job?"

"Notice you're wearing some pretty nice clothes. Let me guess, you saved the money to buy those clothes working as a checker in the local Saintsbury supermarket."

"My new boss bought them for me."

"Is that what we call your pimp these days? A boss."

"You're twisting my words."

"Lady, we've been through this a hundred times with women like you. We chase them down. Bring them to court. Some public defender says it's your word against theirs. Then he pulls out your police records or a diary of your customers, and *puff!* the case goes up in smoke."

A frustrated, dejected and tender Mary was released from the hospital a few hours later. It was now 7 p.m. She had one goal and one goal only–to look presentable by the time she walked into Belfrage and Associates at 9 a.m. the next morning.

~

Considering I got the crap beat out of me yesterday, I don't look half bad, thought Mary as she stared in her mirror after hastily applying makeup and lipstick the next morning. An hour later she was having her first meeting with Belfrage.

"Mary, I've been thinking about the best way to jumpstart your career, help the firm and get you a big commission check," said an initially oblivious Belfrage. "I've talked to some of your old director friends in Brighton. They tell me you can bullshit with the best of them despite your tender age."

"I prefer the term 'persuasively dialogue.'"

"I'm thinking we should have a party at my place and invite all the up-and-coming playwrights and directors in town. I'll introduce you as the firm's hot new associate. You can then work the room, 'persuasively dialogue,' build your own contact data base and ...."

The makeup was starting to wear thin. Belfrage suddenly noticed the bruises on her face and legs. "Mary, whatever happened to you?"

"I had a bit of a run-in."

"With what, a Saintsbury's convoy?"

"No, three bullies down by the docks." She explained her version of the facts, carefully leaving out the Marks bet and rendezvous.

"Obviously, the party went longer than it should. I was having such a great time chatting with all the artsy types. I let the time slip away. Next thing I know, it's pretty late. I'm walking back to my flat alone because the cabbie doesn't know the docks area very well."

"Christ, walking home? In the docks area? Don't tell me you actually plan on living in the dock's area?"

"For a bit. It's really a coming area. And, the views from my flat are quite spectacular."

"Mary, this is London. This isn't some seaside town. That is not the area for an attractive, single woman."

"That's not what the realtor said."

"Mary think about it, what's he going to say? 'I'd like to show you a cute flat in a dangerous neighborhood.'"

"Bill wouldn't lie."

"Who's Bill?"

"My realtor, Bill Bling."

"Bling? You must be joking."

"Do you know him?"

" He's a hack writer. Been trying to make it for years. I wondered what the hell he was doing."

"He mentioned something about the theatre."

"How much does the flat cost?"

"Let's say it's within my budget constraints."

"Stop being coy. How much?"

"£500 a month."

"£500 a month with a water view in London? Does that price include a roof and walls?"

"Really Julian, it's a cute little flat. Tuesday night could have happened to anybody, anywhere in this city."

As she spoke, Belfrage noticed that the new wardrobe, hairdo and makeup had transformed Annabelle Lee's seaside bumpkin from a pseudo-hippie into a sophisticated, sensuous woman with an elegant figure and upscale carriage. The kind of woman who would make a nice addition to the collectibles at his flat.

"How about we make a deal? I'll pay off the apartment lease and you move into my place."

"I hardly think so," said Mary, silently replaying Mark's warning.

"Wait a minute, young lady. I didn't mean what you're thinking. I live by myself in a four- bedroom, 20,000-foot, two-story flat not far from here in Knightsbridge among London's *crème de la crème*. I'm happy to share temporarily with no strings attached. You can come and go as you please while you learn the business and save some money for that ultimate place of your own."

"No strings attached," echoed Mary cautiously.

"Just think of it as the last installment of my Annabelle Lee settlement. After all, she did give me eight great years."

~

Belfrage sensed Mary was weakening, so he went for the close.

"Listen. No pressure. Take a walk through the place by yourself. Make your own decision. I think you'll find the flat large enough that we can go days, maybe weeks without running into each other," said Belfrage sporting a big puppy-dog smile.

Mary looked into his eyes, shrugged her shoulders and nodded acceptance. Belfrage went over to his desk, opened a drawer and handed her a key to his flat. "I think you should make this your first order of business, so we can get down to the business of the business."

As Mary headed for the door, she turned to ask, "About the £3,000 I owe you for my lease. How much time do I have to repay you?"

"Forget it. Think of it as a signing bonus...there's only one condition."

Ahhh, thought Mary, *finally THE catch*!

That name...Mary Jones has got to go. Sounds terribly lowbrow."

"But that's my real name."

"The Theatre has nothing to do with reality."

"Well I did file for a stage name."

"And, it is…."

"Mary Jackson-Peale."

"Lovely, utterly lovely. Who is she?"

"What do you mean who is she?"

"Her personality, her style, her DNA."

"God, I don't know."

"How about we start with self-confident, intuitive in-sightful and sexually alluring but neither braggadocio or over-bearing."

"Goodness, how did we come to compose a dream lady?"

"Guess she's been sequestered in Julian's subconscious."

16

~~~

MARY ARRIVED UNANNOUNCED because Belfrage
inadvertently neglected to alert Sarah to notify his concierge,
Rodney T. Rathman.

"Good morning, Madame, you're here to see whom?"
asked the pompous, gray-haired concierge. Rathman understood full well that protecting the anonymity of the building's
super rich owners was his primary job function. He sensed
Mary, clothes to the contrary, was not of the Knightsbridge
socioeconomic strata.

"Actually, I'm not here to see anyone. I'm Mary Jackson-
Peale. Mr. Belfrage wanted me to have a peek at his flat."

"For what purpose, might I ask?"

"For the purpose of moving in," she snarled impatiently.

The concierge refused to be intimidated. "Are you a partial sublet?"

"No, I'm a friend and business associate."

"Madame, Mr. Belfrage knows the rules. He has not au-
thorized entrance to any friends, paid or otherwise."

She realized he had just inferred she was a paid call girl.
She was furious. "Is this the way you treat all guests of the
owners? Do you have a phone?" He handed her the phone;
she snapped it out of his hands and dialed Belfrage. She explained what had just transpired with a few expletives thrown
in for good measure. "Here, he wants to talk to you. What's
your name?"

"Rodney."

"Julian, here is that rude man Rodney."

Rodney took the phone, eyes bulging and hands shaking.
"Yes, Mr. Belfrage. I understand Mr. Belfrage. Certainly, right
away, Mr. Belfrage."

Rodney hung up the phone. "So sorry, Madame. You understand I was just doing my job. Let me escort you to the
elevator."

"It's okay, Rodney. Really," said Mary graciously.

The elevator arrived and the door opened. "Biddle, please
take Miss Jones to the 12th floor. She is a guest of Mr.
Belfrage. And no stops, please. We've already delayed Madame enough."

"I understand, sir," smiled Biddle. Rodney then smiled
and tipped his hat as the elevator door closed.

Mary glanced around subtly, overwhelmed by the opulent
polished brass, rich walnut burl and gold filigree elevator inte-
rior.

"Here we are, Madame. Twelve."

"Which way is Mr. Belfrage's flat?"

"This is Mr. Belfrage's flat," said Biddle waving his arms
down the halls to his right and left. "The entrance foyer is off
to the left, through those double doors."

Mary opened the doors. In front stood a two-story carved
glass-and-brass marble staircase. Beyond that were floor-to-
ceiling windows, 12 feet high by some 200 feet long. All of
London was in full view. To the right and left on the first
floor was the entertainment complex: a 24 seat dining room,
circular step-down living room, a billiards center, paneled li-

brary and bar to rival the Grosvenor House on Park Lane, and a minitheatre replete with stage and curtains for the impromptu performance, rehearsal or audition. Off the staircase on the second floor were four fully-equipped master suites. In the center was a considerable exercise room filled with the latest electronic gadgetry and a spa that also overlooked the city. Both floors had wide, heated wrap-around balconies with fully stocked wet bars that added another 2,000 square feet to the cramped flat!

~

"So, what do you think?" asked Belfrage when Mary returned to the office.

"The accommodations are a little tight, but I'll make do," she teased.

"When do you want to move in? I'll make arrangements."

"Tomorrow would be lovely."

"When you move in, we celebrate with a catered dinner from Pétrus."

"Pétrus?"

"A neighborhood place I frequent." (In reality, Pétrus was a Michelin three-star-rated restaurant housed in the Berkley Hotel, London's most exclusive hotel.) But Belfrage was partially correct. It was two blocks from his Knightsbridge flat.

Mary spent the next 24 hours reviewing the company database so she could learn the names, preferences and idiosyncrasies of every Belfrage client and prospect.

"Hey, workalcoholic, time to go," said Belfrage.

"But it's only four o'clock," said Mary looking at her watch.

"It's Friday. Nobody in theatre, other than actors and directors, actually perform until Monday morning. Besides, cocktails and canapés arrive at 6 p.m."

~

When the couple arrived at the apartment, each went to their respective suites, as advertised. After Mary showered and shampooed, she went to the closet to select one of the new outfits she had bought at Harrods. There on a padded hanger inside the door was a deliciously low-cut Versace white silk dress with a racy side slit and all the matching accoutrements—shoes, belts, jewelry and perfume. A small white envelope was pinned to the dress that read, "To our new partnership. Enjoy. See you in the library at six. Fondly, Julian."

The dress fit like a glove. She looked every bit a poster model for Versace, Gucci or St. Laurent although she wondered if the ensemble was a little over the top for a delivered meal. That concern was answered the moment she walked into the library. There stood a tuxedoed Julian holding a martini glass and standing next to a tuxedoed *maitre dé*.

"Cosmopolitans or martinis, anyone?" smiled Julian.

"A cosmopolitan would be lovely."

"No, you are lovely. A cosmopolitan is merely refreshing."

"Roger, please accommodate the lady's every wish…I've taken the liberty of ordering dinner; I hope you don't mind."

"I feel as though I'm being terribly spoiled."

"You are. This is my motivational dinner. I expect substantial returns on my investment."

Mary wasn't sure if that was an intentional *double entendre*, but she wasn't about to waste the evening fretting over it. Everything smelled far too scrumptious.

"Roger, perhaps you can explain tonight's fare."

"Very good sir."

"Madame, Chef Marcus Waring has selected a number of off-menu items to surprise and delight you since he wasn't sure how frequently you dine at Pétrus."

"How very thoughtful," said Mary, kicking Belfrage under the table like an excited teenager.

"Tonight's amuse bouche is quail eggs in mini-pastry baskets. Our appetizer is a delightful ham and foie gras terrine. And, the entrée is one of the chef's personal favorites, braised turbot with Welsh rarebit glaze. Hopefully, Madame will save some room for dessert Valrhona chocolate fondue with butterscotch sauce and Devonshire clotted cream. Upon my dismissal, I shall also leave a bon bon trolley should you require a late night intermediary."

Mary had an absolute ball. She felt like a queen. Belfrage remained the perfect gentleman throughout. When the feast ended, Belfrage mentioned Sarah was organizing a "Belfrage" theatre party. He also suggested Mary spend time with Sarah to learn the basics of theatrical finance from the playwright and director's point of view.

"While I don't expect someone to come straight out and ask you about financial terms, it's also better to be prepared for any eventuality. Too many agents take the easy way out and try to do it all on personality and relationships. They haven't read the tea leaves."

It was 1 a.m. Mary couldn't believe Belfrage's focus. She was being given some critical words of wisdom that would one day make her a huge success. She realized then and there, theatrical representation was not all gloss and glitter. It was a business where people continually asked what have you done for me today. Belfrage made himself a major West End Theatre brand by practicing what he preached—although Mary was to discover fairly quickly that his untold riches did not always adhere to the straight and narrow.

At that moment, Mary decided she wanted to be like Belfrage. Only bigger and better..

Dinner and class over, they each retired to their respective suites. No questions asked. No extracurricular activities suggested.

~

"Sarah, Julian said you're working on the guest list for the client-prospect cocktail party."

"You mean Mary's coming-out party, don't you," giggled the outspoken Sarah, who had decided getting cozy with Belfrage's latest fair-haired girl couldn't hurt her chances for advancement. Besides, as an undeclared lesbian, she found Mary's new persona rather exhilarating.

"Mr. B. seems intent on making you the organization's new star *du jour*. I've never seen him wax so about a theatrical assistant. They tend to come and go through here as if there were a swinging door."

"Why so? Is Julian that difficult a taskmaster?"

Sarah wanted to tell her the truth—Belfrage was a dirty old man who duped new employees to his lair—primarily attractive females like Mary—pledging a no-strings, arms-length understanding that eventually became a sex-for-boarding proposition. But Sarah was convinced shocking revelations at this stage of the Mary-Julian relationship would sound like sour grapes on her part, or worse still, jealous rage.

"It's not Julian so much as the business," said Sarah. "The writers and directors all think they are God's gift to the arts. You've got to coddle and spoil them like rotten little misguided children, which they are, of course. Some of the shit—pardon the expression—that passes my desk as submissions...you wouldn't believe it. And they all think they have the next Pulitzer Prize. What directors call avante-garde these days, I label as indecipherable metaphors and symbols concocted while half-stoned in an alternate state of consciousness."

"Sarah," Mary laughed, "you seem to have a feel for the business. Do you have aspirations beyond administrative assistant?"

Sarah couldn't resist a moment of truth. "Not here. That would require a sleep-in with Mr. B. He's definitely not my type."

"I'm not sure you've got him right. I've been living at his flat for two weeks and he has been nothing but the perfect gentleman."

Sarah smiled knowingly. "Don't worry, your night will come. My guess is he's decided you're the type that requires more nurturing than most."

"That's gibberish," responded Mary, thinking Sarah did sound like sour grapes.

"Candidly," said Sarah, "I prefer women. Mr. B. knows that. I just find them more predictable, more sensitive lovers."

Mary thought Sarah a bit brash and certainly less than subtle but quite charming in the way she declared her sexual preference."

"And, what about you?"

"Can't say. I'm partial to either exclusively at this stage of my life although I will confide Elizabeth was head and shoulders above the rest." Mary paused, her mind flashed to those halcyon moments with Elizabeth.

"Who's Elizabeth? I'm all ears," said Sarah. "Let's have a good gossip. What happened?"

"It's a long story, much of which I still don't understand nor have I come to closure. Another time maybe." Mary sat down next to Sarah, not realizing the top two buttons on her blouse had slipped open.

"My, I realize why Elizabeth would be so fond of you," cooed Sarah feeling more comfortable and getting brasher with each passing minute.

"Sarah, is that a nice thing to say to your new boss," responded Mary trying to be demure.

"My dear, who are you kidding?" responded Sarah, crossing her extremely shapely legs. "If you didn't want me to have a gander, wouldn't you have been a teensy bit more conservative?"

Mary shook her head. She was not about to debate the implications of open buttons.

"By the way, Mary Poppins," challenged Sarah, "tell me you weren't scanning my arse when I bent over at the filing cabinet?"

"Those rose colored panties clash terribly with your outer wear," smiled Mary.

"So, I was right," nodded Sarah looking skyward.

A few nearby deskbound employees stared.

"Why don't we finish this conversation over drinks one evening," whispered Mary. "Right now, we really must deal with the party. I need to gather a few clients and start those commission checks rolling in."

"I agree," said Sarah thinking a bit more romantically. "Except, let's make it dinner."

"Deal! The night after the party," said Mary.

Sarah was clearly a crackerjack organizer. She had picked 150 names from the database, got them personally cleared through Belfrage, had invitations designed, printed and mailed. Each with a personally handwritten comment that appeared to come from Julian himself.

Within a week of the mailing, there was an 85 percent RSVP rate. Sarah called the remaining 15 percent herself. Ultimately 95 percent of the invitees attended the party.

17

~~~

"SARAH TELLS ME YOU'VE STUDIED the profiles and pictures of all the invitees, and that you've created some kind of cheat sheet to carry around."

"Let's just say I have been doing my homework. Sarah has been a fantastic help."

"It all sounds terribly organized," said Belfrage. "Be very careful nobody sees you looking at the damn paper during the evening. This is supposed to be a spontaneous party where people laugh, drink and have a good time. Blatant commerciality spoils the stew. And when this is over, I'd like to assign Sarah to you. She's a little too brash and outspoken for my tastes. The other important thing you can accomplish during the next few days is to understand how theatre economics work and what we tell and don't tell our various constituencies. Grab a notepad. Theatre Economics 101 is about to begin in the main conference room."

Moments later, Julian was standing in front of an over-sized, dry, white eraser board in the conference room. He paused and then walked over to the telephone. "Sarah, hold the calls for the next few hours, and have Jason's Deli send up two toasted double-cheese and ham sandwiches and two bottles of Evian."

"You just ordered my favorite sandwich in the whole world."

"I know."

"You know," said Mary incredulously.

"That's sidebar number one, always know your customer's little personal fetishes. Make sure you can do that with everybody who walks through the door next Monday. Now let's deal with my favorite part of the business. Sources of revenue. As a theatrical agent, we have to look at each project as having three, sometimes four, individual revenue streams....for us.

"First and foremost are the investors. They provide the working capital to launch a project. Without them, the greatest script in the world is not going anywhere.

"Since my track record for picking winners is unparalleled in the industry, investors are lined up at the door. We take a finder's fee off the money raised, usually 5 to 10 percent, depending upon how hot the property looks and who's the original cast and/or director. Naturally, I do a little pump-priming with the critics to heighten anticipation. That investment usually returns an extra 5 percent."

Mary thought to herself, *he's arrogant and obnoxious, but he certainly knows his stuff.*

"Surprisingly, the next revenue stream is related to the actual production of the show. We attempt to negotiate approval rights on set design and wardrobe so that wherever possible, we assign the business to our sources, which have previously agreed to pay us a sales commission for including them in the project. That typically is about 7 ½ percent of all gross spending. That item never hits the production's financial statements, if you know what I mean."

"Understood, perfectly," said Mary, thinking off-the-books kickback.

"Then we receive a 'quiet' percentage of the gross from the theatre owners for placing the Belfrage production at their theatre. And, lastly, we receive the street rate agent's commission from the director and actors' gross."

"I assume certain income streams are larger than others?"

"It's not what you think. Everybody focuses on their share from the directors and actors. At Belfrage and Associates, that represents about 20 percent of our total take. It varies from play to play, of course, but when we did a revival of *Coco*, our income from the custom-tailored costumes was worth millions. Our job is to make money in ways others only dream of, confidentially and quietly. Trust me, you can't spend £4,000 a square foot on a flat based upon commissions from actors and directors, no matter how big the hit."

"And what's our financial exposure in each production?"

"None. Zippo. Other than the risk to our reputation if we continually pick clunkers. Using a Yank baseball analogy, one miss in this business and they start warming up replacements in the bullpen; two misses and you're out of the old ball-game."

Mary nodded and wrote as fast as she could.

"Making hits also gives us certain additional opportunities to make money. For example, our lawyers draft all the contracts—-as an expense of the deal, of course. If we have a big hit on our hands, which usually means more than an average occupancy of 75 to 80 percent for nine to twelve months, we include a clause that gives us an option to buy investors out on a predetermined formula and pocket a larger share of the future gross."

"I had no idea."

"Nobody does. What I just explained to you in two hours took me 20 years to develop and market test. The fact that Belfrage and Associates easily makes five to ten times what other theatrical reps gross is our little secret. In fact, I insist

all employees sign an airtight trade secrets nondisclosure."
Belfrage then handed Mary her nondisclosure statement with
a pen. "Just sign here."

"And if I don't?"

"You can leave right now. And I'll still sue you if you try
to use anything I've just told you."

"Julian, you certainly don't mess about."

"Mary, I live by two simple rules: I'm generous to a fault,
but screw me just once and there is no second chance."
Belfrage's stare was blatantly ominous; Mary signed the paper
and moved on. "Doesn't anybody ever question the finances?"

"So long as we keep picking hits, nobody cares. In fact to
insure consumer demand, I insist our public-relations team
gives out more spiff money (bribes) for positive reviews than
the next five firms combined."

"I thought the theatre critics were supposed to be objec-
tive voices of reason?"

"Yeah, and Al Capone is about to be canonized by the
Church of England," responded Belfrage sarcastically.

"How do we position matters to directors and playwrights?"

"We keep it very simple for the artsy types. We tell them
Belfrage always guarantees them, and we do the highest percent of gross available in the market. Plus, we'll bust our butts
to insure their plays are commercial hits. They also get access
to a never-ending stream of life's little vices—men, women,
alcohol or drugs, whatever is their persuasion. My *coup de grace*
is the promise to make them a household word by getting
them feature stories in the newspapers and trade pubs, which,
by the way, always contain prominent inclusions of Belfrage
and Associates as their personal rainmakers.

"Got it," said Mary desperately trying to keep up. She
thought he actually meant Julian Belfrage.

"Then let's storm the beach on Monday," bellowed Belfrage cigar in mouth impersonating Churchill at the Normandy Beach invasion near the end of World War II.

Mary, never a history buff, wondered what beach Belfrage was referring to because London was 63 miles from the nearest coastline.

18

~~~

THE MONOTONOUS DRONE OF au courant techno music permeated every room of Belfrage's flat on tiny but powerful Bose speakers discreetly buried in the walls.

Mary had never been in a social setting with so many trendsetters and pseudo-trendsetters but attempted to blend in. It took all her self-control not to burst out laughing as she overheard the self-indulgent, pompous diatribes spewing from the mouths of the young glitterati, literati, and the older "wanna-be-young-and-outrageous" attired in pants and shirts made out of British flags, wraparound bolts of Japanese silk and sandwich boards comprised of reflective mylar bonded to styrofoam.

"Sounds like James Figurine and The Postal Service with their outrageous new album," offered a thin-as-a-rail dude with waist-length red curly hair, referring to the animated music playing on the dozen or so plasma screens dotting the walls.

"Mistake, Mistake, Mistake, Mistake!" said his thirty-something party mate, waving his arms like a windmill.

"Jonathan, I beg to differ, but I believe Jake is correct." said the third, a stubby, butch guy with a greasy, chopped black hair and black leather studded vest over a bare, shaven chest.

"Did you notice Werner's review in the *Stone*? He really nailed it. And, I quote, 'Figurine's latest is delightful compote of sweet melodies and sonic summersaults that consistently avoid appearing superfluous.'"

"Truth, man. Truth. So hard to come by these days," nodded Jake.

In another corner of the flat, existential painter Rodney Flamont was making like Jackson Pollack splattering canvases with colorful acrylics as guests waited in line to have their abstract portraits completed then blow-dried. From the length of the line, Mary surmised the party was destined to continue into the wee small hours of the morning or perhaps beyond.

Waiters, most of them gay, flamboyantly pranced around serving trays of Knightsbridge pints, a Belfrage concoction that consisted of about eight ounces of garlic flavored Smirnoff, Polish absinthe and few ounces of Cointreau (to mask the dreadful taste and potency) in 16-ounce frosted mugs filled with crushed ice. Behind the waiters trailed lusty, topless female servers offering trays of canapés, assorted party drugs such as freshly rolled joints, crystal meth, blow and PCP and small bondage toys.

Belfrage knew by midnight most of the attendees would be in another zone, so at nine he had the music turned down as he took to his stage. "First of all, thank you all for coming. You are the best and brightest creative minds in all of England."

The crowd gave themselves a big round of applause.

"Do mingle, and get to know your neighbors...while you still can."

The crowd chuckled. "Julian has one favor to ask while you're enjoying yourself. I'd like you to meet our newest theatrical agent, Mary Jackson-Peale," he said as he waved her on stage.

"Look at that, everybody. Mary's bloody shy."

The room understood Belfrage's cue and started chanting, "Mary. Mary. Mary."

Belfrage let the chants continue until Mary joined him on the stage. "You playwrights and directors out there, beware. This lady can take your best property, weave her magic and guarantee it's a commercial hit. Plus, she'll take care of all the investor financing, so your West End show will be up and running in the blink of an eye. Do as you will, but I'd make sure she gets your business card before you leave, pass out or whatever."

The crowd roared. "Suppose we're too cheap to have cards," shouted a voice from the rear.

"Then go in the bathroom and write your contact information on toilet tissue, hand towels, or whatever else you can find around there." He paused for dramatic effect. "Just leave the damn wallpaper alone. Its hand-rolled French tapestry rice paper. I'm not sure I know what the hell that means exactly, but it's obscenely expensive. Use it and I'll charge you another 10 percent of your share of show profits."

Mary, about three Knightsbridge pints into the spirit of the evening played along. "Julian, I thought we agreed 12 percent?"

"Now, Mary, we shouldn't spat in front of our guests; it's not very good business," bantered Belfrage, pleasantly surprised at Mary's quick wit and nimble footwork. "Remember, I am the boss."

"For now, Julian. For now." Mary had them eating out of her hand. Even Belfrage roared. Little did they know Mary was dead serious.

Moments later, the twosome left the stage and the techno was again throbbing. Mary was impressed at how Belfrage was able to pull off such a blatant commercial plug in the middle of this pseudo-hip gathering without anyone taking umbrage. More importantly, within 30 minutes of the announcement two dozen writers and directors stopped by to say hello and provide their business cards. Mary also received six pieces of toilet paper and three paper towels.

After the crowds left Mary's presence, a handsome, unassuming young man with a big broad smile approached. "Looks like I'm going to be in the back of the bus relative to getting a call back," said William Thomas. "Like everybody in the room, I think I have something to say artistically, but unlike most of my affected peers in the room, I am willing to take direction and make changes for the sake of commercial viability."

Mary was instantly attracted to Thomas's light blue eyes, athletic physique and wiry curly blonde hair that gave him the appearance of a Nordic warrior.

"So watcha got?" said Mary, her businesslike candor taking Thomas completely by surprise.

"Are you serious? Here? Now?"

"Why not? Blow me away!"

Thomas accepted the challenge.

"The play is called *Circumstances Yet To Occur*. It's the story of two friends who discover they belong in another order while living in today's world. An order that is both more passionate and more empathetic than our world. They decide to transport themselves to Otherland where they learn how to capture the spirit that makes hearts soar. They are committed to return to our world and make it a better place. I've purposely kept the language simple but metaphorical. I see it as the ultimate 21st Century feel-good play."

Mary paused and thought about what she had just heard. "I think I like it, but I've got some questions."

"Go," said Thomas.

"Give me a feel for set design?"

"Haven't really thought about it," responded Thomas.

Mary tactfully suggested. "I think a child-like allegorical feel might be in order. Like a page out of an *Aesop's Fables*. It will make the premise approachable. But it could be expensive...What about the music score?"

"What music score?" wondered Thomas.

"This premise could also benefit from a music score," said Mary more directly. "Imagine *Phantom* without music. Or *Spamalot*. The audience would be bored to death."

19

~~~

"SO HOW DID WE DO?" inquired Belfrage when he arrived late the next morning.

"Jolly well. After that little stage show, 30 people giving me contact information, telling me they had properties worth reviewing, including some guy with the most esoteric bullshit I've ever heard."

"Oh, you met Will Thomas. He's some piece of work. All his stuff is like that."

"Then why waste the canapés?"

"Because his dad is one of my biggest and most consistent investors. Besides, if just 5 percent of the ideas you review pan out, you'll be a busy lady during the next twelve months."

"Hopefully, with a lot more quid in my pocket."

"It will come, I promise you. It will come. That shindig burnt me out," continued Belfrage. "I'm going over to the Dover coastline for a few days of R&R. I'll be back by the weekend. Do as you will, but I would suggest a day off before you start contacting everybody. Makes your young prospects feel a bit desperate."

"Doesn't that set a terrible example for the rest of the office?"

"Just tell them you plan to work out of the house."

"That's very kind of you, Julian."

"Trust me, it's not about kindness; it's about return on investment. I don't want you to burn out too soon. I plan to make a lot of money with you in the coming years. In this business, everybody burns out at one time or another. The trick is to make it last as long as it can then get the hell out at while you're on top." On his way out, Belfrage stopped by Sarah's desk. "Sarah, I'm going down to Dover for a few days, some R&R. Will be back Tuesday. Same place. You've got the number at the Inn. Take care of Mary, make sure she doesn't work too hard. Ta Ta."

~

Sarah took Belfrage's suggestion literally." "So what is on tap for London's hot new agent this weekend?"

"Nothing, really. Thought I might take a stroll through the National Gallery. I gather there's a Dutch Masters Exhibition."

"Oh, I've heard. I believe there are also some new Rembrandts and Vermeers from the Louvre, the Met and the Rijksmuseum on loan. Mind if I join you?"

~

As usual, the National Gallery was mobbed. It seemed everybody wanted to view the Dutch Masters. After an hour's wait on line and a lot of jostling to get an acceptable look at masterpieces like *Bathsheba*, *Artist in Studio* and *Young Woman with a Water Jug*, the women had had enough.

"My flat's a short cab ride. How about we rest our feet with an afternoon cocktail?' suggested Sarah. At 3 p.m. it was drizzling, and they were unable to secure a cab. "It's not raining that hard, let's just walk along the buildings. Otherwise we could be standing here all afternoon."

Suddenly the heavens opened. Rain started falling in buckets. By the time they reached Sarah's flat they were soaked head to toe.

"You look a ghastly sight," laughed Sarah as they shook off the water in the hallway. "Your mascara is running down your cheeks. I suggest we change clothes. I have plenty, and we're about the same size. Then, as for me, it's a good stiff whiskey."

"Make that two," added Mary. "The stiffer the better."

After handing Mary a dry dress, Sarah poured each of them what amounted to a triple single-malt Laphroaig. They sat quietly across from each other on two white down pillow couches. The liquor was having the desired effect.

It's amazing how whiskey can warm the cockles," said Sarah, moving closer. "I guess that's one of the reasons there are so many alcoholics in this world."

Mary looked into Sarah's eyes. There was that feeling again. The one that Elizabeth....

Sarah's intuition told her Mary's mind was wandering. "You look quite smashing, though my frock is a tad large," offered Sarah, attempting to persuade Mary to return to the here and now.

Sarah laughed. "Too bad your breasts aren't a little larger. You don't quite fill the top appropriately."

"Are you suggesting your breasts are larger than mine?"

"Without question."

"I disagree. Prove it."

Sarah slowly unbuttoned her blouse and revealed her abundance, enveloped in a lightly wired, sheer strapless bra.

"You may have a point," said Mary employing a playful *double entendre*.

The girls embraced tenderly yet cautiously. They could each feel the other's body tremble. Sarah began to slowly unbutton Mary's blouse.

"I'm not sure this is such a good idea," protested Mary mildly. "Mixing business with pleasure is never good business...I'm your boss."

"Suppose I told you, I've wanted you after the first few days."

"Suppose I told you, I felt guilty."

"Guilty of what?"

"I'm still very much in love with Elizabeth."

Sarah kissed Mary, who accepted her moist tender lips. Rebuffs were exhausted. Temptations of the flesh survived and thrived.

They spent the better part of the next two hours as one on the deep, soft billowy couch. Physically and emotionally exhausted, they donned two thick Turkish bathrobes, slithered into Sarah's bed and fell into a deep, restful sleep.

~

Showered and famished, Sarah made the two of them breakfast around 9 a.m.

"My goodness, what a pleasant surprise. You are a wonderful cook," said Mary.

"It's nothing more than steamed eggs, shredded cheddar and some fresh veggies which I season with edamame salt (black sesame seeds and sea salt)."

"I know this may be too early," said Sarah. "But I'm curious. Particularly after yesterday and last evening."

"Curious about what?"

"Elizabeth. I mean where is she? Why aren't you...."

Mary sighed and took a deep breath. It was time to release the pain trapped in uncertainty.

"We were hopelessly in love. Her dad objected strenuously. She left home for somewhere. No forwarding address. Nothing. I searched London. Nothing. It's like she disappeared into thin air."

"Could there have been foul play? Maybe her family didn't want to be embarrassed by your relationship. Not everybody accepts girl on girl."

"Don't be silly. Her parents, friends and staff are broad-minded, aristocratic *crème de la crème* of the Lake Country. Their grandparents housed Wordsworth, Longfellow, Shelly, and Yeats."

"What's that got to do with the family accepting their daughter was a lesbian?"

Sarah saw a conflicted lack of resolution in Mary's eyes. She continued, "What about us?" There's something there. Don't you agree?"

"Agreed," replied Mary with hesitation.

"I know my flat's rather modest, but it is rather convenient to work and play, you know Central London and all that. Why don't you move in?" suggested Sarah.

Mary paused. She wanted to say yes, but couldn't.

"As they say in the cinema, how about I make you an offer you can't refuse?"

"And that is?"

"Should Elizabeth resurface, you can decide with whom you wish to stay, no questions asked."

"I don't think just yet. I've yet to see my first commission checks. Why don't we wait until I'm making a bit more money. We can find ourselves a larger flat."

"So the answer is yes?"

"A pragmatic, qualified yes."

"Shall we continue where we left off then?" said Sarah heading for the bedroom, Mary in tow.

"Not here," interrupted Mary. "Not now. I just had a perfectly wicked thought. An epiphany of sorts. Julian's away for the weekend. Let's consummate our arrangement in his *chambre á coucher.* He's got this mirror on the ceiling…and some very cool….."

"Sterling!" exclaimed Sarah. "And, sooo terribly wicked. I love it."

20

~~~

JULIAN'S TRIP TO DOVER WAS not going quite as well as Mary's stay at Sarah's.

Belfrage had picked up a young gay Basque writer named Marco Swello at Mary's party and suggested a rendezvous in distant Dover, since he wasn't sure how Mary might take to his interest in young men.

In short order, Marco found Belfrage insensitive, too aggressive for his tastes. In civilized fashion, they agreed to disagree and return to London almost immediately. After dropping off Marco, Belfrage arrived at his flat somewhere around 3 p.m. He headed straight for the steam cabinet in his bedroom suite to melt away his Marco frustrations....unaware he was about to encounter a full house.

~

Mary decided to shower before the festivities began in Belfrage's bedroom since she felt it heightened her sensitivities and created a more intense experience.

As Mary showered, Sarah became curious. What kind of wardrobe does a man as rich and influential as Belfrage support? She opened a massive, master-bedroom closet. It was filled with racks and racks of handmade suits, sport coats, pants and ties of every imaginable weight and color. As she caressed the exquisite fabrics, she noticed a tall built-in cabinet discretely tucked in the corner. To her amazement, there sat a store of sex toys including vibrators, bed handcuffs, handcuffs, restraints and such.

Mary entered the closet, clad only in a soft fluffy towel, "What are you doing in there?"

"Our boss certainly has some eclectic tastes…You had your shower. I'd like to be done in these restraints."

"Do we really need such gadgetry?" said Mary, and with a slip of the tongue, "isn't love satisfactory?" She paused for a split second. Was she really in love? Sarah jumped on it. She embraced Mary tightly. "And I love you too."

Caught in the emotion of the moment, Mary put philosophical matters aside and followed her natural urges. Sarah got her wish. Mary took the role of dominatrix. The restraints propelled Sarah's pleasure to unimagined heights.

Unbeknownst to the girls, Belfrage, entered his flat from a second entrance down the hall, went into his bathroom suite, stripped his hairy body nude and was about to enter his steam cabinet. He detected what sounded like moaning and groaning of women originating from his master bedroom. He quietly tip-toed to the bedroom door. "What the hell are you two doing in my bed?" shouted Belfrage. "Get my goddamn restraints off that whore, and get your arses out of here. I should have you arrested for breaking and entering."

"Julian," said Mary boldly."Have you forgotten I live here?"

"I don't remember opening my home to a dirty, lesbian tramp….After the way I treated you. In my own goddamn house, my own bed. That's so fucking sick and disgusting."

"Don't lecture me about sick. Annabelle Lee told me all about the way you laughed at her while you kept screwing that young man!"

Belfrage was horrified that Annabelle had shared such intimacies. He no longer wanted anything to do with Mary. He could see the headlines in the tabloids. He would be ruined and humiliated. "Pack your things and get the hell out of my house right now."

Mary quickly packed her personal belongings, less the wardrobe Belfrage had bought and paid for. "I'll stop by the office and get the rest of my things tomorrow," said Mary.

"Yeah, you do that," sneered Belfrage, stomping over to the bed and removed Sarah's restraints. "You…another tramp. You're also fired! Get the hell out!"

~

The following morning, Mary was packing when Belfrage walked into her office. "Where the hell are you going?"

"I was fired. Remember?"

"And, what are you planning to do?"

"Julian, you're not the only theatrical agent in this town."

"But, I'm the biggest and the best."

"That may be true, so I'll start smaller. Someday we're going to be competitors."

"Over my dead body."

"Now, Julian, don't be childish."

"Let me tell you something, young lady, the agents in this town live off the spoils of Julian Belfrage. Do you think I'm going to teach you all my trade secrets and then let you go to work for one of them?"

Mary started to get angry. "In case you missed it, the London Theatre is not a fucking Belfrage commonwealth run by an enlightened despot. I can do anything and go anywhere I please."

"Bitch, when I get through blacklisting you, you'll have your tail between your legs. I'll have you begging for mercy. So you better save your quid. You're going to need it for the steamer ship to New York cause you ain't never working in London again!"

Mary finished packing her attaché case with her database and financial notes and headed for the door.

"Where the hell do you think you're going with that?" demanded Belfrage as he yanked the attaché case from Mary's hands.

"God damn it, Julian, give that to me, it's mine."

"Bullshit! That's my property. Don't believe me? Take me to court. Now get the hell out of here."

Undaunted and confident, Mary began an accelerated job search. She quickly discovered Belfrage did indeed have her blacklisted. True to his word, Julian personally called every talent agent—big and small in London—to explain Mary was a ruthless liar who couldn't be trusted with clients or employees. That her ultimate goal was to steal somebody's clients and open her own shop.

~

Mary quickly realized there was only one way out. Head to New York and start anew, despite the fact she did not know a single soul in the Big Apple.

Before departing, she was determined to leave Belfrage something to remember her by, with the assistance of Sarah.

"I don't know," said Sarah. "Playing with drugs can be a little dangerous."

"It's not like I'm going to murder him. I just want to mess up his head a little. Look what he did to us. I've got to leave you just to get a job. My plan is to make one stop then head directly to the airport."

"What about me?"

"Once I'm sorted out and have a job, I'll want you to come over and join me."

"I will miss you terribly," said Sarah as she hugged Mary tightly.

"And, I you," said Mary kissing her on the lips, face, neck and nose.

Sarah started to cry. Her mascara started to run.

"Goodness, now who looks a ghastly sight."

"Oh no, said Sarah rubbing her face with a tissue. "This is not how I wish to be remembered."

~

"And to what do I owe this phone call?"

"Julian," said Mary, "You won. I just wanted you to know I was heading to New York. I thought before I left maybe we could have a drink at your flat for old time's sake."

Belfrage assumed Mary had something up her sleeve, he just didn't know what. So he played along. "Sporting of you my dear. I most enjoy a good loser. Does six work for you?"

"Works fine. I don't leave until first thing in the a.m."

Mary arrived at Belfrage's in the most seductive attire she owned: Tight black skirt with generous frontal slit, see-through black blouse and acrylic stiletto heels. She was wearing neither panty nor bra.

"My darling, you look and smell absolutely ravishing. Took the liberty of making a batch of cosmopolitans. I understand the Yanks love 'em." They had a few cosmopolitans, and then Mary turned on some sultry John Coltrane music. "I see you still remember where things are."

"I'll never forget. This is one spectacular place."

"So, what are you going to do?"

"Don't know," purred Mary, "But I'm not angry."

Belfrage thought to himself, *she hasn't pulled out a knife or gun yet, so it won't hurt to act civilized.* "It was nothing personal. Strictly business. You understand?"

"Yes, Julian, I do. Our little *tête á tête* taught me some important lessons."

"Such as…"

"I prefer mature, determined men. And, you certainly are that."

"Thank you."

"Never underestimate your opponent, particularly successful ones."

Belfrage started to let his guard down.

"You know you're going to do fine in New York. Might I give you a piece of advice? Remember when we first met, and you came in with that over-the-top routine."

"Please don't embarrass me again."

"I bet that will work in Yanksville. You do it so well."

"You're putting me on. New York is the cultural capital of the world."

"Sending up Brits in Britain is like laughing at ourselves. We don't take kindly to magnifying our idiosyncrasies. Whereas, in America, they actually believe that exaggerated personality is real. Get my drift?"

"Makes sense."

"How about another cosmo?"

His question restored her focus. It was time to get down to the business at hand. She needed to keep him distracted. She slithered along the enormous sectional until directly under one of the small, high-voltage spots allowing Belfrage to see all. "And why not?" she purred seductively.

He handed her the drink. "How about a line of Charlie?"

"Why not," said Mary.

Belfrage took a small white bag out of the cabinet and made two neat lines on a piece of smoked plexiglas.

"You first," said Mary, cautiously.

"Generally, guests first," smiled Belfrage.

"I'm not a guest, I'm a former employee," laughed Mary. Belfrage obliged, snorting a line.

She hesitated a moment. He was already getting high. She decided the coast was clear and snorted the other line. Seconds later neither was feeling any pain.

"Would you like to dance?" she said opening her arms.

"I'd like to do more than dance with you darling."

"Why don't we? You know, bon voyage and all that."

Moments later they were in Belfrage's suite with their drinks by the side of the bed. Mary knew she needed a few free moments to slip the heroin in her bag into his drink. She undressed enough to tease. "Julian, dear. Don't get offended, but you do smell a bit scruffy. How about you take a quick shower and throw on some of the cologne I adore? Then Mary would love to be tied to the bed, so you can make me gush."

Belfrage was so hot at the prospect he practically dashed into the bathroom. Once the shower was going, Mary reached into her bag and put almost 100 grams of pure heroin into his cosmo, adding some additional Cointreau to mask any possible taste variations. Then she stripped and lay in bed.

Belfrage was delighted to see Mary ready to go. Mistakenly, he assumed it now safe to throw caution to the wind. "Let's have a final toast before we roll in the hay," she said, running her finger around the edge of her glass. "Then I want you to do me again and again."

Belfrage was panting in expectation. He swilled down his cosmopolitan in one gulp and began to tie her outstretched arms to the bedposts. Suddenly Belfrage, who unbeknownst to Mary, was being treated for a serious heart arrhythmia, was overcome by chest pains he had never experienced before. The room was spinning. He tripped and fell, cutting his cheek on the edge of a bureau. He was having a massive cardiac arrest.

"Julian, loosen my wrist, so I can help," she urged, realizing his reaction was more profound than she had planned. Summoning every remaining ounce of energy, Belfrage opened her wrist bands. "Call 999. Hurry. Please." Then he blacked out. She checked his pulse. There was none.

Mary dashed around the flat, removing fingerprints and gathering all her personal effects. Then she dressed quickly, disguising herself in Belfrage's dark overcoat, a long fluffy cashmere scarf, and a wide-brimmed hat. She paused momentarily. Should she or shouldn't she? Finally, she decided to alert 999, deeply masking her voice with a handkerchief. "My friend has just had a heart attack. Please hurry."

She walked casually past the concierge and waved down a passing cab.

The paramedics arrived with oxygen and defibrillators, but Belfrage had long since left for other environs. They saw the two drinks and wondered about foul play.

Scotland Yard arrived minutes later. The only clue was the concierge's observation that an unrecognizable man in trench coat and black felt hat left the lobby at about the same time 999 had been summoned. The police report stated that Belfrage was taking drugs and having bondage sex with another male when he had a massive heart attack. The other male, probably, a male prostitute or a male in another relationship, didn't want the publicity, bolted rather than be associated with the messy details.

"Frankie," said the older male detective to his young female partner, "Like I said on the way over, you work with Scotland Yard long enough and you'll see one of everything."

21

~~~

IT WAS 1 A.M. WHEN SARAH heard a tapping and jiggling at the front door. She assumed it was a break-in and robbery, and made a mad dash for her landline to the police.

"Someone's trying to break into my flat," shouted Sarah. "Come quickly! I'm at 15 Warringer Gardens, Flat B, in Battersea." The jiggling finally stopped and the doorknob turned. Sarah was about to scream.

"Gosh, sorry," said Mary nervously, "I didn't mean to wake you. I was having quite the tussle getting the spare key to work. Does the landlord purposely turn the lights down during the night? I noticed every other bulb in the ceiling was blacked out."

A shaking Sarah took a deep breath. "Dear Jesus, you frightened the living crap out of me; I thought it was a burglar. I just called the police."

Mary's face turned ash white. Her hand was shaking. "Oh God. Stop them. Turn them around."

"I'll try, but it may be too late. For crud sake, relax; it's not exactly the end of the world."

"After tonight, it might well be the end of mine!"

"Whatever are you babbling about? Sit. I'll make some tea. We'll chat."

"Make the damn call," demanded Mary. She went into the bathroom to remove any traces of cocaine on her dress. Sarah called the police to cancel the complaint.

"I understand, Madame, I'll try to radio the detectives assigned to investigate."

No sooner had Sarah hung up the phone when she was greeted by a strong knock on the door. "Police, let us in." She scurried to the door a mite late. Two inspectors, guns in hand, kicked open the door. "Nobody move."

"Don't shoot!" screamed Sarah, hands over her head. "Don't shoot!"

"Is there anyone else in the flat?" asked one of the inspectors.

"Just my roommate in the bathroom."

"Mary, it's the police," said Sarah. "Everything is going to be okay."

"What's your name, Madame?" asked the detective.

"I'm Sarah's roommate, Mary Jones. I was at a party with some friends and got home a trifle late for midweek."

Sarah knew something was wrong since Mary was using her pre-Belfrage name. Sarah and Mary made eye contact. The message was clear. *Be careful.*

"I wouldn't let my daughter wander around the East Side at this hour."

"Sir, I'm 24, so I'm hardly a teenager in need of chaperoning. I had trouble getting the key to work in the lock and began jiggling it quietly so as not to disturb Sarah. Obviously I was noisier than I thought, and so here we are."

"So, you're roommates," said the detective to Sarah.

"It's a rather small place for two adults, no?" said the inspector suspiciously.

Sarah became indignant. "Sir, I'm not sure that's any of your business. It's a temporary situation. My roommate discovered her fiancée was cheating, if you know what I mean. She decided to leave the miserable bloke....There, are you satisfied?"

Feeling somewhat awkward, the inspectors decided to leave. "Sorry to disturb you, ladies."

~

"Where the hell have you been?" demanded Sarah. "It's rather late for a weekday... Even for you."

Mary bit her lip. "I was enraged with Julian after he blackballed me. I invited myself to his flat under the guise of letting bygones be bygones and titillated him into having a goodbye fling. Then I convinced him to shower and cologne before. More romantic and all that. While he was fussing I put two bags of heroin in his drink."

"My Jesus, two bags. Didn't you know he had a heart condition?"

"I didn't mean to kill him. I just wanted him to experience pain like he never felt before."

"You murdered him!"

"It was an accident. He just keeled over by the bed."

"How are we ever going to prove that to the police?"

"I don't plan to. I don't have a choice. From the police standpoint, I've either committed murder or manslaughter. I stick around and I'm off to jail, maybe for life, certainly indefinitely. I was planning on eventually trying my hand in New York theatre. Events just require my residency to begin sooner rather than later."

"New York? What about me? I thought you wanted me."

~

Within minutes, Mary was on the phone with Virgin Atlantic reservations. "I see. Given my emergency...Disappointing"...there was a pause. "Brilliant! I'll take it. And, how much extra is that? My lucky day. Thank you so much for your help. You've made my grandmother very happy."

"What the hell was that all about?"

"Turns out every seat on every airline to New York was booked today. Something about a medical instruments convention at the New York Convention Center. I was about to hang up when the computer identified a last-second cancellation in business class. I gave the bloke a touching story about granny's illness and wound up with the seat at the cost of economy."

"You are a poster child for tall tales!"

"Sarah, dear. I have got to scoot. The plane leaves at 1 p.m. from Heathrow. Between packing, the bank, and discarding all else..."

"What can I do to help?" said Sarah.

"I think it's best you remain detached. The last thing we want is for you to become an accessory after the fact."

Mary and Sarah hugged for what neither realized would be the last time.

"One last thing," said Mary. "Should you find anything I've overlooked, and I mean anything, throw it away. Remember, no clues. Absolutely no clues."

22

~~~

MARY'S UPGRADE DELIVERED important perks ...notably priority check-in and a casual security inspection. Sitting at the cappuccino bar in Virgin's sleek lounge overlooking the passenger terminal, nervously nibbling a sweet roll and a low-fat cappuccino, she picked up a copy of the *Daily Mirror* headlined, "Bats in Belfrage." The story said Belfrage was poisoned by one of his jilted male lovers, and that a search was being conducted throughout London to find "the madman in the raincoat and hat."

Clearly the Belfrage case was a top priority. She assumed it was because of his prominence. Little did she know that the Deputy Commissioner of the Metropolitan Police, i.e., Scotland Yard, had been one of Belfrage's former lovers. He wanted the case solved before that tidbit made its way to the tabloids and destroyed his career.

Mary was a nervous wreck. The coffee cup rattled as she placed it on the saucer. Her mind imagined every airport Johnnie that glanced in her direction was monitoring her behavior. Even the ATM machine was spying on her as she withdrew funds.

Finally, the sweet nothings blared over the microphones: "Virgin Atlantic Flight 826 to JFK in New York City now ready for boarding. May we have those passengers holding business first and families with small children." Mary, dressed in a conservative dark outfit, dashed to the front of the line. In aisle seat 9B, she was practicing yoga belly breathing.

"Drink, Madame, before we depart? "

"Double McCallum on the rocks."

The hostess was a little surprised, given it was only 8:30 a.m., but dutifully obliged. Mary devoured the drink, put her dark glasses on, pushed her seat back, covered herself in a blanket and fell fast asleep. Just before the doors closed, a distinguished, well-dressed gentlemen with gray groomed beard and stylish, titanium-rimmed granny glasses, boarded. "I was wondering if you could move your legs a bit, Madame, so I can get to my seat."

Mary was dead to the world.

The passenger looked at the flight attendant, who shrugged her shoulders. "Your seatmate hasn't moved an inch since her nip."

The man climbed over Mary, pushed her seat upright and placed her newspapers in the seat pocket in front of her. "Maybe we should take off her glasses and put them in her case during takeoff," said the flight attendant.

As he removed Mary's glasses she awoke abruptly, having forgotten for a split second where she was.

"Thief!" she screamed. "Help, thief!. This man is trying to steal my sunglasses!"

"Madame," said the flight attendant, loud enough for the entire business class to hear. "Hardly. You passed out after tossing down the double. I asked this very nice gentleman next to you to assist me in removing your glasses. Air safety and all that sort of thing."

The passengers all had a good chuckle. "I'm so sorry, sir," said Mary, embarrassed. "May I ask what you do," she said, now more relaxed.

"I retired from the corporate world some years ago. My wife and I dabble in residential real estate. We buy interesting buildings, turn them into B&B's, hire staff to operate, then sell them to the Yanks as operating businesses. "

"Why Yanks?"

"My wife's a Yank. We met a long time ago when she was visiting London on holiday. One look in the pub, and I was done. What about you?"

"I'm a theatrical agent. Did my apprenticeship in London. Broadway, here I come."

The man smiled. "Tough go. Never any good at guessing winners, other than Susan. I'll stick to real estate. So where do you live in New York."

"Actually, I'm just in the process of relocating. I don't even have a flat yet."

"New York's not a place for a pretty young girl to just be wandering around. This is also tourist high-season. Could I make a suggestion? There's an area called SoHo near West Greenwich Village. Feels a little like Chelsea. Quiet residential streets, row houses, parks and trees, lots of open air markets, fabulous, cheap ethnic restaurants and oodles of clubs and bars, coffee shops and bookstores where artists read their work. There are also some charming old theatres, like the Cherry Lane and the Minetta Lane that will remind you of the East End."

"Sounds delightful, but it probably costs the earth."

"It just so happens there is a frightfully delightful little bed & breakfast on the edge of the West Village on Horatio Street. Rather peaceful for Manhattan—yet within walking distance of everything. The entire establishment has four rooms and a pleasant rear garden filled with flowers and views of the city lights. The owner, Marjorie Colt, is a painter and lives on the premises. As it happens, she bought the property from Susan. I could call her. I'm sure she'd do me a favor. Could be your lucky day…Marjorie even includes a full English breakfast and afternoon tea. She lived in London for five years and rather enjoys our little traditions."

ACT 2

23

~~~

83 HORATIO STREET WAS exactly as billed: a lovely three-story, red brick, Greek Revival townhouse circa 1840. The quiet, tree-lined street brimmed with colorful window boxes, an urban oasis tucked between two bustling thorough-fares: Greenwich Avenue to the east and 14th Street to the west.

"Mary," you've probably had a long day," said Marjorie, a friendly lady in her mid-50's with curly brown hair and dark brown eyes. "Why not have dinner locally, make yourself a fire and relax by the tv. Maybe take a bath. I'll leave some tea in the kitchen. One of the things that attracted me to the West Village is the interesting neighborhood restaurants within walking distance. I suggest you walk down Greenwich Street, make a right, and then select whatever piques your interest."

"Do you have a favorite?"

"I do. It's a little Northern Italian place called Osteria del Sol. It's reasonably-priced, home-cooked Italian. Marco uses only the freshest ingredients and prepares them with lots of love. Plus, his partner Lester is an absolute hoot."

"Sounds delightful."

"Take Greenwich to Fourth Avenue, make another right and go three blocks to Perry. It's the orange building right on the corner. You can't miss it. Ask Lester to make you an appetizer portion of the gnocchi with truffles, and then you've got to try the oven-roasted branzini. There's nothing quite like it in Manhattan."

"What's branzini?"

"It's his version of European sea bass from the Mediterranean."

That evening Mary had one of the most enjoyable meals of her life. "Ah, Senorina Mary, I am Lester. Margaret asked me to take good care of you. Perfect time to come because the crowds don't arrive till about 8 p.m. We share some wine."

"Wonderful. May I see a menu?"

"All arranged by Marjorie. You no need menu."

Lester returned with two glasses and a bottle of red wine. "Danzante Sangiovese, my favorite. Goes with everything." He filled both glasses, sat down and made a toast, "To a very happy visit."

Mary couldn't quite place Lester's accent. "That is very sweet of you. I don't want to insult you but how much is the wine per glass."

"What how much? First night in New York. No charge. Marco and I want good memories."

Mary decided to make small talk with her tableside visitor. "Where in Italy are you from?"

"Marco from the south of Naples, a little town called Castellammare. Lester not Italian. I'm Hungarian from town of Eszthergum near Danube and Budapest. Unfortunately Eszthergum is the seat of the Roman Catholic Primate of all Hungary and Lester is very gay. Marco and I meet in

Positano. Immediately fall in love, come to America and build this. Now ten years, so we must be doing something right."

The gnocchi were delicate, the truffle and virgin oil sauce gave it just the right hint of nuttiness, and the branzini had the delicacy of Dover sole with the richness of Australian lobster. Dessert was an Italian Vacheran–three thin layers of hazelnut with a feather light zabaglione tucked in between.

That night Mary slept like a baby. When she woke around 8:30 a.m., there was a copy of the *Village Voice*, the *New York Times*, a street map of Manhattan with apartment availabilities covering Midtown West to lower Greenwich Village, at her door. The little yellow post-it note simply said, "This should jumpstart your search. Begin in Midtown and work your way home. Margaret."

Mary did precisely as suggested and made an ambitious schedule of six appointments by 10 a.m. First stop was a "luxury pre-war building" on the southwest corner of 73rd Street and Third Avenue which turned out to be a dark, unremodeled apartment with one small window in a building with a tastefully renovated lobby. *Splashy on the outside, grubby on the inside* thought Mary.

The real estate agent, Robert Edgerton, tried to humiliate Mary into believing the one bedroom was a steal for Manhattan's East Side. "Young lady, you Brits have no idea. The East Side is where it's all happening. This is a fabulous location with generous space. The fact that the landlord wants it rented immediately and is willing to give you one year at just $3,800 a month is your lucky day." Even with a favorable conversion rate, Mary felt the 500 square foot apartment was considerably overpriced. "Mr. Edgerton, it's a lovely place. Just a bit out of my price range."

"My dear," glared the middle aged Edgerton over his granny glasses, "what is your budget?"

"About £1,500 a month."

"What's that in real money?" asked Edgerton impatiently tapping his finger on the Formica countertop.

"About $2,500."

"You're kidding. Child, I'd head below 34th Street. Maybe you can find a small unit in one of those old hotels where those Indian and Pakistani migrants seem to congregate."

After four more equally depressing apartment interviews, Mary was starting to wonder if Manhattan was the right place. But all that changed when she walked into 148 Prince Street at 4 p.m. nibbling on an oven-fresh panini from Vesuvio's Bakery next store.

"I see you gotta piece of Antony's bread? Delicioso, no?" said the heavyset lady with her hair in a bun.

"The bread is yummy, but who's Antony?"

"My son, Antony Dapolito. He run bakery for the past 20 years, like his Papa before him, and his Papa before him— may they rest in peace. We very proud of our little store. Apartment for rent upstairs. Want to see? Antony and his wife, Christine, first floor neighbors."

"Bloody right," said an enthusiastic Mary.

"What bloody? The apartment very clean. No blood."

"Mrs. Dapolito, that's just an expression we use. It just means yes."

"So why not justa say yes? You name?"

"Mary."

"Mother in heaven," said the lady as she raised her eyes to the sky. "Always wanted a daughter named Mary. But God say no, Concetta, you meant to have boys....Antony and Rocco."

"Concetta, a pleasure to meet you." Mary extending her hand.

"No, Concetta, everybody in America calls me Connie," said Mrs. Dapolito.

The sun-filled, fully-furnished, two-bedroom and one-bathroom apartment contained a formal parlor, dining room and roof deck. "Oh, Mrs. Dapolito, it's lovely. But it's probably way over my budget."

Connie didn't want to embarrass Mary, so she avoided asking what her budget was. Connie just assumed the $1,900 below-market rent was too high. But she really liked Mary, so she made her an offer she couldn't refuse. "I understand. But all not lost, let me show you something." Connie led Mary to a rear courtyard via a small walk on the side of the house. There sat a second townhouse, flower boxes brimming over with red geraniums, painted in light green enamel that matched the façade on the landmark bakery. "This place is empty. We no need. Just sits. But inside needs lots of work." They walked through the place. By Lower Manhattan standards, it was huge, some 2,000 square feet with several rooms, three baths, exposed brick walls and wood floors. "Lots of potential, eh?"

"Quite so," said Mary wondering where the conversation was going.

"Make you a deal. You pay me $500 a month plus utilities; fix the place. I get Antony to buy new appliances and nice bed. You take care of the rest of furniture. Stay as long as you want."

"$500," said a delighted Mary.

"You're right," said Connie. "Make it $400. Need lotta work. Antony never ever got around to put plaster on brick walls. Important thing, I get daughter and new friend cheap. Capische?"

"Capische," smiled Mary. "One question. In time, I plan to open my own theatrical agency. Can I use the house for business?"

"Sure. No problem. You get door to open from other side of the building. You take?"

"I take."

Connie called 1-800-Mattress and had a bed and a stick lamp delivered before sunset. Mary packed her bags and dashed over from 83 Horatio. She sat on the floor of what would one day be her dining room with a bottle of Danzante

Sangiovese, some soft ripe brie and a loaf of Vesuvio's crusty round pizziola bread.

~

Mary was energized by the sunlight streaming into her bedroom on this, the first day of the rest of her life. She decided on three initial priorities: purchase a bouquet of sunflowers from the greengrocer on the corner, obtain a listing of Manhattan's theatrical agents at the New York Public Library so she could begin her job search, and have some Indian food for dinner at Salaam Bombay Restaurant, a few blocks north of her apartment.

As she showered, the rickety head began to make a funny, clicking sound...or at least she assumed it was the showerhead. She reached for a towel to dry herself. There climbing up her leg was a giant, striped cockroach. She screamed. Connie came running, assuming Mary had hurt herself. She found Mary standing on the toilet seat cover swatting at what was now two cockroaches dancing around the showerhead.

"I think you dying," laughed Concetta. "They only little itty bitty cockroaches from next store," said Connie, as she squashed each with her hand. "The fresh bread attracts the roaches. These not ordinary New York City roaches. They happy well-fed Italian-American roaches. Next store is treated every week, so spotless. They carry no germs. Just food. Now you live here, we spray this also."

"Today!"

"No problem. Rocco work for Terminex. But Mary," warned Connie, "you gotta be a little tough. You will see much worse. After all, this is New York."

After a piping-hot cappuccino and a crusty, warm fresh roll, she walked up the street to the Korean grocer, Ed Bok Lee, to purchase some of the handsome sunflowers lining the perimeter of his store. Their existence reminded her of the English Romantic Poets and their love of wildflowers. "I'll have a go," she said pointing to the flowers.

"Go?" repeated the confused greengrocer who's English was far from adequate

Mary attempted to help by using simple Brit slang, but she only made matters worse.

"Mate, pack and wrap two to go."

"No mate, me man," responded Bok Lee. "Missy, speak English pleeese."

Mary laughed. "May I please have two bouquets of the big yellow sunflowers?"

"Ahhh," nodded the bald, happy, little man. "Four dollars. Have a nice day."

As she headed back to the apartment to drop off the flowers, she wondered how is it that the most expensive city in the world sold sunflowers at half the going rate in London?

~

Mary was flabbergasted. She had heard about the $200 million Grand Central Station renovation. But hearing was one thing. Jackie Onassis's swansong was breathtaking. The spectacular prepared food and fresh deli arcade, the enormous international food court downstairs with kiosks from 23 different countries, the perfectly restored brass chandeliers and ticket booths, the soaring astrological arched ceiling some 100 feet above the main transportation area and the five formal restaurants ranging from prime steaks at Jordan's Steak House to super fresh seafood at the historical Oyster Bar.

After two hours of browsing, she headed for the main branch of the New York Public Library on 42nd Street and Fifth Avenue. The efficient and courteous staff put the latest annual New York Theatrical Agent's directory into her hands so she could make notes in the main reading room on the third floor. She compiled an extensive database to store in her laptop.

~

The next morning Mary, head buried in the *New York Times* at a small corner table in Vesuvio's, felt a tap on the shoulder. There stood a man with scruffy clothes, a dark beard, shaggy hair and dark, horn-rimmed sunglasses. "Mary, how have you been?"

Mary stared blankly.

"It's me, David Marks. I'm stalking you. You left me high and dry in London."

"What are you doing in New York?" asked Mary.

"If you had actually followed my meager press clippings, you would have known I decided to take Broadway by storm. I've had one play running about 10 months, and I'm polishing another entitled *American Bison*. It's about three Chicago crooks planning a petty heist as they talk in pseudo-meaningful implications, self-serving riffs, and proliferating obscenities. There is Don, owner of a baroquely cluttered junk shop, who acts the circumspect businessman and tries to guide young Bobby into becoming his protégé. And there is Teach, the volatile, violent criminal who keeps mouthing bromides about sound business. It's an entertaining sweep of men who will never climb above the bottom rung of the social ladder. But on a deeper level, you are asked to question a world that allows so many lives to fall between the cracks.

Mary heard nothing beyond 10 months. "David, how long have you been here?"

"On and off for almost a year."

"Has it been that long?"

"I can see, absence did not make your heart grow fonder," laughed David.

"Wish you nothing but good fortune."

"That's a story for another time. What about you?"

"Let's just say I received a crash course on theatrical manners in London. Julian hired me to identify new talent. Befriend them. Nurture their properties. Make them profitable clients. But, you know Julian, he insisted on 100 percent of the credit and about 98 percent of the fees. It didn't take me long to figure it was a real lose-lose situation. So I decided to leverage my experience to see if I could make it in New

York. You know what they say, 'If you can make it here, you can make it anywhere.'"

"I must say, I'm surprised the relationship ended so quickly. The word was that Julian was grooming you to be a partner."

Clearly, David had neither read the morning papers nor heard the news. Mary switched topics. "I'm sorry I never returned your calls... after that night."

Marks looked into Mary's eyes. "I did wonder. Was it me?"

"No, you were good. Very good."

"Then why..."

Mary didn't want to go there. "David, please, let's just move on."

"Fair enough, for now. So where is the world headquarters of Mary Jackson-Peale located?"

"I'm living in the apartment right behind the bakery. The space needs work, but it's quite spacious. I can easily convert the first floor into a suite of offices."

"Ahhh, sweet mysteries of fate," said David, taken by Mary's vision and her sensuous smile. "I live just around the corner."

24

~~~

SARAH WAS BOTH DELIGHTED and disappointed with Mary's phone call. Delighted to hear her voice and her progress report, but disappointed at the response to her proposal.

"Sarah, not yet. I need to get a little more grounded first. This place is a little crazy, everybody seems to be in a hurry, even if they have no place in particular to go. They're also a rather mercurial lot. Everybody seems to be frustrated about something. David said it's like London, only more frenetic."

"David? David who?"

"David Marks, remember, the young Brit playwright. I met him quite by coincidence at the bakery. He's relocated to New York. In fact, we're neighbors. He's working on new play, Bison something or other, he's hoping to launch it Off-Broadway."

"That wanker!" said an angry Sarah. "The play's called *American Bison*. Julian came up with the title. He's still listed as a Belfrage client."

138

"What about the office, post Julian?"

"We had an all-hands-on-deck meeting to try to retain our clients. Our motto is one smart action a day will keep the wolves away. So far, so good. We've retained all but two of our 34 clients. Three, if we include that turncoat Marks."

"Just hang in there," urged Mary. "We'll be together sooner than you think."

Sarah was in a different place. "If we keep the agency growing, the partners have agreed I should be made a vice president. Perhaps you should consider coming back to rejoin the family. I'm happy to move out of my flat and get a larger place."

"You can't be serious. I'm not sure how and why, but at some point the truth about Julian's death will surface. Scotland Yard will come after me with a vengeance. By staying in New York, I remain under the radar screen. And once you join me, they'll never be able to figure out what happened."

"Are you implying that if I stay in England, I'll tattle?"

"I didn't say that. I merely said if we're together in New York, unraveling his murder will be virtually impossible."

"I'm so disappointed with your doubletalk. Don't you realize I'd go to my grave before I would betray you?"

~

Mary mailed a letter of solicitation to 30 of Manhattan's most influential theatrical agencies incorporating exaggerated accomplishments during her Belfrage and Associates tenure. While she thought nobody would check her background across the Atlantic, she listed Sarah as a VP and her immediate supervisor at Belfrage as an insurance policy.

An uneventful week passed as Mary tended to domestic projects—painting, wallpapering, hanging drapes, polishing floors and restoring the exposed brick walls and beamed ceilings. She also browsed the local consignment shops looking for hip Brit outfits that she planned to wear on her forthcoming job interviews. Within ten days, she and the apartment looked smashing. To her dismay, she didn't receive a single phone call or response to her employment queries. She decided to take a more aggressive course of action and call all 30 agencies straight out. While each response was slightly different, they were all shades of the same gray.

"Madame, Darlene Thurgood did receive your resume. While it was impressive and showed an excellent understanding of the business, the fact that you're coming directly from London suggests your American personal contacts are small to nonexistent. Darlene needs someone who can bring clients on board now."

"Well, I am good friends with David Marks. I might be able to convince him…"

"David's good. Very good. An up-and-coming theatre talent. I'm sure if you were to open that door, and Darlene secured his representation, she would find a spot at the agency." The assistant paused. "Where do you know David from?" subtly attempting to validate Mary's claim of friendship.

"Well, he is a Brit you know. We originally met in East London."

"And, he lives here now?"

"Yes. Somewhere in the West Village."

"Somewhere in the West Village. Sounds like you've spent a lot of time together," said the assistant with the proper hint of sarcasm. "Do let us know when you'd like to bring David in for a business discussion."

~

Despite the deep discount in rent, Mary started to run low on cash. Thumbing through the employment section of the *Village Voice*, she noticed a classified ad for a part-time receptionist at the School of Visual Arts. Mary called the number listed in the ad, explained her background, and received an appointment with the human resource director the very next day. The school's avante garde reputation led Mary to dress Brit chic. Pebble gray miniskirt with leather boots, shimmery purple silk blouse and eggbeater hairdo. Her personal chemistry with the director, extensive arts background and funky appearance were a perfect cultural fit.

"Miss Peale, I think you'll enjoy working here and interacting with our creative student body. Should we start Monday?"

"Splendid. What time?"

"Nine will be fine. We'll spend the day doing an orientation so you know your way around the school and our new showcase gallery. That way you'll have a better idea of how to handle the myriad requests that inevitably pop up."

Mary went home to celebrate her good fortune…alone. She began to search for a corkscrew to pop open a bottle of wine. As she searched one of the drawers, she came upon Marks's card. She figured, *what the hell, let me give him a buzz, worst case is he's not home.*

"Hello," said the voice.

"David, is that you?"

"Mary…I thought you'd call once you got settled. But after four weeks of silence, I figured you decided to blow me off…again," said David only half teasing.

"So what are you doing?"

"When?" asked David.

"Right now. I'm celebrating with myself. I just got my first job and popped open a bottle of wine," said Mary hoping.

"What say I scoot around the block and poach some vino?," asked David. "You can tell me all about your job hunting adventures. Then I'll buy you dinner and show you some local night life."

"Wonderful. I'm in the rear house, so I'll wait for you on the steps at 148 Prince." Mary tossed on some makeup, lipstick, straightened her hair and wiggled into a form-fitting miniskirt with a generous center slit. She looked in the mirror. Why did she put on that dress? Why was she so excited? After all, David was a guy and she was…wasn't she?

~

David came down the block with a big smile peeking through his curly black beard. "Mary, it's so good to see you."

She hugged him tightly. "Follow me," she said, grabbing his arm and walking past the attractively lighted inner courtyard. She pushed open the double-Dutch, oak front door of the rear building and said, "Ta da!" as she waved her hand. David was surprised how homey yet elegant the place was. "This is utterly charming. And right in the middle of the Village."

"You know I've been so busy scraping, cleaning, painting and restoring, I've never stepped back to absorb the fruits of my labor. It is pretty smashing isn't it? This is the living room and over there is the dining room. The master suite is off to the left. I haven't touched the second bedroom yet or the second floor, other than the spiral walnut staircase."

"How old is this place?"

"According to Connie, about 1860."

"Wow! Who's Connie?"

"The owners are Concetta Dapolito and her son Antony. But she prefers to be called Connie."

"So this is where Antony lives."

"Do you know him?"

"Only by reputation. He and his family are neighborhood legends. They call him the unofficial mayor of Greenwich Village. Almost single handedly he's maintained the unique character of the area by refusing to allow the national chains like McDonald's, Target and Costco to lease or build. I love everything about the place but the furniture," continued David looking around the empty apartment. "A bit too minimalist for my tastes."

"That's someday," said Mary wistfully as she explained her unique sweat-equity deal.

"Actually, that's not so terrible. So it takes you a little time. Your first check at the theatrical agency should allow you to play catch-up pretty quickly."

"What theatrical agency?"

"You said on the phone you were celebrating your first job."

"I am, but it's merely a part-time receptionist job at the School of Visual Arts. I've sent tons of resumes and followed up with the 30 largest theatrical reps. Not one would give me the time of day unless I could deliver Peter O'Toole or Tom Shoppard. Arrogant wankers!"

"I wouldn't take it personally. That's just New York. They don't sugar-coat their arrogance here like we Brits do. In this town, there are no shortcuts. Everybody has to pay dues. You've got to just keep plugging. Don't get discouraged. Sooner or later, opportunity will appear on your doorstep. You've got to stay sharp so you can seize that moment."

"Thank you, Uncle David," smiled Mary as she innocently curtsied.

"You hungry?" asked David.

They walked over to West Broadway to one of the street's marquee restaurants, Barolo.

"David are you sure you want to go here? I've looked at the menu in the window next to the antipasto platters on more than a few occasions. It looks yummy but very expensive."

"Sounds like you," smiled David devilishly as he took her hand and walked in.

"Ahhh, Mr. David," said a barrel-chested man in a gray sharkskin suit and straight dark hair that appeared to have been dipped in olive oil. "Gud to see ya again. I got your table waiting."

"Sorry about the short notice, but my friend here is just in from England."

"No problemo. The forma occupants of da table were happy to move, if you know what I mean."

"David, you can do the ordering, I eat anything. But let me order the wine. I've been introduced to a reasonably priced Sangiovese. Everybody seems to have it on their wine lists."

"You're not talking about that peasant wine from Danzante?"

"Why, yes."

"That means you've met Oscar. I think he's got stock in the vineyard. For Christ's sake, what does a Hungarian know about Italian wine?'

"So you know Oscar too?"

"Everybody in the neighborhood knows Oscar!"

"Wine, Mr. David?" asked Antony. "I've got a small shipment of the 1992 Produttori del Barbaresco. I want you to try. It's on me. This is like velvet. Goes with anything. What do them faggot connoisseurs know about real food and wine?"

"How about we start with the Raviolo all'vovo, have the zuppa di pesce and finish with an insalata rustica."

"That's my man. *Chi mangia bene*. And thanks for da little ding."

Mary had all she could do not to burst into laughter. "I feel like I was just in an episode of the Sopranos. What's 'da little ding?'" mimicked Mary in her best Italian-American street accent.

"Oh, Antony had this woman on the side, he was trying to impress for the longest time. I told him to tell her he got her a bit part Off-Broadway."

"As what?"

"A dumb blonde in an obscure play called *The Visitor*. She meets the protagonist briefly at a diner. She was perfectly typecast. All she had to do was be herself."

~

Dinner complete, the couple headed down the block to the legendary jazz club, the Blue Note on Bleeker and Third. "It's been in the same place over 40 years," said David. "They book some of the best jazz anywhere in the world. On Friday nights they have what they call 'The Late Night Groove Series' which means they don't start until 12:30."

"When does the place close?"

"About 4 a.m., but the shows end about an hour earlier. Tonight Jim Hall and Ron Carter are doing a bass and guitar gig together for the first time in ten years."

After two double Agraria Grappis each, neither was feeling any pain. "Why don't we have a lie in (sleepover) at my place?" said David placing his hand on Mary's tastefully exposed thigh.. "Then I'll make us breakfast in the morning and send you on your way."

"It's already morning."

"Then later in the morning. Or maybe after brunch," said David.

Mary was conflicted on a number of levels. She was certain she still loved Elizabeth. But hadn't she already cheated with Sarah. Then there was David. He was a man. A man she was clearly attracted to. Why was that, given her avowed preference for same-sex relationships? What if she agreed to have sex with him? She made her decision. "No need to beg. It's rather unbecoming."

~

At David's apartment, the evening's accumulation of alcohol had an undesirable effect on Mary. While she was seductively disrobing on the edge of the bed, the room started to spin. She leaned back and passed out.

25

~~~

MARY AWOKE TO THE SMELL of oven-baked bread from Vesuvio's and freshly brewed Colombian coffee in David's kitchen. Even though she couldn't remember anything specific, she assumed breakfast was a reward for a job well done. She stretched her arms as she kicked the covers off her partially clad body. "It smells delightful."

"David always delivers on his promises."

"I'm famished. Must have been all the exercise last night," she responded assumptively.

"Hardly. You stripped and collapsed. Correction, you partially stripped. That wasn't the half of it...you snore like the dickens!"

Mary playfully grimaced. Neither Elizabeth nor Sarah had ever mentioned it.

"I'm working on the assumption that breakfast in bed at least earns me a raincheck."

~

David's thoughts turned to business. "I have a professional question for you: What kind of experience do you have
with contracts and the financial side of the theatre business?"

Mary sensed a business opportunity.

"Julian gave me an accelerated crash course. He taught
me where all the revenue streams were and how to capture
them, mostly for the firm, sometimes for our investors, and
once in a blue moon for the artists themselves....Why?"

"I think I'm being screwed by my agent, but I don't
know where or how."

"That's a pretty serious accusation."

"My first play, *That Franklin Affair*, has played to favorable reviews and decent audiences from the day we opened ten
months ago. I get weekly accounting statements that look
quite official and show the calculations on my 10 percent of
net, which I'm told is somewhat standard in this country."

"So what's the issue?"

"The expenses against net always seem to be quite high,
so my 10 percent seems more like 1 percent of the gross.
Does that sound right?"

"As a rule of thumb, you should be getting at least 5 percent of gross. The expenses do sound quite out of control.
Have you asked for the back-up documentation?"

"I'm reluctant to upset the applecart. It's hard enough to
get an average theatrical agent in this town. Even at 1 percent
I'm still getting some $3,000 a week. Plus I have no idea what
I'd be looking for."

"What does your agent say about your financial concerns?"

"He says everything is fully audited. It is what it is, get
over it."

"Who is the accounting firm?"

"Lyford and Donald, CPAs. I've never met them. All I
know is one of the partners, William Donald, is my agent,
Dennis' brother. He says they've worked closely for a decade,
and he trusts his brother's numbers implicitly."

Mary smelled a rat. "Tell you what, David, I have a business proposition: Let me go through the contract, analyze your receipts, and meet with the two Donalds. If I find you some additional money, I get 33 percent of the proceeds of everything over the last three month's average weekly distributions."

"And, if there is no recovery?"

"You don't owe me a thing. Other than a dinner and the raincheck."

"Make it 25 percent and we'll call it a deal," said David extending his hand.

"Let's leave it at 33 percent because you have absolutely no risk," said Mary extending her hand.

~

"Dennis, this is my financial advisor from London, Mary Jackson-Peale," said David sitting across the table from Dennis Donald in his 47th floor office in the prestigious Olympic Towers across from St. Patrick's Cathedral.

"Nice to make your acquaintance."

"Likewise," said Donald suspiciously. "David, what happened to your face? I almost didn't recognize you."

"He's now the David I used to know. Looks ten years younger, doesn't he?" said Mary, smiling at David.

Donald sensed Mary was more than just an advisor. "Absolutely. So what can I do for you kids?"

"I've been reviewing David's contract and his disbursement statements. Something seems awry. I believe there may be a few duplicate line items which would increase the overall net and David's weekly disbursement by a rather significant sum."

"Mary, at the risk of seeming rude, what experience do you have in such matters?"

"Well, I used to be Julian Belfrage's right-hand person on all operating and financial matters at Belfrage and Associates in London."

Donald knew Belfrage by reputation. His tone became conciliatory. "Maybe we should get my brother in here. He does the actual numbers."

Brother Frank appeared from an adjoining office suite.

"Frank, this is Mary; she has some questions about your numbers. She used to be the business manager for Julian Belfrage in London," signaled Donald. "It appears some of Dennis's office expenses are in the line items. How much is that?"

"Well it's 10 percent of our overall office."

"Does that estimate include your offices?"

Frank hesitated. "Well, yes."

"Were you aware Dennis office expenses are not an expense of the deal?"

"Where does it say that?"

"Right here in the boilerplate section of page 6. Having done hundreds of these things, I'm sure you can appreciate the rationale. If an agent had 50 clients and each was credited with 10 percent of the office expenses, the agent would stand to make an outrageous supplemental sum at the expense of his clients. I'm sure we wouldn't want that. Word gets around, and before you know it, clients start leaving in droves," said Mary.

"No, you're quite right. I'll do a recalculation straight away."

"The other thing I noticed is that you may have inadvertently added investor disbursements as an expense of the deal, again reducing David's net, rather than treating everybody the same."

"Let me take a look at that," said Frank. "Again, quite right, my dear. My mistake. I apologize. No harm done. The recalculation will take care of that."

Brother Dennis became concerned. "Hang on a minute. Wouldn't I'd have to ask investors for a refund of certain prior disbursements? " Frank was caught in the middle. Dennis continued, "Why raise that kind of red flag, Frank? Can't we just reduce future disbursements until the books balance?"

"Yes, you're right. That is the wiser course of action."

~

"That was a masterful performance," said David upon leaving. Three days later, he received a check for $112,300 from Donald and Associates.

The following day, Mary arrived home from a day of employment interviews. There was an envelope inside the door. It was a check for $37,433.

~

Mary sat back on her bed in the barren apartment with a Cheshire-cat grin on her face. She had never held that much money in her hand before. Her mobile rang. It was David. "Congratulations. Maybe now you can buy yourself some furniture and me an expensive alcohol-free dinner."

"Why alcohol-free?"

"Take a wild guess."

Mary laughed out loud.

"Listen" continued David. "I've been thinking. I have a business proposition for you. Can you meet me at Café Borgia in a half hour or so?"

~

"I want to hire you as my agent. Now that I've cracked Broadway's theatrical curtain, *American Bison* should be easier to market."

"What about Dennis Donald?"

"I fired him yesterday, although he'll continue to get his weekly pound of flesh until *Franklin* closes."

"That still sounds outrageous. People go to jail for less than what he's done to you."

"The New York theatre is a very small club. Never know when I might need him. So I can live with the hosing, as long as I get this new project rolling in the fall."

David was now a very good friend, perhaps her only real friend in New York. She wanted to be certain. "Remember, I'm new to New York. I don't have a full Rolodex just yet."

"That was yesterday. After the Donald brothers meeting, I'm sure you'll figure it out. We can start with the *Franklin* investor group. They've already made a handsome profit on their investment. What I need plays to your strengths—to begin with, some new ideas on how to structure the play to maximize profitability while losing none of its emotional impact. And convince our investors, this project will provide even better returns than *That Franklin Affair* and manage the books so we accurately capture revenues and distribute the appropriate profits."

"Agreed," said Mary. They shook hands.

"Good, now let's talk turkey." Mary stared blankly. "'Talk turkey' is an American colloquialism for let's agree on the financial splits."

"AHHH," said a now enlightened Mary, taking the lead. "Let's just use a standard Belfrage deal. No need to reinvent the wheel. I get 5 percent of the weekly gross, plus a one-time finder's fee of 5 percent on investor funds secured."

"I thought we were going to my *Franklin Affair* investors?"

"We are. That's why I discounted the fee from 10 percent. Plus, I pick up all my own expenses, including fee disbursements. None of that Dennis Donald bogus accounting."

26

~~~

BELLE BART WAS NOT YOUR CLASSIC theatrical investor. Bart, a busty mid-50s Mae West type, was a stage caricature. After a number of menial jobs in West Texas, including local prostitute, pig farmer and carwash caddy, she hit it big at 40 as a bartender at Willie Nelson's *Austin City Limits*. A small-town Texas country girl by birth, Belle became an unofficial sideshow at City Limits Bar because she could mix some pretty potent concoctions—including the infamous Stage 69—that put the local ten-gallon shit-kickers on their heels after two or three rounds. She also carried a Colt 44 on her hip, often making patrons dance for their drinks by demonstrating her famous two-shot-hop around their boots.

Somewhere along the way, a rich international news magnate, Rupert Bart, visited City Limits to celebrate his acquisition of the *Dallas Morning Herald* to add to his collection of tv, radio and newspaper properties. He belted down two Stage 69s, then invited her to his suite at the five-star Turtle Creek Mansion. Rupert was Belle's ticket out.

They made love and shopped for a week nonstop and then got married. It was a first marriage for both. It lasted 389 days. The 61-year-old Rupert died of a massive heart attack at 3 a.m. while riding Belle. There were two relevant themes at the funeral attended by hundreds of the rich and famous. "Rupert died in the saddle" and "Belle now owns big beans and breasts."

To everyone's surprise, the street-savvy Belle turned Rupert's millions into billions, making her Manhattan's crudest and richest dame. While she bought the trapping of sophistication—34-room Park Avenue apartment, a collection of French Impressionist masterpieces,etc—she never quite cracked the in crowd until she started investing in theatrical productions.

~

MARY ARRIVED ALONE. She was greeted coldly at Bart's massive apartment door by her young, sassy administrative watchdog, Samantha Hodges, who immediately reminded Mary of Sarah Fender in demeanor and appearance.

"I have nothing on the schedule for a Mary Jackson."

"It's Mary Jackson-Peale."

"You say the appointment was made directly by Mr. Marks with Mrs. Bart. Let me check."

"No problem. David also asked if you would be so kind as to give this note to Mrs. Bart."

The small sealed white envelope read, "Personal and confidential. Fondly, David."

Samantha was dying to open the envelope, but the manner in which it was addressed, she wouldn't dare. Mary realized David had experienced Samantha's strident gatekeeper mentality when he told her to write precisely as he dictated. The handwritten card inside read, "We did well on the *Franklin Affair*. I will be forever in your debt. Listen to what Mary has to say. This investment will make you the toast of Broadway."

The door to Belle's office opened. "Mrs. Bart will see you now," smiled Samantha.

Even though Mary had never made an investor pitch, David's unique relationship gave her complete confidence that the money was there for the taking. "Thank you for seeing me. David says you're the patron saint of emerging playwrights."

"Only if I think I can make a buck."

"It's quite different in London."

"How so, dearie?"

"We have an extensive series of government grants and tax incentives to stimulate new theatre development, but there's no profit in successful East End plays. The real money is strictly West End. Directors and playwrights take the view that risk at the development stage bids prices up when properties deemed commercial open on the West End."

"What's this East End-West End stuff you keep referring to?"

"The East End is roughly equivalent of America's Off-Broadway while the West End is a mirror image of your Broadway."

"So what's my handsome young Brit got?"

"David's latest play is called *American Bison*. Personally, I believe it has the potential to gross Off-Broadway, then after a short run and some favorable reviews, become a Broadway smash with a long, profitable run."

"Dearie, you sure? You look a little green," observed Bart.

"Green?" said Mary quizzically.

"No experience at picking winners. Got my drift?"

"Not so," said Mary determined to exaggerate her accomplishments in her most pronounced British. "I was the lead agent at Belfrage and Associates, London's largest theatrical organization. I had a streak of eight straight West End hits and employed the best of the best actors and directors.

"So what are you doing here?"

"Succeeding in the New York theatre has been an important professional goal for years. Plus, I have other interests here."

"David can do that to you. He is one hunk of a man. How much do we need to build the box?" laughed Bart heartily.

"I've penciled it out at about a million, given the custom set."

"That's a lot of custom set for Off-Broadway."

"We'll be able to reuse it on Broadway."

"How do the returns 'pencil' out?" mimicked Bart.

"Assuming a conservative audience gross, I estimate about 10 percent Off-Broadway and about 25 percent on Broadway."

"Sounds pretty good. Assume you've got the money. Send me the contracts."

"Don't you want to hear a synopsis or read the script?"

"Naaaw, save it for the rest of the group. David does this esoteric stuff I rarely understand. All I know is if David likes it, the critics will like it, and hopefully the audiences will follow. The more I meddle, the more confused I get."

"Not even a tinsy, winsy bit about the storyline?" said Mary incredulously.

"Oh, go ahead, I've got five minutes."

"*Bison* is an existential metaphor for a world that lets so many unfortunate souls to slip through the cracks...The three main characters are..."

"That's enough," said Belle. "Save it for the cocktail party. Like always, I expect you to deliver David in the flesh to meet and greet my investor friends at the apartment. Shall we say, Friday next?"

~

Mary figured she had just made about $50,000 on the capital raise and another $20,000 on the set kickback, plus yet-to-be-defined supplemental revenue streams. At minimum, David deserved a phone call and a dinner invite. "David, that Belle's a hoot."

"Does that mean you got a financial commitment?"

"Commitment? I'm going home to prepare contracts right now and put them in the mail. She even told me to pick the set designer."

"She liked the play that much."

"She loved the metaphor," said Mary without hesitation. "Now there is just the matter of the cocktail party."

"What cocktail party?" asked David.

"Belle told me, same as you did the last time, with her investor group."

"There was no last time."

"Well, there is now. You'll come meet and greet at her apartment."

"You are one piece of work. One meet and greet coming up."

27

~ ~ ~

London, about the same time....

A SECOND SCOTLAND YARD AUTOPSY identified the real cause of Belfrage's death. "It appears a 'friendly' third party spiked the deceased's drink with a rather large dose of heroin," said Yard Coroner, Dr. James Paulus.

"Who would be stupid enough to mix that stuff in a cosmopolitan?" asked Johnny's partner, Inspector Harrick.

"Probably someone who wasn't actually planning on killing him."

"You suggesting we have a second-degree manslaughter on our hands?"

"I believe so," responded Paulus.

~

The detectives concluded their investigation should begin with the victim's family and friends. After all, there were no signs of a break-in at Belfrage's flat, and the doorman reported an unidentified man in a trench coat hurriedly exited the building about the time of the phone call to the police. "Why don't we start with Belfrage's assistant?" said Harrick."She's got to have some kind of database and a feeling about the guy's romantic interests. That should give us an initial list of suspects."

~

Sarah had become increasingly concerned Belfrage and Associates would quickly collapse and was in the middle of an off-site job interview when the inspectors paid a visit to the Belfrage offices.

Harrick asked the human resource director if Mr. Belfrage really relied on Miss Fender.

"She did everything. She was Mr. Belfrage's fair-haired girl. She could do no wrong."

"Did she also handle Mr. Belfrage's personal affairs?"

"As I said, she did everything. In fact, once Mr. Belfrage passed, Sarah held the office together single-handedly. She has been a tower of strength."

"Thanks for your help. Tell Miss Bender we're anxious to take her statement. We are looking for close business associates and friends of Mr. Belfrage."

"Best you talk to Sarah about all of that directly."

Harrick's cell phone vibrated. He had an urgent text message from Paulus.

"A few strands of a red hair were found under the victim's bed."

"Just out of curiosity," said Harrick, "what color is Miss Fender's hair."

"Strange question, officer. But, as you will see, Sarah is a most attractive young lady with rather long black hair."

"We have a hunch, said Harrick, "someone with red hair may have been involved in the case."

"I can't say for sure, but I think Mr. Belfrage shied away from redheads after the first Mrs. Belfrage."

"The first Mrs. Belfrage?"

"That was a long, long time ago."

~

The interview went so well that Sarah's new boss, Franklin Margoles, invited her to lunch.

Afterward, Sarah called the h.r. director. "Helen, I'm sorry to abandon you, but I have just agreed to a new position."

"Can't say I blame you. Where?"

"Margoles and Company."

"Dear old Julian would roll over in his grave. He hated that man. Ever since they stole Bill Nighty (famous theatrical writer director) right from under his nose."

"It was nothing personal. It's just business."

"Is this then you're official notice."

"I think it best. I was planning to stop by tomorrow, pick up my personal things, and then take a few days off before I started at Margoles."

"See you in the morning then...By the way dear, two very nice gentlemen from Scotland Yard stopped by today. They wanted to talk to you about Mr. Belfrage's demise. Some routine questions, I assume, to close the case. They left their phone number."

"What did you tell them?" said a suddenly alarmed Sarah.

"About what?"

"Me?"

"They were interested in getting a list of Julian's close friends and contacts. I told them you were the one person best equipped to answer a question like that."

~

Sarah was not about to call Scotland Yard.

She was convinced the delicate web she and Mary had woven would not stand the test of time. She also knew going to the police was fraught with peril. As the daughter of a solicitor, she knew, if caught, she could be convicted and imprisoned as an accessory to manslaughter. Even if all the stars lineup appropriately, she was, at minimum, guilty of obstructing justice, another major felony.

Circumstances created the only logical course of action. She would flee to America. She emptied her bank account, packed a selected wardrobe and bought a ticket on the first plane to New York the following morning. To calm her nerves and get a few hours sleep, she took 20 mg of Valium. When she arrived at the British Airways counter the next morning, she was bleary eyed and quite loopy.

"Miss Bender, seems all is in order," said the clerk behind the counter. "Enjoy the club, we'll call your flight."

"The club?"

"The business class lounge…you do realize you are holding a business-class seat."

"Sorry," said Sarah, "my mind was wondering."

She decided there would be no more mistakes, no drawing attention to herself, no calls, even to Mary.

Three days later, every client bailed at Belfrage and Associates. After 28 years, the firm closed its doors forever.

28

~ ~ ~

UPON ARRIVAL, SARAH WENT directly to Mary's apartment. About 6 p.m., she knocked and knocked to no avail. Unbeknownst to her, Mary was hosting an investors' dinner with Belle Bart and a few of her well-heeled buddies.

Sarah recalled prior telephone conversations about Mary's fondness for her landlord and neighbor, Connie Dapolito, in the adjoining building. "I'm frightfully sorry to bother you at this late hour," said Sarah with bag in hand, "My name is Sarah Bender, I'm a friend of Mary's, I was wondering if..."

"Say no more, Mary talk about you all the time. I can tell you from London, have that funny accent," joked Connie. Sarah wondered who had the stranger accent. "I give you key to apartment. You rest after that long trip. Your friend just work, work, work."

Nothing has changed, thought Sarah.

161

"Nice for her to have a best friend visit. She like the daughter I never had. Maybe you can help her find right man. She deserve that."

Sarah wondered what all this 'best friend' crap was? Either Mary was embarrassed to tell Connie the real truth, or something had changed during their time apart. She took herself on a self-guided tour of the apartment. She was pleased by the possibilities As Mary had suggested, there was plenty of space for them to live on the second floor while creating a trendy yet welcoming first-floor office.

She was appalled at the scarcity of furnishings. Mary had neither suggested, hinted nor implied her entire furniture collection consisted of a queen-sized bed and stick lamp in the bedroom, and a single canvas director's chair in the kitchen. Sarah tried Mary's cell a few times but to no avail. Exhausted, she fell fast asleep on the bed. Early in the morning, she was awakened by Mary's return. "Sarah. What a wonderful surprise. When did you get here?"

"About 6 p.m. last night. I tried your mobile, but it just went to voice mail."

"So sorry about that. I was courting some potential investors."

"Till 4 a.m.?" said Sarah looking at her watch.

"Well I had to tell my first client that we had his play financed."

"And, who might that be?"

"David Marks."

Mary saw the suspicious look in Sarah's expression.

"David and I just hung out a bit. After all, it's not every day investors make that kind of financial commitment."

"Hung out?" challenged Sarah, jealousy seeping through.

"Love, we just talked shop. The bars here close at four. Before we knew it, the sun was rising. So I walked home."

"Walked home. In New York?

"David lives around the block."

"How terribly convenient."

Mary realized she needed to walk on eggshells.

"Why don't I shower, take a little nap, and then invite David to lunch so you can say hello again. There's nothing to fret about."

Mary held Sarah gently and kissed her.

"How about after lunch," smiled Sarah, "we go furniture shopping. This place needs absolutely everything."

~

"My significant other has just arrived from London," said Mary with Sarah listening intently. "I believe you have met. Sarah Fender from Julian's office." From the business-like tone of Mary's voice, David realized things had changed from the night before. "She's going to be my office manager and since you're my first client, I thought we should meet. What are you doing for lunch?"

At noon, Mary and Sarah were holding hands at a corner table at Osteria del Sole awaiting David.

Oscar approached. "Oscar, this is my dear friend Sarah," she said holding up the clasped hands. Oscar, who had waited on Mary and David on several intimate occasions, was confused.

"No Dee today."

"Yes Dee," smiled Mary, "Mr. Marks will be joining us shortly. Why not open a bottle of that wonderful Sangiovese?"

Now Oscar was totally confused.

So was Sarah. "No Dee, what was that all about?"

"Oscar is Hungarian. His English is sporadic. He wanted us to know there was no Fra Diablo today. The chef insists on preparing only fresh line-caught fish. I guess he didn't like what was available at the Fulton Fish Market this morning. Oscar's calls the dish 'Dee.'" The whole thing indeed sounded fishy to Sarah.

Minutes later David arrived. "David, I almost didn't recognize you without the beard."

"Funny," said Mary. "When I met David in New York, I said exactly the opposite."

"Totally serendipitous," laughed David.

Within minutes, the threesome had consumed one bottle and ordered a second. The conversation became decidedly less formal. "Where did you two meet?"asked David.

"We met at Julian," said Sarah holding Mary's hand. "Mind if I tell you something? she added staring at David's beardless face. Sarah looked at Mary. "Promise you won't get mad?"

"Promise."

"Blame it on the wine or jet lag," giggled Sarah.

"Out with it, already," urged Mary.

"The girls at the office used to have it on about what it would be like to have oral sex with your curly wire beard."

"My god," said a shocked and displeased Mary. "What a god-awful thing to say."

"And when did we become such a prude?" responded Sarah.

As the girls bantered, an increasingly horny David's hand slid under the table.

The conversation also made Sarah horny. She decided to slip her hand under the table and rub Mary's thigh in apology.

There she met David's.

Lunch was over.

29

~~~

"THAT WAS UNBELIEVABLY embarrassing!" said Sarah. "I'm surprised you didn't get on the table and let him do you in front of the entire restaurant."

"Petty jealousy does not become you. It didn't mean anything."

"Hogwash."

For the next four days and nights Sarah refused to engage in conversation of any sort. To occupy the silence, Mary focused on her work—finishing Belle's contract details and identifying the appropriate Off-Broadway theatre locale.

Belle got Mary an appointment with Marty Balan, owner of the landmark Cherry Lane Playhouse, New York's oldest theatre, and a converted turn-of-the-century box factory. Mary made the meeting a slamdunk by studying her history.

"Martin, your gracious old place is tailor made for a genre-breaking work like *American Bison*. The karma is overwhelming. When you think of the playwrights who have graced this stage—Scott Fitzgerald, Dos Passos, O'Neil, Odets, Gertrude

Stein, Albee, Pinter, Saroyan…the list goes on and on. David is destined to be another of those long lived lights."

"Mary, I gotta compliment you. You know your stuff. Let's hope the play does as well as you just did. I'll have my attorneys prepare the engagement contracts."

"No curveballs?"

"Marty Balan doesn't throw curve balls. My family has been here since 1924, and, god willing, we'll be here another 50 years."

"How do you handle the agent's finder's fee?"

"It's just a standard line item in the contract. I hope you're not trying to negotiate more than the 5 percent," glared Balan.

"No, no," smiled Mary. She had the answer she wanted. "Remember, I'm a Brit. This is my first New York production. Whatever is the going custom is fine with me." She shook hands with Balan and left. As she walked back to her place, she began to think about the last four miserably awkward days. Decision time with respect to David and Sarah was rapidly approaching. She adored David professionally. He was a never-ending font of creativity. Personally, he was also a lot of fun. Romantic, sensitive, and quite smashing in bed . But did she want to live with him, a man? Any man? Her Mum's humiliating experience with Riley, Annabelle Lee's devastating marriage to Belfrage, and her own intuitions suggested otherwise.

Then there was Sarah, a bundle of pent-up insecurities. There was clearly a fondness. But was it bells-and-whistles love like Elizabeth? Regardless, didn't she owe Sarah, who out of sheer affection and loyalty, hid their terrible secret with no strings attached? Shouldn't that kind of love be rewarded? In the end, the decision was no decision—Mary subconsciously accepted her inevitable destiny.

~

Mary decided David should be the first to know. She arranged lunch.

David was more than just a friend. He was her first and only client. The lynchpin upon which her aspirations to be somebody in New York theatre rested. That association had to flourish. On a purely personal level, informing him of her decision would add a certain irreversible punctuation to the parameters of their future relationship. Her public pledge to Sarah would also provide Mary the closure she so desperately needed for own sanity.

"Congratulations. We now have a landmark venue to launch the *Bison*," she announced to David.

"You're kidding. The Cherry Lane agreed?"

"Why so surprised? You lucky sod. You do have the best agent in New York."

"Love, this deserves another one of our titanic celebrations…, and it's my treat all the way," retorted David in his Sunday-best *double entendre*.

Mary was well prepared. "I can't."

"You mean you won't."

"I mean I can't and I won't." Mary took a deep breath. "Life has changed post-Sarah."

"No, life has just returned to the way it was, pre-David."

"Whatever." Mary didn't want to argue. It was painful enough. "I'd still want to represent you."

"I wouldn't have it any other way. If I can't have your body, I still want your mind."

"This is important," said Mary. "Can you separate the professional from the personal?"

David wasn't sure, but he knew the answer Mary wanted to hear. "I've invested a lot of time and energy into helping Mary Jackson-Peale become a noted "A" list agent. It makes no sense to ditch her when my investment is about to be realized."

"Spoken like the unscrupulous, coldhearted, brazen New Yorker you've become," smiled Mary. "Thank you for understanding."

A relieved Mary called Sarah. The weight of the world had been removed from her shoulders. The phone rang and rang until the voice mail clicked in. Mary had no way of knowing Sarah was in the shower.

"Sarah, honey. Please pick up the phone." She waited a few moments. "Please pick up the phone. We've got to stop this belabored silence. I love you very much. I've told David and he understands. Plus, I just made a fabulous deal on a theatre that will make us oodles. We're going to make it big time. The opening is right around the corner, so I'll be a little late tonight. Wrapping up contracts and such at Belle's place. What say we celebrate with a nice romantic dinner tomorrow evening. Just the two of us. On my way home, I'll tell Oscar to whip us up something special…From now on, Osteria will be our place," said Mary, subtly implying she was sorry about the luncheon mishap, and that it would never happen again.

~

A broken-hearted Sarah never received the voicemail.

Tears streamed down her face as she showered. Running into David's groping hand was the final straw. Money had changed Mary. David had changed Mary. New York had changed Mary. She knew she couldn't return to London or anywhere in England for that matter. And she certainly had no interest in remaining in the West Village. There was no way out. She browsed Mary's closet searching for just the right outfit, since they were about the same size. She applied her makeup and blow dried her hair, and looked quite smashing.

She then walked up to Greenwich Avenue and hailed a cab. Along the way, she turned heads…both male and female.

Once inside the cab, the scent of Hermes Caléche filled the cabin.

"Lady, I ain't tryin' to be fresh or anything, but you look and smell great. I hope that guy realizes what a catch he's got. Where to?"

Sarah smiled. "The Brooklyn Bridge."

"The Brooklyn Bridge. You sure?" said the cabbie questioning the strange request. "Where at the bridge?"

"I don't know. Isn't there a place people trod across?"

"There is. They just don't usually do it after dark." The cabbie stopped at the traffic light and looked in the rearview mirror. Sarah was fumbling, trying to take a cigarette out of her case. "Lady, you okay?"

"Fine, fine. I just want to see the skyline. We don't have anything like this in London."

The cab driver was not convinced. He dropped Sarah at the base of the bridge on the Manhattan side near Canal Street then pulled around the corner and stopped the first patrolmen he saw. "Officer, a well dressed lady just insisted I drop her at the base of da bridge. It don't make no sense. I think you better check it out."

The policeman headed to the bridge walk...but it was already too late.

~

Sarah stood at the midpoint on the bridge and looked at the swirling currents of the East River some 280 feet below.

She held the railing tightly as her inner self battled—-to do or not to do. She glanced upward at the twinkling Manhattan skyline and the clear, star-filled sky. To a rational mind, it was an almost perfect New York summer night. A night filled with possibilities, no matter how small, no matter how grand. But to Sarah it was a sky filled with dark, heavy clouds and endless tumult. A sky dominated by David's dour face peering through imaginary layers of white chiffon. She hesitated as the misty air gently swirled around her long black hair. It was her moment of cleansing. She had passed the point.

She climbed up on the railing, looked into the deep abyss, asked God's forgiveness and jumped. The air rushed past her contorted face as her body collided with choppy seas. The rip tides then flushed her limp remains out of the East River, past the Statue of Liberty and into the channel leading to the

Atlantic Ocean. The only marker that showed Sarah once visited here was a small piece of Mary's dress snagged by the jagged rocks along the water's edge.

~

Mary arrived home about midnight.

"Sarah, dear, no need to jingle the police, it's just me," shouted an excited Mary, recalling the London incident. She began to search the apartment looking for Sarah then went downstairs to the office. There was no sign of her anywhere, and no clues to where she had gone. There was nothing else Mary could do but trod on until she resurfaced.

Three weeks went by and still no Sarah. While she waited for some kind of contact, Mary occupied her days and nights with the launch of David's play.

30

~~~

INITIAL REACTION TO *American Bison,* billed as the British wunderkind playwright and director David Marks's second American invasion, was at best disappointing and depressing.

Attendance didn't meet expectations. The Cherry Lane Theatre was only half full (including investor comps and VIP guests) for its traditional Friday preview night. The few critics that were cajoled into attending wrote scathing reviews.

> "Brit import David Marks brought his intellect across the Atlantic but left all else floating on the Thames."
>
> —-Clive Hagstrom,
> *New York Times*

> "The Cherry Lane's longstanding reputation as champion of the avant-garde was brought to its knees last evening."
>
> —Walter Sinue,
> *Village Voice*

"The Bison's self-indulgent stage design created dark new standards for the words excessive and self indulgent, while play's storyline vacillated from obtuse to oblique."

—Edward Hampton,
Newsweek

"Derivative drivel. David Mamet should be furious. Marks and his stage design imposters irreparably tarnished the sparkle of *The Old Neighbor.*"

—James Mathias,
USA Today

And the hallway buzz—generally considered an informal measurement of a play's audience receptivity—ranged from stunned silence to utter disdain. As one exiting theatre goer described, "I feel like I've just finished my weekly session with my shrink—completely confused, intellectually unsatisfied and a hell of a lot poorer!"

To add insult to injury, one of the leads —John Sampson—inexplicably forgot key dialogue at a critical juncture in the play just before the end of the first act. Their game attempt to improvise was both obvious and monstrously shallow, leading the lounge critics to skewer the couple as "Gus—The Theatre Cat and his Alzheimer Mistress."

~

"I think I'll slit my wrists and ride off into the sunset bleeding to death," said the always intense Marks at the somber opening-night party later that evening.

"Paring knife or steak knife," smiled a cool, collected Mary.

"How can you joke at a moment like this?"

"Listen, David," said Mary, dragging the playwright to a quiet corner and looking him straight in the eye. "We've come too far for you to have a meltdown in front of our investors. We'll fix the damn thing and make it even better. Do you hear what I'm saying?" Her confidence neutralized his doom and gloom.

David silently shook his head yes.

"So, Mary," said Belle with a Grey Goose Cosmopolitan in hand. "Looks like we're off to a hell of a bumpy start. Reminds me of my first marriage." Belle looked straight into David's eyes. "You know time is a wastin', and time is money."

David was mortified and tongue-tied, but Mary came to the rescue.

"Belle daaarling, David and I were just discussing the matter. He's already decided to rewrite certain bridge passages to make the script a tad more audience accessible."

David nodded, hoping Belle wouldn't ask for a more detailed explanation of whatever the hell Mary had just promised.

Mary was on a roll. "Also, David, I think your notion of adding sociological entendres to cool the play's searing intensity is also a bloody good fix."

David shook his head. He wanted some of Mary's hallucinogens!

"David's also thinking the stage and sound design of Otto's set may need to be a bit more allegorical, perhaps even a little over the top. But that's why you have previews, to hone and polish for opening night."

Belle paused and stared silently at Mary for about five seconds, although it felt like an hour to David. His pulse pounding.

"We might even change the name."

David wanted to scream.

"Sounds good to me, dearie, although I don't have a clue what the hell you're talking about."

Belle then patted David on the rump. "Just pack the house and everything will take care of itself."

Mary wanted to burst over Belle's seemingly endless ste-
reotypical mannerisms. "To paraphrase you Yanks... 'no
problemo!'"

Belle chuckled. "I think we stole the phrase from them
Wops, but I know what you mean." She turned to David. "So
playwright, when do we see the changes on the stage?"

"I'm guessing around...." Mary interrupted, "Day after
tomorrow," she said confidently. "We'll incorporate what we
can into Saturday night's performance."

"Atta girl," said Belle. "I'm counting on you to stay the
course with our resident creative genius."

David—eyes ready to burst from their sockets—now
bore a strong resemblance to Marty Feldman of *Young Frank-
enstein.*

"Hey, Igor," chuckled Belle, noticing the similarity. "You
look like a porcupine slithered up your derriere. Stick with
this girl, she's a winner."

Once Belle was out of earshot, David wigged out. "What
the bloody hell was that all about? Accessible dialogue? Enhanced stage and sound design? Your diatribe was absolutely
astounding."

Mary was at a critical juncture in her development as a
theatrical agent. She was confident she had the necessary creative sensitivity and commercial instincts to resuscitate a
troubled stage property. But... recognizing and communi-
cating what needed to be done versus motivating the playwright to action were two entirely different issues. How could
she get Marks to trust her suggestions? How could she
achieve the ultimate Trifecta...script revisions that would
please the critics, the public and her investors, a set change
and a new name...in 48 hours? And assuming the play was
successfully sliced and diced, how could she persuade Marks
that he remained the play's artistic soul? "Do you disagree
with my comments?" asked Mary

"I heard the audience just like you"

"You have any better ideas?"

"No. Not at the moment."

"So, when do we go back to your place to revise the script?"

"How about tomorrow morning after breakfast? I'll be in a better mood."

"Rehearsals have got to start by 10 a.m. if we're going to in-corporate any changes into Saturday night's performance."

"That means an all-night rewrite, then all-day and night rehearsals."

"Sounds right."

"Let's assume you can bully a lily-livered sod like myself. What about Otto's stage and sound design?" asked Marks, now increasingly aware he was executing commands rather than creating possibilities. "When do we expect Otto to work on the fixes?"

Mary knew she had made a huge mistake by insisting Otto replicate *The Old Neighborhood* set design concept so he could focus on his first love, sound design. Otto needed to perform immediate damage control—no more "derivative drivel" critical commentaries. He had to recast the set design with the props at hand and then reinvent a completely new design in the coming weeks, assuming the play ran that long and the budget would allow. "Like everybody else.... tonight," insisted Mary.

"Suppose he balks. Those Scandinavians are a fearless lot."

"And suppose I don't authorize payment of his supplier bills for the shitty set design we currently own?"

Marks nodded and took out his mobile phone. "Otto, this is David....."

~

One important item remained. A title change.

"My title's perfect," argued David.

"My instinct doesn't agree," responded Mary.

"Give me a break, for Christ's sake, how many plays have you represented?"

"Doesn't matter. This is make it or break it time."

David was confronted with the decision of his professional life. He glared. Mary stared right back.

"Okay, you win. Let me guess…you already have a suggestion."

"Lost In Life."

"Because?"

"Isn't that what it's really about?"

David stood quietly, thinking. "Actually, I rather like it."

Mary kissed him on the cheek and sent him on his way.

~

While David and Otto burned the midnight oil, Mary's focus turned to increasing last-minute box-office traffic.

First step was to alert the local Kinko's that they would be open all night designing window posters to herald an exciting new play at the Cherry Lane. "I need an experienced mate, so don't give me one of those interns in training."

"But, Madame, this is so last-minute."

"You gentleman spend a fortune advertising 24-hour service. I merely wish what you promise. I'm prepared to call your Dallas World Headquarters if necessary. I'm sure they will be frightfully interested in your personal deviations from customer-service philosophy," threatened Mary in a most proper, aloof British accent. Minutes later one of the store's most experienced designers was working with Mary terminal to terminal on the initial poster design.

The main visual was the unusual set with a headline, "The Critics are talking about *Lost In Life*," which was technically true. The visual was surrounded by glowing quotes, taken completely out of context. For example, Marks became the "Brit Import. The play design contained "new standards," and the riveting dialogue "brought reality to its knees." "Mary Jackson-Peale Productions Presents" was also prominently displayed.

"What size do we want?"

"About 20 by 28 and dry mounted so they fit comfortably in local store windows."

"No problem," said the clerk. "How many do you need?"

"I'm guessing a hundred."

"That's impossible by 9 a.m.

"How many can you deliver?"

"About half."

"Fine. Have the first half ready at nine and the second batch by noon."

Production underway, it was time to tackle distribution and posting.

"Mama Concetta," said Mary to a surprised Connie Dapolito at 4:30 a.m. while she and her family were baking the sesame pizziolas, crusty loaves of Tuscan olive bread, 24-inch Grissini breadsticks and stacks of La Foccaccia Liquore for the early morning crowds. "This place smells heavenly."

"You no come here before dawn to tell me bread smells good."

"You're right, Mama. Remember how you told me, if I needed a favor…"

"I remember. What you need?"

"My friend's play—the one he worked so hard on—is not going well. We need a bigger audience or it will never get to Broadway. I'm having a poster made for store windows. I was wondering if you and Antony knew some neighborhood kids who could talk the store owners into putting the signs in their windows first thing in the morning.?"

She smiled knowingly. "Si, Si, it is done."

"Are you sure? Because if we don't get a good showing tomorrow night at the Cherry Lane, the owner might close the show. That would devastate my friend David."

"The good looking boyfriend with the curly hair and blue eyes?"

"He's not my boyfriend. He's just a friend."

"I see the way he looks. Trust me he thinking more than good friend." Mama paused. "He good in bed?"

"Now Mama, that's a terribly private question!"

"Hey," smiled Mama raising her hands and eyebrows. "You like family. This America in the 21st Century. No be a stuffy Brit."

"He's very good in bed," smiled Mary.

"I thought so."

"Mama, the posters."

"Ahhh, sorry. Like I say before, lots of people in the Village owe Antony favors. We call them in. All the local shopkeepers will put the signs in their windows today and tomorrow as well as buy tickets to attend. Concetta word is her bond."

Mama Concetta paused. There was more. "We should make the play worthwhile for the shopkeepers. Everybody loves a raffle. Let our friends pick a name out of a hat. Free. The winner gets a new laptop computer."

"I'm not sure I've got the budget or the time to organize...."

"No budget. Free. Antony has a warehouse full of new computers that 'fell off truck,'" smiled Concetta.

Mary frowned. "Suppose the computer was damaged in the fall. Aren't we opening Pandora's Box?"

Concetta realized Mary didn't understand her idiomatic expression. "In America 'fell off the truck' is an expression we use to mean 'we borrow.' The computer is perfect condition, have original warranties."

Mary stared blankly. Concetta decided the less Mary understood the better. "Mary, just leave everything to the Dapolitos. We have full house tomorrow night."

~

The Saturday performance went as Concetta predicted. A full house with thundering applause— sometimes even at the right moment.

Antony's influence spread to other relevant areas of the entertainment industry. A number of critics from *Newsday*, *The Daily News* and the *New York Post*, not only attended the performance, but also wrote sterling reviews. Those reviews, the plethora of posters throughout the Village and the periodic "off the truck" consumer promotions, filled the house for 30 straight days.

David was ecstatic. He assumed his revisions were the driving force behind the show's newfound popularity. His reputation as an up-and-coming playwright and director had been salvaged.

Lost In Life taught Mary a valuable lesson. Ground-breaking esoteric was a wasted concept in the Colonies. She also became a fan of performing and collecting favors.

Concetta was actually the only one who knew the real story behind the play's sudden success and the change in critical attitude. But she saw no reason to divulge the subtleties of the Mafioso's how and when.

In time—four months to be exact—word-of-mouth momentum began to attract non-Villagers to the Cherry Lane. By the sixth month, *Lost In Life* was Off-Broadway's hardest ticket to acquire at face value.

Mary was so grateful to Mama and the Dapolito family that, against Otto and David's wishes, the play's set was painted Vesuvio green, the imaginary company used in the play was renamed The Vesuvio Corporation. Coincidentally, it was founded in 1920, the same year as the bakery. Mama was so proud of the bakery's prominence in the play that she sent pictures of her and Antony in front of the set back to their family in the little hill town of Calrizzano, about 30 kilometers north east of Naples.

31

~ ~ ~

THE GRASSROOTS SUCCESS OF *Lost In Life* created a flood of administrative details that had little personal appeal to Mary—investor queries, press interviews, bookkeeping reports, supplier sales calls and poster updates. Clearly, the time had come.

"Eileen, this is Mary Jackson-Peale. We met recently at…"

"The Tribecca Festival. I remember it vividly," interrupted Eileen, one of the New York theatres most successful headhunters. "You dropped some of your single malt gasoline on my dress."

"Frightfully sorry," giggled Mary.

"To what do I owe the pleasure of a call from the queen of Off-Broadway?

"Aren't we exaggerating a bit?"

"No…One can't walk around Greenwich Village without seeing your name on a poster."

"I need a girl Friday. Somebody who'll run the backroom, so I can concentrate on business and client development."

"Do you have a compensation package in mind?"

"No, I figured that's one of the reasons I want to engage you. I'm willing to pay fair market rates and benefits, whatever that is. She would be my alter ego regarding any and all office details. I'd like someone who has the skills to prepare financial reports for investors and performers and at the same time has no issue with rolling up her sleeves to make sure a live voice always answers the phones."

"Normally," said Eileen, "I deal in locating young people who want to become actors, actresses, playwrights and directors. Administrative staff is not my bag. But it just so happens, a very bright young lady named Allison Edwards from Smith College left her resume."

"What's Smith, a trade school?"

"No," chuckled Eileen, assuming Mary was having her on.

"Do you know how many Smiths there are in England?"

Eileen realized a little relevant background would make things right. "Smith College in Northampton, Massachusetts, is one of America's most prestigious and progressive women's colleges. It was founded in 1871 and specializes in graduates who want to break new ground."

Mary was still a little skeptical. "You know this is a dream job for anyone who wants to break into show business. There must be a million girls in New York who'd want the opportunity."

"Mary, at the risk of being a tad rude, Smith graduates are not accustomed to working in start-ups. Daddy spends upwards of $75,000 a year for daughters to attend. Daughters like Barbara Bush, Nancy Reagan, Betty Friedan, Gloria Steinem and Julia Child. So you're going to have to do a little selling."

"I'm not a start up!" responded Mary indignantly.

"I beg your pardon," said Eileen. "Including yourself, how many employees do you currently have?"

"One."

~

"I'm Allison Edwards," said the red-haired beauty with light blue eyes, dressed to the nines in a Giorgio Armani striped blue pants suit, looking around the partially finished office in the rear of Vesuvio's Bake Shop. "This isn't really the Peale and Associates Theatrical Agency, is it?"

Mary was already up to her ears in Smith College pedigree. Plus the phones were ringing off the hooks. She wasn't in the mood. "Listen, Allison. I'm busting my butt to build a first class theatrical agency. I'm really not interested in some snooty Smith sod staring me down. Around here, you have to roll up your sleeves and get your hands dirty. This is not a holding station for someone planning to marry Prince William or Harry."

Allison stood her ground. "Shall I assume you're Mary Jackson-Peale?"

"You should."

"Eileen said you might be a little high-strung."

"Oh, really!"

"Is there anything I can say that won't set you off? I'm just here for a job interview, not a debate."

"What else did Eileen tell you?"

"She said it might be an unusual and challenging opportunity for me to use my diverse skill base," chuckled the sassy Allison. "I have a heavy accounting and statistics background and extensive experience establishing, maintaining, and analyzing company as well as individual investor partnership books and records. I also have a minor in marketing and promotion and have run numerous college alumni events...all of which, I might add, have been money-makers. I'm also pretty damn good with people, and as former editor of the college paper, I have a fair sense of what makes a good literary product and or a public relation story."

Mary was impressed by her credentials, her articulateness and, most of all, her poise under pressure. "Maybe we should start over again?"

"Only if you want to engage in civil discourse. If I wish to be shit upon, I can always talk to my father," grinned Allison.

Mary was convinced Allison might be a perfect fit. But there were concerns. Allison went to expensive schools, wore expensive clothes and clearly had a taste for the good life. Mary was planning on paying $30,000 a year with some modest health benefits. Could Allison afford to accept that number? Would she bolt at the first opportunity?

Allison was surprisingly flexible with regard to compensation. She sensed the opportunity. "I'm willing to accept whatever salary you are offering, assuming, if I prove my worth, there is more in the wings. Plus, if I like it here and we can build something, particularly after we decorate the place, I'd like a taste of equity."

"Done," said Mary. "Assuming David agrees."

"David?"

"I have one major client at the moment, playwright and friend David Marks. The chemistry has to be right. After all, you would be working closely with him."

"Never been a problem before," responded Allison confidently. "American men are rather easy to direct. Most are still grappling with the intellectual capacity of the contemporary woman. They're rather Elizabethan in that respect."

"David's not most guys, and he's not American." said Mary defensively. "He's that one-in-a-million male. He's not the least bit threatened by the smart and edgy, but you might be a little overwhelming even for...".

"Why don't we let David decide that? Let's do lunch. It will be a little less confrontational. Yes?"

Mary jumped at the idea. "What works for you? I see you live in Connecticut?"

"Sorry about that," said Allison looking at her resume. "My parents live on a farm in Norfolk, Connecticut. I live in the city, so I can pop by when it is convenient for you and David."

Mary stared at Allison for almost 30 seconds. She put her index finger on her lips. She was thinking. *Let's do that.*

Call it woman's intuition, Allison sensed David was more than just a client.

~

"Mary, what do I know about interviewing prospective employees?" protested David. "I'm a playwright because I couldn't hold down a real job."

Mary wouldn't take no. "How about we just do breakfast at Vesuvio's? At least you get a cappuccino, Mama's panini toast, and you can still run home if you don't like…."

David smiled. "You buying?"

"When was the last time you paid for anything?" teased Mary.

"I'm the client."

Allison turned heads when she arrived. Her red hair was waist length, her dress was short and form fitting. Mary and David were sitting at a corner table. She walked up to the table with a big grin on her face. "And you must be David." As she began to sit down, she continued. "I've never been interviewed by a successful playwright before. It was rather unusual preparing to meet you. So I Googled you and went to see *Lost In Life* twice, Saturday matinee and Tuesday evening."

"You Googled me. Is that good or bad?"

"It means I got some of your background on the internet. I noticed you graduated from Exeter with a degree in biosciences. That's very impressive; your alma mater has some terribly well-known alumni in nuclear science, geo politics, and mathematical theory."

Mary sat stunned. She realized she knew nothing of David's background…other than he was a great lay and playwright, not necessarily in that order.

"I graduated from Smith. My *grandmum* spent her junior year in the Exeter-Smith study abroad program. She absolutely loved London. She still talks about dancing the weekend away at Annabelle's."

"It's long since closed. Annabelle made a fortune from her 'A' list patrons and bought a mansion in Monte Carlo. She didn't want anybody else using her brand name."

"Pity, grandmum said the VIP accoutrements were to die for."

David was mesmerized by her intellect, dazzled by her sheer beauty. "No worries. There are a number of cool replacements I can show you next time we're in London."

Mary thought to herself, *I can't believe it; the bastard is hitting on my job applicant right in front of me.*

"And how did you switch from bioscience to playwriting? What a fascinating evolution," said a genuinely smitten Allison.

"Actually, it wasn't all that dramatic. Isn't there a direct correlation between studying the ocean's sea mammals and the personality defects of human beings on the stage?" David commented wryly.

Allison burst into delicious laughter.

Mary needed a time-out. "How about we order some breakfast? If it's okay with both of you, I love Mama's toasted panini." Mary assumed Allison had Googled that also.

"What a coincidence," smiled David. "I was about to order the same thing." He turned to Mary. "As far as I'm concerned, Allison would be a perfect addition to your staff."

Allison started the next day.

32

~~~

BY THE END OF FIRST WEEK, Allison had organized a series of efficient, user-friendly protocols and processes and created a basic accounting system for Peale and Associates financial statements, individual playwright, director and investor distributions, as well as individual P&L's for individual theatrical projects.

She also had certain features added and removed from the phone system, so that no call was left unattended, while at the same time lowering their overall phone costs. Every morning when Mary arrived, she had a log of her days' activities, incoming calls and calls to be made.

"Now that we've got operations under control," said Allison, "I think it's time to tackle the office design and decor. Give it a contemporary theatrical feeling."

"I appreciate everything you've done, Allison, and while I'd like to do the office, I have to watch my expenses until we add some additional clients."

The ever-resourceful Allison had a few more tricks up her sleeve. "I quite agree, Mary. But it just so happens some first-class architects and builders owe my father a few favors. While you've been out working on business development, I took the liberty of asking them to create some preliminary blueprints." She handed Mary three sets of plans based upon restoration of the exposed brick walls, antique knotty wood floors, and rich walnut ceiling beams, plus an artful blending of technologically enhanced modern cabinetry with highly functional antique furnishings.

"Allison, it's beautiful. But I'm afraid to ask."

"The answer is zero."

"How can that be?"

"As I said, Daddy is owed a few favors."

"That's the same speech Mrs. Dapolito gave me."

Allison smiled. "That's a different kind of favor. Daddy's quite legitimate. He is an experienced theatrical investor, and he also happens to be a huge benefactor at Cooper Union on 7th Street. They are only too happy to have their students and suppliers design and execute a real world project for Daddy."

Mary wondered. *How does one define legitimate? And, who ever heard of a trade union (i.e., Cooper Union) with students instead of members?*

~

With the office design underway, Allison's focus turned to helping Mary increase her client base. Step one was to put the squeeze on Marks. "So, David, are you happy with Mary's representation?"

"Absolutely."

"You know she's working diligently on moving *Lost In Life* to Broadway as we speak."

"That would be a dream come true."

"David, I don't mean to insult you, but if Peale and Associates is ever going to be a theatrical powerhouse, we need more properties."

"Well, I told you I'm working on an interesting new play. Allison, nothing personal, but I have a philosophy of never discussing a project in progress till I have the entire first draft. That way I'm confident we have soup. I abhor all the bullshit in this business."

"Bullshit is the currency of business. You just can't be that naive."

"You sound like Lord Byron," smiled David. "You know those famous lines from the *Ancient Mariner*, 'Bullshit, bullshit everywhere, but not a drop to drink.'"

"That is absolutely gross!" said Allison.

David chuckled. "I thought it was rather base and comedic. I've certainly heard worse at Lord Shipley's Pub in East London at four in the morning."

Allison adored the mischievous "little boy" twinkle in David's eyes. But that was for another time. She responded on point, with just a touch of Jewish guilt "Don't you think it's time for you to do something *for* Mary without her having to ask? You have friends, don't you?"

"Yes."

"And some of them are aspiring playwrights?"

"Most."

"Are they talented?"

"No, they're all deadbeats."

"Be serious."

"That was a dumb question. Most of my friends are far more talented than I, they just haven't gotten that big break yet."

"So, why don't we have them meet Mary? She can decide if they have something worth representing, and they can decide if they like her."

"They're not going to respond to a Mary inquisition."

"I quite agree. The tone should be casual, so why don't we set up a get-to-know-you coffee clutch at Vesuvio's?"

"Sounds right."

"Give Mary a head's up, and we'll see what happens," said Allison.

"Me give Mary a head's up? It was your idea."

"I think the suggestion would be better received coming from you. After all, they're your friends, not mine."

~

David and four young British playwrights—a macho, wire-haired lesbian named Marianne Kaufman; a cerebral, heavily bearded Arthur Ingram; an angry black Kenyan named Nigel Oboto; and a debonair historian/writer named Darien Manners sat around Vesuvio's largest table. The smell of fresh bread permeated the place.

"As I think you all know, Mary has been instrumental in making *Lost In Life* a critical and commercial success for me. It's just a matter of time before we're Broadway-bound. I wanted her to meet all of you because I've seen most of your work, and, frankly, I think it's better than mine."

"I would tend to agree," smiled Ingram.

"As far as I'm concerned, the key to getting anywhere in this business is to have a good agent in your corner to do the heavy lifting. Our job is to concentrate on the creative product."

David waved his hand at Mary as if to say, you're on.

"Before we get started, does everybody have a cappuccino and toasted panini?" smiled Mary as she stood up. "As you know, Brit ramblings on an empty stomach can be dodgy." Her self-depreciatory humor struck a chord. She knew playwrights loathe to let anyone—other than themselves—take matters super seriously. Mary's seemingly casual comment was, as always, part of a master plan. She intended to disarm their psyches on the way to identifying the diamonds in the rough before adroitly discarding the rest before the toast was cold and the cappuccino finished. "Peale and Associates has a simple mission: To help the best and brightest young theatrical minds achieve all their dreams."

The cynical Oboto retorted immediately. "You white people talk in such lofty, conceptual terms. I write to put food on the table and give myself a sense of achievement and self-worth. Remember, while you've been feasting topside these past 200 years, we've been fed scraps down in the belly of the slave ship."

The room was still. Mary put her hands on her hips. "Do you enjoy Sandburg?"

"Very much so. But, Lady, what has that got to do with societal inequality."

"Do you know what drove Sandburg to accomplish? His driving force was about fulfilling his dreams. Sandburg said 'Nothing happens unless first a dream.'" Mary stared deeply in Oboto's dark brown eyes. "I would challenge you, Nigel Oboto, stand up, find your dream, believe in your dream, and live your dream. The past does not portend the future. You hold the power to make your own future."

There was dead silence. The room was now Mary's.

~

"I'd like to talk creative philosophy," said Mary. "Okay?"

The group nodded. Even David now realized Mary had captured the group's undivided attention.

"Peale and Associates is not looking for clichés. We are looking for writers with something important to say. The message need not be maudlin or intellectually droll, it can contain humor, irony, pathos, wit. However, we are not looking for likeable fluff, neatly repackaged for commercial success. That's just not my cup of tea."

Nobody moved.

Mary wondered what they were thinking. "Does anybody have a question?"

"What's your process," asked Marianne Kaufman, finally breaking the silence.

"Quite simple. If you have a property that fits our profile, I'd appreciate a one or two-page synopsis. If I think it has merit, I'll request the full script. That's also your signal to schedule an appointment with my assistant Allison. By the time we meet, I'll have read the property in its entirety, so we can have a meaningful conversation about content, including my suggestions.

"What about contracts and finances," queried Manners.

"Unless we see eye to eye creatively, that is probably not a useful exercise. You need to be committed to your work first, the money will come. Suffice to say, I handle everything from contract development and actual negotiations to monitoring, collecting and distributing your proper share."

"Based on my experience with Mary, she's an ace," David chimed in.

"I want to thank you all for spending the time with me. I will respect whatever decision you make."

Mary then went for the close as only Mary could. "I would like to leave you with a final thought. Never forget, the theatre business is a series of intellectual contradictions: creatively challenging, unmercifully cutthroat and coyly self-indulgent. Peale and Associates only represents those willing to create to their convictions, not commerciality." She quoted a reinforcing passage from Frost:

> *Two roads diverged in a wood,*
> *and I took the one less traveled by,*
> *And that has made all the difference.*

Game. Set. Match.

~

Mary walked back to her office, David not far behind.

"Tough crowd," said Mary.

As they walked through the door, Allison was there with a big Cheshire grin. "Whatever did you say to those poor people? They practically knocked down the door to leave their synopses."

"Congratulations," said David.

"It's a little early for that. Let's see if we actually have anything to celebrate."

~ ~ ~

MARY WAS PLEASANTLY SURPRISED by the innovative nature of each synopsis.

Marianne Kaufman's project, *Little Fanny Coscia*, was the
tender and tragic personal journey of an eight-year-old boy
named Charlie Imperale and a seven-year-old girl named
Fanny Coscia who fell in love on Mulberry Street in Little
Italy at the turn of the 20th Century. They loved each other
for another 79 years but somehow never married. In the process, Charlie married twice, Fanny once, but never to each
other. "It's based on a true story I discovered while talking
to my father in Nottingham."

"How so?" asked Mary.

"Father loved to play the accordion. Perhaps more than
that, he was a historian of the instrument. From what he told
me the world's greatest accordionist in the 20th century was
an Italian-American named Imperale."

"The Charlie in your story."

"Yes."

"And was Fanny a fabrication?"

"No, she really existed. In fact, the more I researched their relationship, the more certain I became that they were destined for each other. But on the way to achieving his musical stardom, Charlie made conscious choices. Temporarily abandoning Fanny for fleeting fame was his ultimate mistake. Despite his professional success, his personal life was a maze of failed marriages, prescription drug-abuse and wanton affairs. Through it all, he still managed to find ways to stay in touch with Fanny, his anchor to reality. In the end, he realized he never stopped loving Fanny. Although Charlie died ten years before Fanny, they are buried near each other in the same cemetery in New York City."

"What a lovely story," said Mary, tears forming in her eyes. "It's jam packed with heart-wrenching counterpoints which should make for a powerful theatre experience. But I do have an issue with the ending."

"Issue?" responded Marianne stiffly.

"The ending is so sad. People prefer positive resolution," said Mary, thinking commercial appeal.

"How is that possible, given the truth of the storyline?"

"Daaarling, don't get encumbered by the truth," volunteered Mary deftly.

Marianne remained more than a touch resistant.

"Suppose, just suppose," said Mary, "Charlie comes back to visit Fanny during her last ten years, almost like a dream sequence. They talk. He apologizes for all the mistakes. Tells her he will be waiting for her when her time comes. May be they even have a last dance before he returns to the spiritual realm."

Marianne sought affirmation of Mary's suggestions from her peers. Heads began to nod.

"That's good, Luv, very good," said David. "Actually, it's stunningly brilliant."

Marianne made all the revisions—to Mary's precise specs. A few days, later a Peale and Associates contract arrived in

Marianne's mailbox, which she promptly signed and returned, no questions asked about weekly gross distributions and other such boring financial details.

~

The second property, *J.L & The Beak* by Oboto, was biting, angry, ironic and yet humorous and sensitive. The play's premise was a bit surprising—given the recent election of an African-American to the Presidency. Oboto believed racism remained deeply embedded in the fabric of American society. He sensitively exposed this latent racism through the day-to-day experiences of two best friends, J.L. (short for Jayson Lether), an impoverished black boy with a stutter, and Mark McKinney, a well-to-do white child who had it all, including a big pointed nose, hence the nickname "The Beak." In Oboto's play, J.L. became disenfranchised, wandered from menial job to menial job, ultimately conceiving a son out of wedlock with a woman who disappeared with the baby shortly after birth. By contrast, The Beak became a successful hotel developer and was a multi-millionaire by the time he reached thirty. "It's partially autobiographical," revealed Oboto.

"Do you stay in touch with Mark?"

"What makes you ask that?"

"I just assumed," said Mary.

"There you white people go again…assuming," said an agitated Oboto.

"Nigel," counseled Mary firmly, "please."

Marianne was curious about J.L.'s identity. "So are you or aren't you?"

"None of your business."

"Juvenile outbursts do not make for representation. Life is too short," counseled Mary sternly.

"Does that mean you'd consider representing me?"

"It depends."

"On what?"

"What really happened to the boys?"

"Actually, J.L. worked his ass off to become a model citizen. He's a supervisor at the Post Office and hasn't missed a day of work in 12 years. He married a sweet telephone receptionist named Donna Marie. They have a four-year-old son named Zack. J.L. and The Beak remain best friends to this day. In fact, The Beak is Zack's godfather."

"This is more than just a story," observed Mary sensitively.

"J.L. is my younger brother who moved to the States with my grandmother during the Nigerian civil war in the Eighties."

"What about you?"

"My father insisted that he, Mom and I remain in our hometown of Sokoto, Northern Nigeria, to protect our modest farm from the violent roaming thugs called the Niger Delta People's Volunteer Force. One night while we were sleeping, the rebels entered our house, dragged my mother and father out the door and hanged them from a tree in front of our home... In the chaos and confusion, I was able to hide in the darkness of a nearby hollow where I watched."

~

Darien Manners was gay.

While working in the claims processing department of a Fortune 500 company, he befriended an unscrupulous, mid-management female executive, who confided she was on the brink of performance dismissal. One evening, in a moment of drunken candor at a neighbor pub, the woman revealed her "100 percent foolproof plan" to enhance her severance package by two million dollars.

Manners fashioned his play, *Alexandria Plummet & Friends*," on the intimate details she had shared....a married, middle-aged man seeking companionship for all the wrong reasons, befriended a female coworker. They saw each on numerous occasions after hours but never consummated a sexual relationship. The woman convinced another co-worker to support a different, juicier version of the facts in exchange for a share of the settlement. The pair hired an unscrupulous lawyer and sued the worker and the company. In the end, to avoid a tabloid scandal and keep the male executive's marriage whole, the worker and the company's insurance carrier agreed to a generous financial settlement without admission of guilt in exchange for a gag order on the matter.

"Darien, you have the trappings of an unusual story," analyzed Mary. "But it screams for a less obvious ending."

Manners stared quizzically, restating the obvious. "The ending is the payoffs, and everybody gets on with their lives."

"Think!" challenged Mary. "There has to be more."

All eyes were on Manners. "How about the woman decides to start life anew, moves back to her roots and falls in love with a genuinely decent sort, perhaps a recent widower, from her past. Just when we think all's well that ends well, the couple is killed in some kind of terrible auto or airplane tragedy."

"Now we're getting somewhere. What else?"

"What else? retorted Manners waving his hands effeminately.

"What else. Think retribution. Think eye for an eye. "

Manners enjoyed being challenged intellectually. "I've got it. The guy's wife, a health care professional, falls in love with a male doctor confidant during her emotional travail. Maybe a socially-conscious doctor with whom she works, and they ride off into an eternal sunset together."

"I like it. It's still needs a little polish. But you can work on that privately."

~

Mary had a visceral dislike for the cerebral Arthur Ingram from the moment their paths crossed. There was something in his arrogant body language. But he was Marks's friend, and a deal was a deal. Unlike the others, his synopsis was almost indecipherable, but his script concept, *27 Million Dead and Nobody Remembers,* was heart-wrenching.

Ingram's family was Russian. Their original name was Jovanovich. They migrated from Vladivostok, which sat strategically on the Sea of Japan and was the home of the Russian Pacific Fleet during World War II. As the Germans pushed into Russia from the west, his Dad decided his family would be safer in the English hillside, so they fled to the tiny rural town of Scunthorpe in the eastern county of Lincolnshire..

Ingram's family research unearthed one of World War II's great tragedies, largely unrecognized among the Western allies. Twenty-seven million Russian civilians were ferociously murdered in their own towns and villages to quench the insatiably violent thirst of the Nazis for Russian trophies.

" I decided to employ the technique used in the French opera *Lakmè*. The play is entitled *27 Million Dead and Nobody Remembers*. In its totality, it is a moving litany of the terrible tragedies that befell ordinary Russian families, through eleven mini-stories incorporated into the overall story."

"I think I get it, but, just to be sure, give me a quick synopsis of one of the mini-stories."

"Lilia Litvyak was an unassuming, little girl from Central Moscow who eventually became the battalion chief of a ragtag woman's flying squadron the Germans named *Nachthexen* (Women Witches), whose mission was to create supply disruptions by dropping bombs in the middle of the night at the German front, from old, World War I wooden-frame and canvas planes. The ladies readily understood their missions would ultimately lead to certain death. Lilia even created a song that the women sang as they plummeted groundward. Lilia completed 183 missions, the most in Russian history, before her death at age 21."

"That is gripping stuff, old man."

"My thought is to create a multi-scene, photographic backdrop with minimalist stage props—furniture to visually enhance each mini-story, rather than waste money on elaborate sets and moving equipment. I've been to Russia in the course of my research and have some amazing pictures, which will help the visual impact of each story."

"I don't know about that picture as set technique," said Mary, certain she was not going to allow herself to get critically roasted over set design again. "It's been a bit overdone since *The Old Neighborhood*."

"My dear, technology has come a long way since Mamet's feat. I'm talking animated graphics, sophisticated multidimensional 3D imaging. The set will be illusionary in nature, but absolute and concrete to the eye."

~

At five o'clock, a bleary-eyed Mary had been meeting, talking and evaluating for seven straight hours. No lunch, no coffee breaks, no toasted panini.

"So how did we do today?" smiled a perky, fresh Allison.

"Potentially, we have three, maybe four winners. They're all going to want to polish their scripts and push me to get them into production ASAP."

"So…"

"That will take an enormous amount of investor capital. You don't happen to have a few million in your pocketbook, do you?" said Mary.

"Actually…. I do have a thought," volunteered Allison…"We can run an advertisement seeking theatrical investment capital."

"And you seriously think that will attract genuine prospects?"

"If we make the proposition enticing, place the advertisement in the right section on the right day, I think you might be surprised. Daddy always says there's plenty of opportunity capital out there, you just need to know how to access it."

"They'd laugh us out of London if I ran such an advert."

"In case you didn't notice," said Allison the proper hint of indignation, "we're not in London. We're in the uncivilized colonies."

"I'll willing to bite…but just once… now who's going to create this magical advert?"

"Why don't you take a script or two down to Vesuvio's and have a cappuccino," said Allison. "Come back in a half hour."

"Silly me," laughed Mary.

Thirty minutes later, Allison placed an ad mockup on Mary's desk.

RARE BROADWAY
INVESTMENT OPPORTUNITY

Earn 25% Or More Per Annum On Your Investment Plus Exclusive Investor VIP Perks Too Numerous To Detail. Minimum Capital Required $500,000. Send Qualifications To New York's Theatrical Legend, Peale And Associates, P.O. Box 102, Church Street Station, NY 10010, To Find Out If You Qualify.

"This is grossly misleading," said Mary.

"How so?"

"A few things here and there," said Mary sarcastically. "We're not on Broadway yet, not even close....The 25 per cent is an unreasonable expectation. If we have a super smash, half of that is the more likely scenario...We're not New York's leading anything...There are no VIP perks... And you've got to be daft if you think people with $500,000 or more in spare change will send their personal information to a PO Box number."

"Mere details. By the time we hold the investor presentations, we'll have everything buttoned up."

"Investor presentations?"

"The idea is to create a competitive frenzy by getting expressions of interest from as many people as possible."

"Expressions of interest. Whatever are you talking about?"

"Not to worry, I've seen Daddy raise angel capital like this a hundred times. Mary, let me worry the details."

"Pray tell, fair maiden, do I get a vote in where we place the advert, since it's my money?"

"The suggestion box is open."

"I suggest *Variety, Playbill* and *Advertising Age.*"

"Too obvious. We'll use *Barron's,* the *New York Law Journal* and *Investor's Daily.*"

"What the hell are they?"

"Places where people who make deals go to look for deals. Trust me, we'll stand out."

"I get the feeling I don't have the final vote."

"Mary, with all due respect, in matters such as this, you have no vote."

Mary didn't know whether to fire Allison because of her insolence or applaud her iconoclastic initiative.

She decided to roll the dice.

~

Four days later the answer arrived en masse. Their modest PO Box was stuffed with some 200 responses.

"Hey lady," said the postal clerk behind the counter, "I don't know what you're giving away, but for crying out loud, the next time you run your ad, rent a bigger PO box." He then pulled a tray from under the counter with perhaps another 200 responses.

The women hugged each other then returned to the office with a burlap sack. "I don't think there is any shortcut," said Allison. "We need to look at every letter and decide if they are "A" or "B" prospects."

"How do we tell the difference?" said Mary beginning to accept the reality that Allison just might be the business partner she sorely needed.

"An 'A' prospect is ready to invest now. 'B' prospects have questions or considerations they want answered," responded a confident Allison. "Based on my calculations we have 196 'A' prospects. We need to attack them ASAP while continuing to stroke the 'B's' in the event we don't raise at least two million from the 'A's.'"

"Allie, Allie," said a bleary-eyed Mary. "I'm toast. I'm sure you've already got a detailed program ready to go for the 196."

"Naturally."

"Not tonight. Remember, this lady's pushing 30. It's 7 o'clock, and as you Yanks say, there's no gas left in the tank. I need sustenance. I need some R&R."

"I bet Lester can whip up something. Then we'll get you beddy bye."

Mary wasn't sure if Allison had made a pass or was just matching colloquialisms.

Two glasses of wine later, they were feeling no pain. Mary started to visually explore Allison's sensuous assets. She realized, perhaps for the first time that Allison was not only was strikingly beautiful but also earthy, sultry. With Sarah disappearing off the face of the earth, Mary had been celibate for the longest time. She was getting more aroused by the minute.

Should she or shouldn't she? She decided she should. She gently squeezed Allison's hand. There was no response. Mary took that to mean "continue." Mary discreetly placed her hand on Allison's thigh under the table. "You know you're quite stunning."

"Mary, you're witty and charming. I love working with you. But, no disrespect intended....I'm really not into women. Call me old-fashioned, but I just prefer guys."

"Tell me you're a virgin?" said Mary.

"Certainly not when it comes to men."

"You mean to tell me you've never had it on with another woman?" asked Mary incredulously.

"It's not something that piques my interest. Frankly, I find it off-putting."

"How can you be put off by something you've never tried?" challenged an emotionally-bruised Mary.

Allison sensed the need to move lest their blossoming relationship become irreparably harmed.

"Let's just say I'm already in a relationship. AC/DC behavior is not his cup of tea."

Mary quickly put two and two together. The stares, the fawning.

"I rather suspect we're talking about David."

Allison was shocked. How did she know? David told her about his past relationship with Mary but swore he had said nothing to Mary just yet. There was no point. The situation was awkward enough with all the business intersects. Unbeknownst to Mary, Allison and David were secretly engaged and planned to marry at the right time. Allison wondered...*does Mary still have romantic designs on David?*

The fact was, Mary couldn't care less about David. What was over was over. But she was deeply scarred by the tone of Allison's descriptor "AC/DC," and the implication that a woman who preferred a woman was less of a woman. She wanted to scream. But to what avail? Instead, she bit her stiff British upper lip.

"Let me make it easy for you. David and I had our fling. It didn't work out. He was having a little trouble with my, as you put it, AC/DC proclivities. He owes me nothing personally. Our relationship is now strictly business. My hope is that, no matter what happens with you two, we can all remain friends and business associates."

"I appreciate your candor," said Allison. "I'm simply mad about the man."

34

~~~

THE NEXT ORDER OF BUSINESS WAS to meet, greet and entice 196 prospects. As usual, Allison had a plan. "I see breaking the database into ten meetings of roughly 20 prospects."

"That sounds a trifle impersonal."

"Daddy always says a good business person separates the shoppers from the buyers." Allison went into pitch mode. "The numbers are irrelevant. It's more a matter of how special we make the experience...I'm thinking we open with cocktails and canapés and finish with dinner after our presentation. At that point, I reintroduce you, and you introduce the playwrights and discuss the properties and then turn it back to me."

"For...."

"Money. I'll do financial projections, contracts and collect initial expressions of interest and binder deposits. Maybe $50,000 with a 72-hour cancellation clause."

"You don't seriously..."

"I do. The Smith Foundation did it all the time."

"That was charitable gift giving."

"And, we're about obscene returns, ego gratifying perks and hobnobbing with New York's creative intelligentsia.

"What about the nays?"

"We'll politely show them the door."

"Boss lady"…laughed Mary at Allison's confident brashness. "One more question."

"Madame, I await your utterance," teased Allison in her best Brit.

"This presentation, how do you think *we* should structure it?"

"You know what they say, 'a picture is worth a thousand words.'" Allison walked over to her computer and called up a slickly produced PowerPoint slide show with embedded audio and video clips and financial projections using flash animation.

"This thing is incredible. Who did it?"

"Me."

"Let me guess. They're just like Daddy's."

Allison smiled. "I merely borrowed one of Daddy's road show templates and customized the content.

"'Road show?'"

"Just a Yank term for raising investor capital from qualified investors." Allison sensed Mary was in foreign waters. "Witness," said Allison, pointing at a gray color slide captioned, "Introducing the Peale and Associates' Platinum Perk Program."

Mary's smile returned.

"I call this our investor psychology section. Investors think the sun rises and sets on their money. We reserve the first two rows of the center orchestra for investors and their families. They just call a private number up to 48 hours prior. No costs, no muss, no fuss…They also receive two backstage passes upon request. We host a monthly educational cocktail party with the cast to inform our investors about the refinements we're planning to make."

"Suppose there aren't any changes?"

"The cast can make something up….after all, they are actors."

~

Twenty minutes later, a cab stopped in front of 1170 Park Avenue near the corner of 84th Street.

"Good afternoon, Miss Edwards," said the doorman.

"Eric, this is my business associate and very good friend, Mary Jackson-Peale. We are launching a rather complicated project that will involve a lot of coming and going."

Mary couldn't help but notice how proper Allison's tone and manner had become.

"I want you to treat Miss Peale as you would any other homeowner. Give her the extra set of keys and notify the rest of the building staff that when Miss Peale calls, they should come running. One more thing: This project involves a series of meetings with highly qualified investors. Miss Peale and I will give you the list. No one else should be permitted entry. No exceptions."

"Very good, Madame."

The elevator opened to the 24th floor entry hall. As Mary was to learn, Allison's 8,000 square foot apartment spanned the entire floor. "I was thinking cocktails in the drawing rooms and library, maybe a little harp music over here in the corner. That leaves you the living room and a number of little nooks and crannies around the floor to smooze and hold mini meetings. I'm thinking the office is where we sign up expressions of interests and deposits," she said.

"Daddy has offered his corporate attorney, Tom Kruger of Paul Hastings. Daddy says Tom is the best dealmaker in town. I'm thinking that's a pretty good idea. Don't you agree?"

Mary was as silent as a church mouse.

"Behind these double doors is the ballroom. With a few modifications, it should work fine as our presentation room. It comfortably holds 50 to 75 and contains a state-of-the-art projection and theater system, so everybody should be able to see the ten-foot screen. I think we should install some flat screens every 20 feet to make sure our investors see their checkbooks!" laughed Allison. "Okay with you?"

Mary again just silently nodded.

"Let me show you the bedroom suites down the hall for our overnight guests. Allison opened a series of doors that led to four 750 square foot master suites. "This is my suite on the northwest corner. As you can see, the other ones usually go unused. Each has its own theme and is about the same size as the suites in the garishly renovated St. Regis Hotel."

Mary thought, *forget the guests. What about me?*

Allison pointed to the walls. "I'm guessing even if our guests aren't art aficionados, they should at least recognize the names Rauschenberg, Pollack, Johns, Chagall, Picasso, Dali, Miro, Pissarro and Seurat. Allison looked at Mary. "Questions?....suggestions?"

"Just one," smiled Mary. "How do you afford all this on $30,000 a year?"

~

"We'd like to thank all of you for stopping by," said Allison. "Whether you realize it or not, you have been identified as savvy investors who demand above average returns yet appreciate the cultural importance of one of America's great institutions, the Broadway Theatre."

Mary had all she could do to keep a straight face.

"A number of you may have recognized my last name is Edwards. I am indeed the daughter of James Edwards of Norfolk, who many of you know personally or have seen featured in *Forbes* and *Business Week*. He has dedicated his entire career to making sure his investors are satisfied investors." Allison had the crowd, mostly male, eating out of her hand. "Consequently, we've revised the order of our little presentation. While I'm sure you'll enjoy hearing about the stage properties and meeting our wonderful playwrights and directors, I know the critical question is, 'What's in it for me?'"

Allison went through a series of projections that showed investors a return of 10 percent by month three, 20 per cent by month six with 60 per cent of the seats filled. Then Allison raised the ante. "Mary's plan is to do something that has never been done before. To debut all four plays in the same season using blockbuster ads with quotes from all of you who attend the previews. It will be your chance to influence your own investment. That will leave you two investment options. $200,000 will give you five points in a single show, and $750,000 will give you five points in all four shows. Whichever package you pick is up to you; the perks are the same. We have a special investor hotline that will allow you to receive, the complimentary, VIP orchestra seats in the first two rows. You also have the right to reserve one of the suites in daddy's humble *pied á terre*. Again, at absolutely no cost. After a back-stage visit to say hello to the stars, it's off to your three-course meal in the Pool Room at the Four Seasons on Park Avenue."

Every head in the room nodded.

"Any questions on how the investment works?"

No one raised a hand.

"Why don't we take a little break while Mary and her team set up? Grab another drink, make yourselves at home, and take a cook's tour of the guest suites."

As the group wandered away, Mary grabbed Allison by the arm. From the look in Mary's eyes, she figured she was pissed about her impromptu reordering of the presentation.

"I thought this was your apartment, not daddy's *pied á terre*?"

"It is."

"But that's not what you said."

"Mary, stop with that holier-than-thou attitude. You're going to tell me you've never stretched the truth?"

Mary was dead silent.

"I rest my case. Besides, do we really want a bunch of cutthroat investors to know a spoiled 22-year-old princess extracted a ten-million-dollar apartment from big, bad James Edwards?"

~

Allison was a hard act to follow, but Mary more than held her own. "Ladies and Gentlemen," said Mary in a side room to her four playwrights, "it's show time." And show time it was. Each presentation was succinct yet engaging; passionate yet friendly and accessible.

"*Little Fanny Coscia, J.L. & The Beak and Alexandria Plummet* were unanimously liked while the majority of investors struggled with *27 Million Dead*.

The most vocal of the naysayers was Sol Levine, a former rug merchant from the seaport town of Ashdod, about 40 miles from Judea, who emigrated to the United States in 1967 and had made his fortune selling European designer seconds and overstocks to underdeveloped countries. Both his parents died in Auschwitz, so he took particular offense to *27 Million Dead* and got into a heated debate with Arthur Ingram.

"Why should I help you tell that story? You diminish my family's suffering."

"What about *my* family's suffering?"

"The world doesn't care about uneducated peasants?"

"A grossly erroneous characterization fostered by our ultra left, Jewish-dominated media."

"You're on thin ice," shouted Levine, "without support of the critics, you and your morality play are going nowhere."

"What's that got to do with the Nazis terrorizing every town, village and city in Russia, slaughtering tens of millions of innocent men, women and children?"

"My parents died in gas chambers," said Levine expecting empathy.

"My grandfather was hanged from a telephone pole in the town square at Orem. The Nazis laughed and threw tomatoes at him while he choked to death in front of his own children."

"I don't give a shit!"

"How are twenty-seven million innocent people dying less important than six million?"

"I don't give a shit," said Levine who left in a huff.

~

Despite the Levine flap, that first evening raised two million in commitments from five different investors.

"I must say I learned a lot about American financing," said Mary after everyone had left.

"Thank you," smiled Allison.

"I gather we may have already reached our goal."

"What goal?"

"The two million, remember?"

"I just made that up. By the time we finish our entire road show, we should raise at least ten million. I'm figuring you use the two on whatever you need to do to get the shows up and running successfully. We put the other eight million in six month T-bills that return about 6 percent. That gives *us* about two and a half million in distributions before investors are expecting to see a dime."

"That should make them very happy," said Mary.

"Make who happy?"

"The investors."

"I said *us*."

Mary could see Belfrage rolling over in his grave. A supplemental income stream he missed!

35

~~~

WITH MONEY AND THREE QUALITY properties in hand (to the dismay of James Ingram, she decided to hold onto *27 Million Dead*) Mary was able to negotiate deals with the crème de la crème of Off-Broadway theatres. *Fanny Coscia* found a home at the Cherry Lane; *Plummet & Friends* at the Atlantic Theatre on West 20th, *J.L. & The Beak* at the Union Square Theatre on East 17th Street. She also succeeded in premiering all three plays at the beginning of the high season, making her the talk of the theatrical community.

Fanny Coscia and *Plummet & Friends* received outstanding critical reviews as highly engaging, inventive and insightful. By month eight, word of mouth had spread and performances typically played to near sold-out houses, six nights a week.

J.L. & The Beak hit a sociological nerve. Blacks boycotted the show as unrealistic. Whites did likewise because they felt the issue of racism passé. The critics either thought the direction "too strident" given the mellow conclusion or the conclusion too mellow given the strident direction. Mary realized she only had herself to blame. Tackling a long-standing and complicated American cultural issue may have been a bit too ambitious.

But two out of three successes and her innovative road-block strategy branded her "The Playwrights Agent" in the trade press. "Princess Mary," as the press dubbed her, was now the never-say-die Brit, who could turn a sow's ear into the proverbial silk purse."

Peale and Associates was deluged with requests for press interviews and unsolicited manuscripts. Mary and Allison were awash in a sea of details. Their "excess" income stream strategy allowed Mary to hire additional staff. Within a matter of months, the office exploded. Peale and Associates employed eight full-timers and four part-timers. Mary thrived on the place's energy. Everybody walked around smiling.

The women also finished designing and furnishing the office, pretty much to Allison's original vision—fashionable, shabby chic. *New York Magazine* and *Vanity Fair* both did features on the place.

MP Jackson and Associates, the firm's new name, was the place to be if you were young, passionate about the theatre and wanted to make connections. It also didn't hurt if you were drop-dead gorgeous. Mary and Allison were convinced they made for higher investor interest among New York's predominately male power elite, where the easy money appeared to reside.

Every playwright in town wanted Mary to review and analyze his script. Those with whom she worked were extremely gracious about attributing their success to Mary's unique ability to nurture the creative process, raise production capital and then let them do their thing.

She also became a master at toying with the press.

"Mary, Jonathan Thomas, *Village Voice* on one," shouted Allison over the office din.

"Jonathan dear, how's my favorite critic."

"I'm only your favorite since my scathing review about that J.L. bomb."

"Well, then we must make certain that never happens again," said Mary confidently.

"I'm calling because my editor had an interesting idea he wanted me to run by you. We think our readers would enjoy a color story about the Brit who burst upon the Off-Broadway scene. We've even got the headline, "The Brit that Burst Off-Broadway's Bubble.""

"Do you boys sit up all night abusing illegal substances to derive your alliterative brainstorms?"

"The idea is to trace your history from the day you walked in and out of the door at Belfrage in London, to your success in converting aspiring Brit playwrights into New York powerhouses."

Mary saw red flags in the Belfrage connection. "I like the idea Jonathan and I'm happy to do the piece, but I think you need to tell your editor he's mixing apples and oranges."

"What do you mean?"

"I may be wrong, but I can't imagine your readers actually care about what I did and didn't do in London. I think the interesting insight from the *Village Voice's* standpoint is how I moved from familiar surroundings to the theatrical capital of the world and helped a talented bunch of British writers convert their raw ideas into commercial success on the American stage. I'm thinking your readers would find that angle more relevant."

The story appeared in the *Voice* a fortnight later to widespread acclaim.

And thus Mary dodged another bullet.

~

Allison decided the women needed the afternoon off.

"This pace is crazy," said Allison. "We live, eat and sleep theatre."

"So?" responded Mary, who found the 16-hour business days and evenings exhilarating.

"Don't you have any other interests?"

"I like men *and* women."

"I didn't mean that. I meant like hobbies, diversions, you know," said Allison. "Other things."

Mary was not like other women. "I like to read poetry."

Allison realized she needed to take matters into her own hands. "How about we just go shopping?"

"For what?" asked Mary. "My wardrobe is fine. My flat is decorated. I'm not about to buy a car in Manhattan."

"What about shoes? Or maybe a new bag?"

"I've got plenty," said Mary.

"Mary," chuckled Allison, getting absolutely nowhere, "you're a woman, women love to shop. You can always use an extra something. This is Manhattan, the shopping capital of the world. Women come from all over to shop on Madison and Fifth Avenues. The best part is you can afford it."

"Allison, I appreciate the gesture. But in case you didn't notice, I'm not wired like other women. I absolutely love my job, my avocation... it's my hobby. When I need something, I just go and buy it. One list. One trip. In and out."

"Mary, that's what a guy would say."

"I wouldn't know about that. I've never gone shopping with a guy. They're just for sex."

"Wow, talk about jaded," responded Allison.

"I'm not jaded. I'm just pragmatic."

Mary did close the office for the afternoon. Allison went shopping, most of the other employees went home to rest, and Mary wandered over to Café La Fête on Thompson seeking a low-fat cappuccino and a friendly face.

She got the cappuccino.

~

"You are not going to believe this!" said an excited Allison, placing a copy of the *Village Voice* on Mary's desk.

"Pray tell," said Mary. "A Friday edition of the *Voice* on Friday."

"Don't be a twit, page three, page four, page five."

"Let me guess, that's your impersonation of a stuttering Brit."

"The Obies! The Obies! Peale properties had bee nominated for 10 Obies, Off-Broadway's annual awards, similar to Broadway's Tony Awards.

Fanny and Plummet had been nominated for best drama and best original play awards plus best design and best performances by a lead actor and actress. Mary went from pleased to stunned as she read the nominations—Nigel Oboto has received a nomination for best new playwright.

"Oh my God, I don't believe it."

Mary had the article reprinted and framed for the office. She also sent a brief note with a copy of the article to her entire investor group. The note read in part, "I'd like to thank all of you for supporting our endeavors. These nominations are proof positive that substantive theatre can be created and recognized by its peers without limitation. Peale and Associates will prepare and run advertisements supporting our collective accomplishments, which, over the long term, should enhance your return on investment."

Allison read the note and smiled. Mary was now becoming adroit at both sides of the business.

"When is the actual ceremony?" asked Allison.

"April 20th at the New World Theater."

"Why don't we throw a post ceremony party?"

"Suppose we don't win?" worried Mary.

"It really doesn't matter. We've been open for business less than two years and look what you've accomplished. The party's about making a statement to the entire theatrical community that Mary Jackson-Peale will be a force to be reckoned with for years to come."

"Let me guess, you've already found a place and selected a menu."

"I hope you don't mind," smiled Allison.

"At this point, I'm just one of the hired help. My job is to read scripts. Just send me the invitation so I know where to go."

Allison did just that.

~

The award ceremony was a perfect introduction to those who didn't know Mary Jackson-Peale. Her clients took home five Obies. *Fanny* won for Best Drama and Director, *Plummet* gathered awards for Set Direction and Best Lead Actor and Set Direction. The upset of the evening was Oboto winning the Best New Playwright Obie.

As Oboto went on stage, he looked at Mary and said, "I am overwhelmed. I don't know what to say. Perhaps my story did have resonance after all. Normally, at this point, the winner thanks a host of associates, sometimes disingenuously. In my case, there is only one person who believed. One person who actually owns a piece of this award, my agent, Mary Jackson-Peale."

Mary nodded. Nigel wasn't finished. "Mary, stand up so everyone can place a face with the name." Mary, dressed in what would become her signature frock, a low-cut, leopard-skin pattern, tight silk dress, stood and waved.

Oboto then made the blunder of the evening in front of 800 people he didn't know. "Mary's hosting a little post-ceremony blast at the Tribecca Grill. You're all invited."

Allison stiffened like a board. "Dear Jesus, what a schmuck. Imagine if most of this crowd actually shows up? The cops will shut the place down."

"I have larger concerns," said Mary."Imagine the god damn liquor bill!"

The ceremonies ended about 11 p.m. It took Mary almost an hour to congratulate her ecstatic clients. Then she and Allison were off to the Tribecca Grill where Obie guests were hanging from the rafters. A bouncer stopped them at the door as they tried to enter. "Sorry Madame this is a private party."

"It's my god damn party," said an incensed Mary.

"Nice try, Madame, but that excuse has been tried about a dozen times already."

"This is outrageous…I'm Mary Jackson-Peale, my clients are in there spending my money…"

"…and I'm Prince Charles," said the bouncer. "I'm just doing this gig for a few extra pounds. The Queen forgot to approve my stipend for the month."

Allison stepped in front of Mary. "Listen you big buffoon. Get Bob on that walkie-talkie. Tell him Allison Edwards is outside and smoking mad."

"You want me to call Mr. DeNiro? You crazy, lady?"

"He's channel 34 on that damn thing. I suggest you call him before I have your ass skewered."

Mary was seeing another dimension of the surprising Allison.

"Mr. D., there's some red-haired broad out here who said she knows you…an Allison something or other." The bouncer's face turned beet red. I understand. Totally, Mr. D." The bouncer then stretched out his enormous arms to keep the pushing and shoving crowd away from the ladies. "Somebody will be here in a minute," he smiled. "Sorry."

Two obese, barrel-chested bodyguards who looked like something out of *The Sopranos* whisked the girls through a private entrance into a spacious rear office and lounge. "Allie, Allie, how many times have I told you to use the other entrance," joked DeNiro with his usual facial contortions.

"It's Tuesday night, I never imagined."

DeNiro smiled at Mary and extended his hand. "I assume you're the crazy agent who invited all the freeloaders."

"I'm so sorry, Mr. DeNiro."

"What's to be sorry? It's your tab, not mine."

"I'm terribly aware."

"Hey, what to worry? You can afford it. I hear you've got the Midas touch."

"Beginner's luck, Mr. DeNiro," modestly replied a star-struck Mary.

"It's Bob."

36

~~~

DAYS LATER, MARY'S MAGIC carpet ride made another unscheduled stop.

"Mary, this is Luce Jason Thomas III. I don't think we've ever met. I'm the owner of the Walter Kerr Theatre. I've read an awful lot about you. In fact, I was so intrigued, I spent last week Off-Broadway watching your client productions. Very impressive."

"Thank you."

"I think we should talk. Are you free for breakfast on Thursday?"

"Yes."

"How about Berger's on West 47th around eight thirty."

She reached for her calendar. There was a conflict. It didn't matter. It wasn't everyday you got a call from Luce Jason Thomas III.

"Done."

"That's what I like, a person who doesn't vacillate. This business is full of phonies who try to impress you with the old let me check my schedule. I say you either do or don't."

"Where are you meeting?" asked Allison.

"Berger's on 47th....Were you listening?"

"Berger's? You mean Berger's Deli on West 47th?"

"I guess so. Why?"

"I'm afraid you weren't listening. That's the busiest deli in New York. Grand Central Station at rush hour is like a library reading room compared to that place."

"You must be thinking of another Berger's."

"Breakfast, lunch or dinner?"

Mary paused. "Breaky."

"That's the place."

~

Berger's was exactly as billed. A raucous scene.

Messengers with multi-colored mohawks screamed orders over a glass steam tray. A single row of customers sat elbow to elbow on plastic leather stools circling a brown Formica counter that ran the length of the restaurant.

"Jack, I need my turkey club with mayo. The man called twice" screamed the messenger to the Mexican take-out chief.

"How many times I tell you no, Jack. It's Guillermo to you. You tell man, go fuck himself."

"Fuck you, he's a guaranteed fin. That's why he's the man, Jack."

"Guillermo," said the chief, slamming his knife through the sandwich on the butcher-block cutting board.

The messenger turned to scan Mary in her miniskirt and stiletto heels. He assumed she was a prostitute on the prowl. "Ho, ho, ho, what's a babe like you doing tricks in a place like this...especially at eight thirty. Aren't nooners more rewarding?"

Mary, angry as hell, took a swing. "Hey, we got a feisty one here, Jack."

A small gray-haired man with a mustache and red cardigan began to pull her away. She started to push back. "Easy, Mary. I'm Luce Thomas."

"Did you see how that pig treated me? It's outrageous!" said Mary.

The soft-spoken, gravelly-voiced man chuckled. "You've got to understand. This is Berger's. You're not exactly dressed like *Breakfast At Tiffany's*."

Mary wasn't sure what that was supposed to mean, but she knew it wasn't a compliment. She restrained her anger. You do that in business. Particularly, if you're an up-and-coming theatrical agent trying to do a deal with a Broadway titan.

"I'm at our table in the rear. It's more private." She saw three other middle aged men waving. "I hope you don't mind. This is Sam Shubert from the Shubert Theatre and Lynn Margoles from the Ambassador."

Quite an auspicious little group, thought Mary. She was sitting elbow to elbow with three of the boards of directors of the elite League of New York Theatres. They were the ultimate decision-makers at three of Broadway's most influential theatres and had dear friends who controlled what appeared at virtually all the other important theatres from West 43rd to 51st Street.

"I told them we were going to do a deal. They all like deals. Sammy had a wonderful idea. But we can do business in a few minutes. Let's order breakfast first."

The extraordinary down-to-earth Thomas was nothing like she expected. He was warm, easy going and a real gentleman, although slightly rough at the edges.

"Good morning, boys," said the sassy diminutive Hispanic waitress. "The usual?"

"You've got it," smiled Lynn.

"I'm surprised after all these years, you guys don't have blocked arteries."

"How long have you 'boys' been coming here?" asked Mary, trying to make conversation.

"Maria, how many years?" asked Thomas.

"Ten years, five days a week, bologna omelets, sesame bagels with cream cheese and hash brown patties."

"Maria, let's keep it simple, just make it five orders."

"You sure, lady?"

"Don't listen to her," chuckled Sam. "She's from Puerto Rico. They don't have bologna there. Guillermo makes the best bologna omelets in New York. You know with all the health shit going around, it isn't that easy to get a really good bologna omelet."

Maria returned with a mountain of food. The omelet alone weighted almost 12 ounces. Then there was the modest eight-ounce hash brown patty and the biggest sesame bagel smothered in cream cheese that Mary had ever seen.

"Told ya," said the waitress smiling at Mary. "Want something to wash all that down?"

"How about a fire truck filled with coffee?"

~

Sam looked at Mary's three quarter empty plate. "You did good for a first time."

"I know you boys didn't drag me to Berger's to see how much bologna I could eat."

"Lane talked to you on the phone, right? Did he tell you we all went to see your plays?"

"Yes," impressed that they all apparently took the time.

"We liked most of the stuff. I want *Plummet* for the Shubert. Lane, our resident romantic wants *Fanny*, and Lynn wants to take a chance on that *Beak* thing."

Luce shrugged his shoulders. "It's his money."

"Did I get it right, fellas?"

Mary was pleased but concerned. "Lynn," she said respectfully, "May I call you Lynn? You know *The Beak* didn't do well Off-Broadway. It was 30 performances and out."

"Young lady, I appreciate your concern, but just because New York liberals say racism is passé doesn't make it so. Ask those people in Harlem how easy it is to get into a good school and get a good job. Ask Mayor Bloomberg why Black unemployment is still four times the rate of whites?"

"You realize supporting a social cause and producing a play for profit are entirely different matters," said Mary.

"Like Luce said, it's my money."

~

It was time to talk terms.

"We estimate our current shows may run out of steam before next season, so we'd like to be ready by fall. With a little luck, we get some nice publicity and a few packed houses. We all make some money, and maybe your crowd wins a Tony or two."

"How do you see the deal structured?" asked Mary.

They all looked at each other. "What do you mean?" said Thomas.

"The terms."

"Same as always. You raise the money, have full artistic license, all book and movie rights, we put up our theatres, staff and publicity houses, and you get 25 percent of the net."

The operative word was "net." From Mary's standpoint, the boys were trying to slip one by. They'd load all their expenses and some hidden profits into the net, and then she'd be stuck accounting for actor salaries and director distribution out of her share. The proposed deal had all the earmarks of a financial disaster. But she wanted the opportunity to have presence on Broadway, if for no other reason, so she could shove the programs up Johnson's ass at the *New York Times*.

"How do you define net?"

"Net is net," stated Thomas. "We pay all the theatre expenses, the actor's salaries and playwright and director distribution, investor shares and interest due, and then split the rest 25 – 75. As our partner, you get to approve all major expenses and can use your own set designers and suppliers.

That's your business, if you know what I mean. Do we have a deal?"

"Deal," said Mary.

"Good. We'll send the papers over in the next few days. Now finish your bologna, Mary; that's good bologna. It's Hebrew National."

37

~ ~ ~

SUCCESS TRANSFORMED MARY'S life into a whirl-wind existence. More scripts than she could possibly evaluate, more requests for business lunches and dinners, more interviews than she could ever accommodate and more investors demanding reports and presentations.

More...more...more...

The broader her network of business associates, the narrower her circle of trusted friends. Namely, Allison and David Marks. Her social life became virtually nonexistent since she lacked the one thing necessary to seek and cultivate meaningful new relationships—time. The crush of it all created a conflicted personality. Mary "A" found the challenges and notoriety emotionally exhilarating and intellectually stimulating. It was truly a magic carpet ride. Mary "B" found the pace stifling, the people dreary and the trappings of success suffocating and lonely.

While her daily commute was virtually nonexistent—about 30 steps down the stairs to her office—the virtual 24/7 merging of the home and office confused her increasingly fragile psyche. Her cluttered mind was transformed into a voice mailbox that was always full while her body seemed strapped to a treadmill that never stopped moving.

Mary's primary release from the pressures of her maddening world—a good night's sleep—had all but vanished, replaced by an arduous struggle to capture a few tranquil hours in the lonely darkness of her bedroom. To overcome her battle with insomnia, Mary devised a series of self-help strategies.

She played mind games intended to soothe her body and soul. In one, Mary imagined herself drinking a glass of warm milk then feeling the liquid calm her body as it weaved its way through her system. Sometimes she'd create a list of the next day's activities on her imaginary yellow post-it notes by the side of her bed, and then prioritize and re-prioritize until she gradually slipped into a first or second-level sleep state. But, she rarely, if ever, achieved a deep, night-long rest.

Despite battling gamely, she was losing ground. She routinely woke three or four times a night to soothe her dry, parched throat, to void, or to decipher some imaginary noise.

Eventually a more alarming set of symptoms arrived. Moments after slipping into a first level sleep, she imagined herself suffocating, unable to breathe. She bolted to a standing position at the side of the bed, holding onto a nearby dresser for balance and gasping for air. At first, she thought her blockages were somehow related to the apartment's dry forced air heating system. By the third evening, an exhausted Mary dozed in bed—propped up on pillows—waiting for a relapse, which, like clockwork, ultimately reared its head.

~

The battle with sleep deprivation almost lost, she sought professional help. After an Internet search that included reference checks and patient feedback, she settled on a gentle, soft- spoken doctor named Leonard DiRe, a well-known internist who specialized in sleep disorders. DiRe, affiliated with the world-class Lenox Hill Hospital on Park Avenue, maintained offices a block from Allison's apartment.

DiRe's waiting room oozed comfort and tranquility. Billowy couches, wingback chairs and antique furnishings occupied every nook and cranny. As she was to quickly learn, the accoutrements reflected the man. To her amazement, DiRe was also time-conscious. She was ushered into DiRe's inner sanctum for her 3 p.m. appointment at precisely 3 p.m.

"I must say, I'm impressed," said Mary to the bald, slightly overweight and cordial man across the desk. "Based on my past experience, a timely doctor is almost as rare as the playwright who delivers a script within the agreed deadline."

"It's not often this office is graced by the presence of such an important member of the American Theatre," volleyed DiRe right back. "I chased all my other patients out the back door and told them to come back after you left."

Mary grinned. He made her feel terribly special. By the time the consult was over, some two hours later, patient and doctor had bonded. After two days of extensive tests, Mary was ushered back into DiRe's office. He decided to start with the good news. "Mary...I have some excellent news. The tests all came back negative. There is absolutely nothing wrong with you... physically."

"Does that mean I'm crazy?"

"I didn't say that. But I do think your lack of sleep is making you a bit depressed which in turn gives rise to a subsequent bout of insomnia. Clinically, this cycle is called intermittent insomnia."

"But what about the chronic shortness of breath?"

"I'm quite certain it's stress induced." The reality was that Mary was in the acute phase of intermittent insomnia, and fragile as a piece of fine Venetian glass. "Absolutely, it's merely a malady of our 21st Century lifestyles."

"What do you suggest?"

"Well, you might want to visit a psychiatrist. With all your artistic successes, there is no logical reason for you to be depressed. Tackling that condition first might reduce the insomnia."

Mary bristled at the thought. "Doctor, can't you just give me a prescription for something?"

DiRe became a bit more firm. "Mary, it's not that easy. It is true that depressive states can be stabilized or reversed when a suitable antidepressant is administered. But, what works for one person has enormous side-effects for another. We're all different physiologically and psychologically. Even then, I'm fairly certain there is no single silver bullet for your situation. Those damn drug company television commercials generate inappropriate expectations. The notion that one Ambien, Lunesta or Rozerem a day and you'll be jumping over fences with sheep is nonsense. They're playing to desperate minds with unrealistic expectations.

"The other issue is those medications are habit forming. They are meant to provide temporary relief; they are not a long-term solution. The reason I suggested a psychiatrist is not because you're crazy, but rather to keep you from becoming so. He or she will work with you to determine the root cause of the depression. Insomnia is just a byproduct of a bigger issue."

"Let me think about it," said Mary dismissively.

~

It had been almost a year since Chloe last spoke to her daughter.

"I've been reading about your Off-Broadway successes. I guess it keeps you busy."

"Mum, what can I say? I'm sorry."

"So what do I owe the honor of this call," said Chloe with the proper hint of indignation.

"I just wanted you to be the first to know—before it hits the press—your daughter is Broadway bound."

"What does that mean exactly?"

"Recently, I had the good fortune to sign a deal with three of Broadway's most influential theatre owners to house three of the plays I represent on their stages, pending financing, of course."

"I know nothing about play financing. Is that a big pending?"

"Don't think so. I hired this lady, Allison, who has amazing family contacts. I think we'll be all right."

"This lady...is she your latest new friend?"

"Mum, it's nothing like that. In fact, Allison's head-over-heels in love with David Marks, the director. Remember the flat I rented in East London?"

"Didn't you say something about a fling..."

"Mum, that was a long time ago. I was lonely. Elizabeth had disappeared. I was confused. I needed companionship."

"How terribly convenient."

"That's cruel."

"Each of us has our own way of post rationalizing. Truth is one of life's most difficult realities...it took me 15 years with your father to realize that."

Mary didn't know on what level to respond. "Fact is, David and I are still friends. Quite coincidentally, he moved to New York and became my client. I'm the one who introduced him to Allison."

There was a long pause....

"Have there been any developments?" asked Mary.

Chloe sensed a searching in Mary's tone.

"Best I can tell, the police have never identified the old boy's murderer."

"And Elizabeth?"

"I don't believe she has ever surfaced."

"I just don't understand it. We were so..."

"The impression I had when last we spoke was that you had moved on. Wasn't it a Sarah something?"

"That was a mistake."

"Why?"

"I never really loved her. She loved me. I didn't want to be cruel. What was the point?" Mary realized for the first time the reality of her relationship with Sarah. "Mum." Mary began to sob uncontrollably.

"It's all right my child, let it out."

"I'm so lonely. It's hard to internalize much less articulate. By all conventional standards, I'm awash in success. Everybody wants my ear, all the time. I can't be that good. I'm not that good. What have I done to deserve all this success?"

38

~~~

MARY'S INNER TURMOIL began to affect her daily behavior.

She functioned quite normally prior to noon—at least initially. The office staff lovingly characterized Mary as the whirlwind multi-tasker on steroids. After putting in no less than five hours around the office, lunch was either feast or famine—a languid meal at a proper restaurant with a client or prospective client, or the hasty gobbling of a freshly baked, crusty Vesuvio's roll, washed down with one, sometimes two, of Mama's supercharged *doppia* espresso.

The onset of Mary's daily depression usually set in around 3 p.m., perhaps a bit later. A heavy gloom would hover over her head until it morphed into dread and alienation, and eventually, a stifling anxiety. When the sensations became unbearable, she'd retreat to her office, close the door, and begin a series of deep belly breaths with her eyes closed. While not classical Yoga, her self-designed exercise generally gave her a measure of temporary relief.

Mary also began to research the web in the privacy of her apartment to learn about other techniques to manage her depression. She remained confident that her strong sense of logic and self-determination and a few holistic solutions would somehow prevail.

As she slipped deeper and deeper into depression, she discovered two things: there were millions of words written about the onset of depression, but few that specifically captured what she was feeling, and, despite all logic to the contrary, she remained deeply resistant to the reality that she was losing control of her mental faculties.

~

Allison, more sensitive to Mary's patterns than the other employees, knew something was up, and that it was getting worse by the day. She offered Mary a unique weekend of rest and relaxation among the rich and super rich on Eastern Long Island where Scott and Zelda Fitzgerald once romped in sophisticated towns and quaint villages named Quogue, Water Mill, East Hampton, Southampton and Amagansett. "It's supposed to be a lovely weekend. Haven't we earned a little R&R," suggested Allison one Friday in July.

"I don't disagree," said the emotionally drained Mary, thinking excuses. "But what about David?"

"David's buried in play revisions. You know Mr. Intensity. If you even breathe while he's creating, he becomes rather ornery. What do you say?"

"Even we Brits know it's prime time out there. I'm sure there are no reservations to be had."

"Taken care of. We'll stay at my parents' place."

"Are you sure that won't be an imposition?"

"I'm Daddy's little girl. I have a standing invitation."

"Won't daddy's little girl plus one be an invasion of their privacy?"

"Trust me, they've got the space."

Mary was out of excuses...save one. "Sounds great. But the traffic. It's already Friday noon. It will take us six hours on that damn, unpleasant Long Island Expressway."

"No worries," said Allison. "Daddy can take care of that with one phone call."

Mary finally nodded yes although she was curious about the 'one phone call.'"

"Time's a wasting. We've got twenty minutes to get to Thirty-fifth Street."

"Thirty-fifth Street? I've got to get some clothes."

Again Allison had a solution. "We're about the same size. I've got a closet full of clothes. And whatever you're missing, we can buy out there. Eastern Long Island is not exactly like the Siberian tundra."

~

They were standing next to a big, white circle on a stationery dock at the East 35th Street heliport. "Stand back," directed Allison, pointing to the huge, hovering helicopter preparing to land, "Here comes Stanley."

Once on the ground, chopper blades coming to a still position, a handsome young pilot who looked like Leonardo DiCaprio popped out the door. "Allie, ready to go? It's an absolutely gorgeous day for flying."

Mary's jaw dropped. The cabin was ultra-luxurious, housing the creature comforts of a small jet liner: two quiet turbo-thrust Rolls Royce engines, six individually heated reclining bucket seats and a tiny galley with a refrigerator and a coffee and tea-maker. Overhead were two satellite-controlled combination television-DVDs.

"Look at that mess," said Stanley, once airborne, pointing to the bumper-to-bumper expressway traffic as far as the eye could see. Stanley did a 360° swing above the Manhattan skyline and headed east toward the white, sandy beaches of Long Island.

Mary began to perspire profusely. Allison laughed. "So the boss is acrophobic?" Her heart started to pound. She was in the early stages of a panic attack. "Tell him to land. I've got to get out!"

"Easy, easy," said Allison, removing a small blue bottle from her pocketbook. "Take one of these, it will calm your nerves."

Mary grabbed two and swallowed them before Allison could say no.

"Take some deep breaths," instructed Allison, "and don't look down."

Within a matter of minutes Mary was on the way to dreamland. When she woke, Stanley was setting the craft down on a private helicopter pad next to a magnificent stone structure with ten double chimney flues, formal gardens and an abundance of decks with direct ocean views.

"Home sweet home," chuckled Allison.

"Good glory," said Mary, "this place is the size of Bodiam Castle in East Sussex." She noticed Allison's bottle on the floor. She quickly scooped it up and placed it in her purse.

"Good afternoon," said a chubby, elegantly dressed bald man helping the ladies out of the copter. "Does your friend have any bags?"

"Jonathan, we came foot loose and fancy free." This is my very good friend, Mary," said Allison.

"A pleasure to make your acquaintance. As for clothing, Marion should have no trouble rustling up an outfit or two for the weekend from your wardrobe room."

`Mary thought to herself, *wardrobe room, castles, and private helicopters. What next?*

"Jonathan, I detect a bit of a Northern accent, some-where near Cumbria County, I suspect."

"Town of Keswick. Very good, Madame," realizing Mary was also a Brit. "And, yourself?"

"Opposite direction, Brighton."

"Lovely beaches and such but nothing the likes of East-ern Long Island. First visit to the shore?"

"Matter of fact yes. I've read about it and seen pictures, but with the crush of business, never been."

Mary sensed an odd coincidence. Had she met Jonathan before, at another time, perhaps another life? Did Jonathan have anything to do with Elizabeth's William? "Jonathan, I have this strange sense, we've met before."

"I hardly think so. I'd remember."

"Did you by any chance know a Sir James and Lady Anne Clifford of Ullswater?"

Jonathan stood frozen in the sand. "I didn't know them personally, but my twin brother worked for them."

"Worked for them. What does he do now?"

"He mysteriously disappeared a few years back. I haven't heard from him since."

"What did the Cliffords say?"

"They had no idea where he went. One day he was just gone. No notes. No forwarding address. No remaining wardrobe or personal effects... It was like he never passed here."

~

As Mary and Allison made their way to the massive rear veranda, they were greeted by a well-dressed middle-aged couple straight out of *GQ Magazine*.

"You must be Mary," said the smiling, tanned, red-haired woman with a porcelain complexion and elegant shapely figure. "I'm Allison's mother, Margaret. We've heard so much about you. We're really looking forward to a nice weekend together. We were thinking dinner at home this evening then tomorrow perhaps..."

An equally handsome and well-dressed man with a distinctive square jaw and a full head of wavy gray hair tapped Margaret on the shoulder and nodded.

"Oh goodness, I'm sorry, Franklin."

"Welcome to Southampton. I'm Allison's father, Franklin, otherwise known as the lone male in the brood. Why don't you ladies come in and freshen up, change into something more Long Island. We'll have the drinks waiting on the veranda. How does that sound?"

"Dad, I'm sure Mary would love one of your cook's tours."

Mary wondered why Allison wanted to do a tour of the kitchen. She certainly knew Mary just hated to cook!

"How about we get a little sloshed first? The tour can wait. But, that having been said, Mary, you're the guest."

"I vote for the sloshed idea."

"Now, that's my girl," smiled Franklin.

As Mary finished her fourth margarita and was feeling no pain, the foursome watched the sun set. "So Franklin, Allison has only told me bits and pieces about what you do."

"I've had good run. Without getting too technical, I buy and sell undervalued companies domestically and internationally."

"From the looks of your modest abode, you've obviously done very well."

Franklin looked up at the house with pride. "When Margaret and I were married, we didn't have a dime. Just two kids with a couple of college degrees and a lot of dreams. Right, Margaret? Everything you see, we earned. For the first few years, Margaret was the entire backroom operations and I even swept the floors. We've been fortunate to buy right about eight times, which had allowed us to expand around the world. We have six offices in the world's money capitals, London, Dubai, Zurich, New York, Liechtenstein and Moscow. "

"Eight offices, Daddy. You always forget Sydney and Singapore."

"You're right, dear. It's eight offices," smiled Franklin. "We've got all we need for ten lifetimes. So I've been grooming Allison to take over the family business since she was a teenager. It's getting about that time, would you say, Allie?"

Mary wondered, based on Allison's natural feel for theatre administration, did she really want to do what dad was suggesting?

"So Mary, what is it that you do?"

"I'm involved in a small theatrical agency."

"Tough business. Picking a winning play is so subjective. Not like evaluating companies. That's all black and white. What do you do there?"

"One of my main jobs is evaluating properties."

"Atta girl, good for you. Have you got a plan after that?"

"Not just yet."

"Well, there's plenty of time. Plus maybe you'll meet a rich Islander and decide to chuck it in for a life of opulent leisure and play."

"Daddy, that's a terrible thing to say to somebody you've just met."

"Here goes my feisty daughter with that politically correct stuff again. Why is it so repulsive for a woman to think about just living a life of leisure if she has the means? There are lots of worthwhile causes to fill one's time. But no, everybody's got to go somewhere and make something out of themselves, otherwise, they're failures. No wonder the shrinks have lines out the doors."

"Daddy, I think we should move on."

"Margaret, you should be proud of this young lady. She's just like you. She knows how to put the old man in his place with just a few words." Franklin looked at his watch. "Mary, we have about twenty minutes before dinner. How would you like to see something really unusual?"

"I'm always game for a challenge."

"Franklin, no" said a horrified Margaret. "You're *not*."

Franklin opened a large wooden door and turned on the spotlights. "What you see in front of you," proudly announced Franklin, "is the largest private collection of New Guinea primitive art in the world. The Metropolitan Museum of Art will be transporting it in the fall to prepare the works for a major exhibition during the winter months."

Mary made two 360° revolutions, experiencing another eerie coincidence during her little journey some 3,000 miles away. Sir James and Anne Clifford owned a similar, if smaller, collection of New Guinea artifacts!

The four-course meal was splendid and distinctly Eastern Shore. Fresh Blue Point oysters, three-pound locally caught lobsters steamed in fennel, ears of white sugar corn, tender snap peas and local beefsteak tomatoes sitting atop freshly-made buffalo mozzarella, and mountains of local blueberries and blackberries topped with fresh homemade whipped cream.

"Mr. and Mrs. Edwards, I am absolutely stuffed. That was fabulous."

"It's a gorgeous night," said Margaret Edwards. "Maybe you and Allison should take a walk along the beach. Fabulous natural digestive, and it doesn't cost the earth."

~

As Mary and Allison walked along the Atlantic shore, waves crashing, Mary's mind shaped a loving remembrance. There stood a serene Elizabeth Clifford leaning over the railing of the family steamer on a peaceful shimmering Lake Ullswater pointing to Wordsworth's endless fields of wild yellow and purple flowers.

"Mary, I don't think I've ever seen you so pensive."

Mary looked in Allison's eyes, not sure what to say. Her mouth began to speak what filled her heart. "I don't know where to begin. There's so much you don't know about me."

"You can say as little or as much as you care to," said Allison gently.

"I was once totally and completely in love."

"So what happened to him?"

"He was a she. This is the only picture of the two of us that exists," said Mary as she carefully removed her torn picture from her purse. "We went to a photo booth on a board-walk and did four poses. She kept two and I kept two."

"She's very pretty. What happened to her?"

"I don't know. She was to join me in London, but she vanished completely."

"What did her parents say?"

"They were a royal couple, some distant relative to Prince Philip. They didn't want their daughter involved with a lesbian."

"Did you go to the police?"

"They essentially told me to get lost. The Cliffords were the most prominent citizens in the Lake Country. But I kept trying to get information. I even tried to contact the butler William, who also mysteriously disappeared."

"I'm so sorry, I had no idea."

"What's really spooky is that while talking to your Jonathan, I learned he's the twin brother of the Clifford's William."

Chills ran down Allison's spine. "My god."

"There's more."

"I noticed your father's Papua New Guinea primitive art collection."

"What could that ghastly stuff possibly have to do with anything?"

"Sir James also collected the stuff. It resided in a separate room just like your father's and was displayed in almost the same way. Last time we spoke, his collection was about to be exhibited in London at one of the museums."

"Good Christ."

That evening, Mary had a hellish nightmare. She was trapped in a labyrinth with no apparent exit. As she identified one potential escape route after another, she was blocked by the same angry, lunatic gargoyle.

~~~

SINCE DAVID MARKS RARELY, if ever, paid for dinner, Mary knew something was up.

"Thanks for meeting on such short notice."

"Your picking up the dinner tab is about as rare as the 1859 British Guinea half-cent stamp," laughed Mary. "Besides, you made it sound like a frightful emergency."

"Well, you are my agent, my advisor….And hopefully, my very close friend."

"How close?" teased Mary, subconsciously curious.

"Not that close…By the way, you look sensational, given your weekend."

"I gather Allison spoke to you," retorted Mary, feeling emotionally violated.

David proudly placed a manila envelope on the table. "I put the final touches on my latest and greatest while you two were hobnobbing with the Eastern Long Island's nouveau riche."

As the Yanks say, "Give me the elevator pitch."

"The play is the unholy partnership of a fast track Wall Street entrepreneur and classic overextended corporate exec. On the way to becoming filthy rich they destroy everyone and everything in their way."

"Good, but not great," said Mary prematurely.

"Have a minute there. You haven't even heard the play's central the twist" responded Marks confidently. "The organization guy becomes more evil than his immoral partner. I modeled the transition on transformation of strength between Scott and Zelda Fitzgerald, except my transformation is raw, natural, unfiltered and uncompromising. In the end, you actually dislike the whole lot. Properly, they all burn in their individual hells."

Mary had no idea if the premise fit reality. "What does a Brit writer know about the American way of business?"

"If you want to become obscenely rich, there's no better role model in the world than the greedy Yank executives."

"So true,…so true," laughed Mary, thinking about the prior weekend's garish display of wealth. It does sound intriguing. Does it have a title?"

"Yes. *And Pigs Get Slaughtered.*"

"What is that supposed to mean?"

"Comes from a well-known Wall-Street commandment, "Hogs get rich, and pigs get slaughtered.""

"Let me read it. But at first blush, if feels strictly Off-Broadway."

"I think we're both beyond that."

"You 're thinking straight to Broadway?"

Marks nodded.

"My, have our aspirations become grandiose."

"My agent made me that way," smiled Marks.

"Let me read the story and think about it. There's something missing; I'm just not sure what."

"You know most playwrights would tell you to jack off. But after what I've seen you do, I wouldn't dare."

"Paying for dinner, offering compliments. Did you get hit by a truck on the way over?"

"By the way, I think I can make your critique a little friendlier. Turns out Allie's parents are good friends with Robert DeNiro."

"I know. I've already seen that movie."

"Franklin organized a meeting for me while you guys were cavorting all over Long Island."

"He told me he knew nothing about the theatre."

"He absolutely positively doesn't. When I told him a bit about the play, he laughed. He said it could have been a biography of at least a half dozen of his buddies."

"You showed him before me?"

"I didn't show him anything. I just told him the storyline. He's the one who insisted I meet with Bob."

"So now it's Bob."

"Why are you being so petty? We hit it off. He wants to star in the play. Do you realize what that could mean at box office?"

Mary knew. "Are you sure?"

"Sure. The guy calls Andy Garcia right on the spot, and he agrees to be the organization man."

Mary could hear the cash registers ringing. "My, we are just full of surprises today."

"I've got one more little one," said David. "Let me guess," quipped Mary. "Steven Spielberg has agreed to direct."

"No," laughed David. "But that's not such a bad idea." David paused. "I've fallen head over heels in love... Me, Mister Intensity."

"Is this the part where you tell me about Allison?"

"How did you know?"

"Girlfriends share. It's something you blokes have never learned."

"So, what has she told you?"

"That she's madly in love and hopes one day to engage."

"Good, then she doesn't suspect."

"Suspect what?"

"That's what I wanted to share. Look at this"

David pulled a small, blue Tiffany box from his pocket and showed Mary a most exquisite pear-shaped diamond ring. "I've decided to ask her to marry me, sooner than later."

Mary smiled. She was truly happy for David. Plus another chapter of her life had reached closure...almost.

Mary was still curious. "Where are you going to live? I'm guessing your apartment is a little tight for your future wife's tastes...to say nothing of the macho clutter everywhere?"

Mary was on a roll. "Even that mattress is lumpy...."

David shook his head laughing. "Mary, Mary, think."

"Let me guess, you're moving into her Park Avenue palace."

"She's already asked on a number of occasions. So, why not?"

"David, may I ask you a very personal question?"

"Fire away."

"How come you never asked me to move in with you?"

40

~~~

ONE YEAR LATER......6,000 people filled Radio City Musical Hall for the 58th Annual Tony Awards Ceremony with millions more tuned in via national television.

For Mary and her clan—David Marks, Nigel Oboto, Marianne Kaufman and Darien Manners—it was the first time they had rubbed elbows with Broadway's legends.

"You nervous?" asked Mary.

"Piece of cake," nervously smiled Marks, "I've been nominated for so many Tonys, it's starting to get a little passé..."Oh, my god, is that really Sidney Poitier?"

As Luce predicted, it had been a very good year for Mary. *Fanny* and *Plummet* had been nominated for six Tonys in the categories of Best Play, Best Performance by a Leading Actor, Best Direction, Best Scene Design and Best Book.

While *J.L. & The Beak* was a surprising commercial success, to Oboto's consternation, the play received no nominations, allowing him to cry "racist foul."

Since *Fanny* and *Plummet* were written by first-time play-wrights, they were considered long, long shots, garnering little pre-ceremony press. As far as the press was concerned, the story of the year was "Princess Mary and Her Midas Touch." Her opening trifecta—three intellectually challenging properties just reaching Broadway in the same season—and her larger-than-life dress and manner, quickly transformed her from a youthful, energetic Brit curiosity into one of the legitimate theatre's most influential agents.

The first upset of the evening was in Set Design. *Fanny* bested such celebrated properties as *The History Boys* and *The Constant Wife*. Manners also collected a Tony for writing *Plummet*, while *Fanny* garnered Kaufman a Tony for Best Direction and Original Drama.

As Broadway newcomers and long shots, Mary's group was seated halfway back in the orchestra. So each time one of her clients won a Tony, the little group stood and applauded while the other 5,994 people waited for the winner to reach the stage.

Probably the biggest upset of the evening was Marianne Kaufmann's Best Director Tony, since this was not only her first Broadway play, it was also the first time she had ever directed a play, anywhere.

Kaufmann was overwhelmed as she walked onto the stage. "When I think of the legends who have received this prestigious award—Arthur Miller, Edward Albee, Tennessee Williams and Arthur Penn to just name a few, it is unfathomable to me that a Brit from London's East End could write a bittersweet love story about a boy and a girl from Mulberry Street and find herself in this fabulous place at this exciting moment.

"Certainly, lots of people helped win this award, but there is only one person who fought for the opportunity for us to even open on Broadway. She has been the most important influence in my short, professional career. My Candle in the

Wind, my agent, Broadway's agent par excellence, Mary Jackson-Peale."

Mary stood and waved. The cameras cut to her.

She was a theatrical icon.

~

Later that evening, Jason Lane Thomas and his New York theatre-owner buddies held a private party in the Rainbow Room atop Rockefeller Center to thank Mary and her group for filling their theatres during the past year. Lane spared no expense as Michael Feinstein warbled some of his favorite Gershwin tunes, *Embraceable You, S' Wonderful,* and *They Can't Take that Away From Me.*

"Thank you, Michael, that was *S' Wonderful,*" smiled Lane on the stage. As the crowd hushed, Thomas decided it was time to make a toast.

"If I could please get everybody's attention…Mary, come on up here. I'd like to toast this remarkable young lady before you swill every last drop of my Dom. One thousand of Broadway's elite generously chuckled then raised their glasses. Mary curtsied like a loyal subject in front of Thomas, purposely exposing her firm, shapely assets. He smiled knowingly at her naughty bravado. "My dear, you are a breath of fresh air to a community that prides itself on being conservative, stuffy and taken with itself. We commend your unique ability to identify diamonds in the rough and to coach, cajole and challenge your clients to achieve the highest levels of artistic excellence."

~

The party started to wind down about 3 a.m. Thomas grabbed the microphone for the last time. "It occurred to me before you all start to stumble home, you might want a sneak preview of the press release that the Board of New York Theatre Owners will be emailing to the *New York Times* and *Variety* first thing in the morning." Thomas looked at his watch. "I mean right after we leave here." The crowd chuckled. Mary, would you come up here and be the voiceover?"

Thomas handed her the press release. "Headline: DeNiro, Garcia and Tony playwright, Marks, to collaborate on new play, *And Pigs Get Slaughtered.* Subhead: The play, an insider's exploration of the greed and excesses of Wall Street, promises to be Broadway's blockbuster of the decade."

The crowd gasped with excitement.

"The Mary Jackson-Peale Theatrical Agency announced today that Tony award-winning playwright, David Marks, and two Academy Award winners, Robert DeNiro and Andy Garcia, *And Pigs Get Slaughtered,* will open September 28th. Mr. Marks will also serve as director, while Mr. Garcia and Mr. DeNiro, in addition to performing the lead roles, will also be the show's executive producers."

The crowd gave Mary and Jason Lane Thomas a two-minute standing ovation. "As you can imagine, we think *Pigs* will be the hottest ticket in town next season." Thomas spotted Mel Brooks. "Yes, Mel, it will even surpass *The Producers,*" predicted Thomas.

The crowd roared.

"In fact, to accommodate the crowds and to achieve the larger-than-life emotions the play will generate, myself, and my dear friend, Sol Mitchum, have created a general partnership to stage the play at New York's largest live theatrical venue, the Wintergarden.

The next day, the Arts Section of the *New York Times* declared the Mary Jackson-Peale Agency was now "the Great White Way's brightest light."

41

~~~

Lake Country, England….

"THAT'S RIDICULOUS," BARKED SIR JAMES when told the going rate for replacement staff. "Hardy and Baker Employment Recruiters come highly recommended and have a reputation for identifying precisely the proper help," rebutted Lady Clifford. "And, while they may charge a bit more up front, their recommendations come with a 12-month replacement guarantee, which I find frightfully commendable. God knows we have to watch every pound," teased the Lady.

"Respectfully my dear, I don't agree. People always seem to revel in taking advantage of the well-to-do. I am quite certain an advert in the local paper, explaining the position's requirements, salary and benefits, signed by us, will generate more William replacements than we'll ever require. How often do you think a member of the common class gets an opportunity to work for a Clifford?"

~

Sir James was right…and, in this case, also wrong.

A young third-generation hog farmer named Michael Tobin from nearby Grange-over-Sands spotted the advert in the
local newspaper. Tobin despised the family occupation and
consumed his waking hours trying to figure out how to leave
Dad and his hog farm with enough money in his pocket to
begin life anew in London. Dad wanted to maintain his modest way of life plus stash a few quid away for the later years,
just as his father before him. The dashing 22-year-old Tobin
spent every pound he earned on wine, women and revelry.
He was confident the advert offered him the way out.

He had heard of the Cliffords and Sir James's philanthropic activities in London. He did some research and determined the physical part of the job would certainly be less
strenuous than his current existence as an apprentice hog
farmer. He also vaguely remembered hearing the Cliffords
had an attractive daughter named Elizabeth which could be
an interesting test of his upper class wooing skills, a skill he
hypothesized would be particularly useful in London. He
called to schedule an interview, only to discover he was candidate number 16. "We've been surprised at the overwhelming response," said Lady Clifford, doing her best impersonation of the family's administrative aide until William's replacement was hired.

Tobin took the last remaining time slot but he knew an
impassioned speech about being a hard worker and loyal employee was just a starting point at his interview. He had two
days to identify his unique point of difference. He went to the
local library and researched all he could about the Cliffords.
He discovered Sir James was an avid equestrian, while Lady
Ann loved poetry, particularly the English Romantics from
around the Lake Country.

Hence, his pitch to Sir James. He was the empathetic
young horse lover who wanted to save his earnings to open a
first-class tack shop for the local aristocracy. "As the son of a
hog farmer, I didn't have the spare quid to own me own
horse, so I took second jobs at the local stables and the sta-

bles of—if you don't mind me saying so—fine gentleman like yourself. I took to learning all there was to know about horse tack. My goal is to save enough to start my own shop near the Century Training Grounds in Cumbria."

"Noble goal. But that could be an expensive endeavor," said Sir James.

Tobin blew smoke like an expert. "Clearly. But I think I've figured out how to merchandise the shop to appear larger than it is while still giving me customers what they want. I'll stock and display the best of the best—Silver Fox All Purpose Saddles, the Crosby Prex De Nation, the Black 21 inch Cutback Show and probably the Stubben Siegfried. "I'd post pictures of basics like the all-purpose Jumping Saddles and wide English Endurance Saddles because they can be ordered on demand quite efficiently through the internet.

"I also figure I'll need to carry some riding apparel. The ladies love their shopping."

"Young man, you certainly know your tack."

"Thank you sir. I'm sorry, I get a little passionate."

"Nothing wrong with a little passion," said Sir James.

"From your standpoint sir, I'll bump me old rump—pardon the language, Madame—to fulfill whatever tasks are required. And since I have no romantic interests to encumber me, I can be available twenty-four seven. I'm desperate to become a shopkeeper and have that business of me own."

Sir James was utterly enamored.

It was now time to charm the lady of the castle.

~

"Me lady, when Sir James is out riding, what are your interests?"

"Besides my little daughter, just one. I love to read poetry."

"Amazing coincidence! As do I when not tending to the hogs," said Tobin innocently. "If you've got a poem within you today, I can guarantee you a tomorrow."

"Ahhh, Terri Guillemets," said Lady Clifford, gleefully identifying the quote. "Do you have a preference?" asked Lady Clifford.

"My tastes run wide and deep. I even think that Sandburg has surprising depth—for a Yank. I believe it is he who said 'Poetry is an echo, asking a shadow to dance.' But I must confess, I am most fond of the English Movement."

"The coincidence continues," remarked Lady Clifford seemingly unaware she was being had. "So am I. By chance, do you have one favorite?"

Do I have a favorite? thought Tobin. *Why the hell do you think I did all that research!* "So hard to choose but"…Tobin paused for dramatic effect. In reality, he had actually memorized and rehearsed but one poem, *On the Sea*, by John Keats, which he believed to be Lady Clifford's favorite verse. Tobin dramatically raised his eyes heaven bound and stretched out his hands.

> *It keeps eternal whisperings around*
> *Desolate shores, and with its mighty swell*
> *Gluts twice ten thousand caverns,*
> *till the spell of Hecate*
> *leaves them their old shadowy sound…..*

"That was wonderful," cooed Lady Clifford. "Such emotion! Bravo! I could feel Keats listening intently."

Sir James smiled at Lady Clifford. She nodded back. "Thank you for visiting with us," said Sir James. "I think I speak for the two of us when I say it was a real pleasure to meet such a grounded young man in this day and age of video games and eternal frivolity. We will be back to you with our response shortly. Very shortly."

"Very good sir. Is there any need to meet your daughter? Does she have a vote, if I might be so brash?"

"She does and would, if we knew where the dear was. But unfortunately, one day she up and left. Bit of a statement of independence to her father, I suspect," mused Sir James in his Sunday-best acting performance.

"Oh a bit of time on the road, and she'll realize what fine parents and lineage she has. I'm sure she'll be back before you know it," said Tobin, who now couldn't care less since her vote no longer mattered.

"Rather not like her," said a saddened Lady Clifford.

"Well, if I get the job, maybe I can help there a bit."

"Very generous, Tobin," said Sir James. "But I think we'll leave that to the police."

~

Sir James and Lady Clifford had the briefest of candidate discussions over dinner.

"I have a feeling this is a short conversation," said Sir James looking at Lady Clifford to declare her preference.

"Tobin."

"Me, too."

"He's the kind of man that would be perfect for Elizabeth."

"He's a commoner, my dear."

"Even so, this is the 21st Century."

"No matter, till Elizabeth comes to her senses."

"That day will come," said Lady Clifford. "I miss her so."

"I'll call the young man in the morning and tell him he can start immediately. He can live in the rear quarters."

"And the wage?" asked Lady Clifford.

"As discussed in the advert, £400 a month plus room and board."

"But he's such a fine young man. How will he ever save for that tack shop on that wage? Let's make it six."

"My dear, that's London scale. But, it is your money. I'm merely your financial enabler."

"And, such a noble one," smiled Lady Clifford reaching her hand across the table to clasp Sir James's.

"Might you indulge my whims in one more matter? Would you not agree this castle has more rooms than we could ever use personally? I think we should consider treating young Master Tobin as a member of the family. Why not offer him a choice... suite in the servants' quarters or a room in the main castle?"

"For his convenience or yours, my dear?"

"James, what a terrible thing to say!"

"I was just having you on a bit. I rather like the idea. It would be nice to have some young blood in this old place again...at least until Elizabeth returns."

~

Sir James rang Tobin. He was ecstatic with the unexpected raise and the offer to live in the main castle down the hall from Lady and Sir Clifford.

He could tell from the way she looked at him the prior evening. Besides, she was "a bit of awright"—well put-together and preserved for a woman of 52—despite her snobby breeding. That evening, as Tobin slept at the hog farm for what would be the last time ever, he fantasized what it would be like to straddle the loins of the super rich, middle aged wench.

~

Tobin moved his limited belongings into the upstairs bedroom under the watchful eye of Lady Clifford. She noticed him place a guitar by the side of his bed.

"You play the guitar?" asked Lady Clifford.

"A bit. Mostly 19th Century ballads. I find them interesting. They are quite like one-part poetry, one-part music."

"Would you play something for us after dinner tonight?"

Dinner ended, Sir James was about to retire to the study.

"Dear James, before you go, I learned something new about Michael when he was moving in today. He's also a musician."

"Let me guess. He sing to hogs to fatten their yield."

"James, be serious."

"I thought that was rather funny."

"As did I," interrupted Tobin to insure family harmony.

"Well, go on."

Tobin went to retrieve his guitar. "I'll do just one."

"My sentiments precisely," said Sir James. "I have a long two days ahead of me in London with our estate solicitors, accountants and bankers."

"I didn't realize you were going to London," said Lady Clifford.

"I apologize, my Lady, a variety of issues have arisen since that damn minister and Parliament enacted those new statutes to further tax people of means. We need to re-evaluate and modify our entire long-term strategy."

"Sounds dreadfully boring."

"It's even worse. The Grosvenor is absolutely booked. Some damn American technology convention."

"Wherever will you stay?"

"Our agent called around. I've gotten a frightfully small room at an exorbitant rate at Claridge's. Another reason why I didn't want to drag you into town."

"Thank you James. So thoughtful."

~

"Perhaps one song before we all retire?"

"It's called *The Lass That Loves A Sailor*. It was written by Charles Didbin around 1808. He was born in Southampton, the eighteenth son of a poor silver-maker."

"Eighteen sons. I can see why he was poor," smiled Sir James.

Gently and tenderly Michael Tobin strummed and sang. He was good, very good, thought Lady Clifford.

> *The moon on the ocean*
> *Was dimmed by a ripple....*
> *But the standing toast*
> *That pleased the most,*
> *Was 'The wind that blows,*
> *The Ship that goes,*
> *And the lass that loves a sailor!'....*

Michael's romantic tones resurrected James's latent desires. As he and Lady Clifford entered their bedroom, James softly purred his wish that they engage in a round of "physical delight."

42

~~~

THE NEXT MORNING, Tobin drove Sir James to the helicopter pad on the other side of the lake. On the way back, he marveled at the verdant hillside painted in shades of yellow, lavender, blue and red. As he drove up the long driveway, he could see Lady Clifford standing at the front entrance to the castle in a cheerful, terribly modest, yellow summer dress. By her side was a wicker picnic basket. "I thought it such a lovely day we should go for a spin on the Lake in our steamer. I had the chef pack a little lunch."

Tobin misunderstood the Lady's generosity. He assumed she was trying to seduce him. The conceited young man thought to himself, *just this once I'll play hard to get, women love men who tease, particularly those as handsome and fit as he.* "Love to Madame, but Sir James has given me a list of errands to complete over the next 48 hours."

"Look, Michael, I'm a little long in the tooth to pretend. I know the main reason you took the job is to have access to

Sir James's business contacts. That's fine with me. But as the lady of the house, I also need to be pleased."

It was an unfortunate set of words.

Tobin was rather charmed by the lady's forthrightness. He smiled and took the picnic basket. "Now, where is the steamer I heard so much about last evening. I warn you, my lady, I've never driven a powered water vessel." They walked through the rear gardens to the dock where the handsome teak and chrome steamer rested.

"It's a beauty," said Tobin.

"Untie the boat," directed Lady Clifford, "then jump aboard. I'll give you your first driving lesson." She was indeed an expert sailor. "Grasp the steering wheel firmly, place the gears in reverse and gently throttle out of the cove."

Tobin was enjoying the expensive toy as he headed toward the middle of the lake.

"Michael, be careful. You're terribly close to water's edge. The tides are low and craggy rock formations rest just below the water line. Let's not turn our maiden voyage into Titanic II."

Michael held the steering wheel and carefully captained the boat to open waters, far afield from shore.

"Well, at least you listened. That is more than I can say for my daughter's first run. I told her to take care steering, stay in open waters. I turned my head for an instant, and she lost control, bringing us aground in the muddy cove. We had to call for help. The tugboat service had a devil of a time freeing us. It took bloody hours. You should have seen Sir James when the bill arrived."

Tobin smiled. It was close to that time. "It is quite beautiful out here."

Lady Clifford misunderstood Tobin's subtle advances. "Quite so. The colors of these rolling hills are quite stunning. So vibrant, so alive. Makes you understand why the Romantic Movement began here. Would you mind if I read something?" Lady Clifford removed a small volume from her basket and started to read William Wordsworth's *Ode To May*, as the sea breezes gently flowed through her hair.

> *While from the purpling east departs*
> *The star that led the dawn,*
> *Blithe Flora from her couch upstarts,*
> *For May is on the lawn*
> *A quickening hope, a freshening glee,*
> *Foreran the expected Power,*
> *Whose first-drawn breath, from bush and tree,*
> *Awake to silent joy:*
> *Queen art thou still for each gay plant*
> *Where the slim wild deer roves;*
> *And served in depths where fishes haunt*
> *Their own mysterious groves.*

> *Cloud-piercing peak, and trackless heath,*
> *Instinctive homage pay;*
> *Nor wants the dim-lit cave a wreath*
> *To honour thee, sweet May! ....*

"That was lovely," responded Tobin, ever so gently.

"Let's drop anchor in the next cove and have a spot of lunch."

"Yes, My Lady. And how do I anchor this fine vessel."

"Once inside the cove, hog farmer, turn the throttle to zero. That will stop the boat. Then remove the anchor from the front well—over there on your left—and throw it overboard, making sure it grabs the lake's bottom."

"Trust me to anchor?"

"Any idiot can anchor," she smiled and began to set the lunch table at the rear of the boat.

~

Tobin crashed the steamer ashore and was stuck in the mud. His face turned red with embarrassment. "Relax, young man, no damage has been done. I'll show you how to release from shore after lunch."

"I'm so sorry, my Lady."

She smiled. "I guess I was wrong. Not any idiot can anchor. The idiot requires at least a modicum of common sense."

~

The afternoon flew by. It was time to leave. Lady Clifford tired to reverse the boat, but the rudder seemed to be caught on something. Tobin jumped into the shallow water with a flashlight to free the entanglement. "We're in luck," he said. "The rudder is merely caught on some cloth. Hand me a knife, I'll have us freed in a jiff." He returned to the side of the boat with a big smile on his face. He held up a clump of colored fabric. "This was the culprit. We're now good to go."

Lady Clifford looked at the fabric and started to scream. "AHHHHH, no. Dear God!"

Tobin jumped in the boat, unsure of what the problem was. He held the shaking, shuddering Lady Clifford. "What the hell is the matter? Did I say something to offend?"

"That fabric. That's a piece of my daughter's dress." She continued to sob and cry uncontrollably. "We've got to get back to the Castle. I've must call Sir James straight away. Let him know that somebody has done something terrible to our daughter."

43

~ ~ ~

"WELCOME BACK, SIR JAMES. So good to see you and Lady Clifford again," said Jonathan, the hotel clerk. We have your usual corner suite. How long might you and the Lady be staying with us?"

"Unfortunately, this is just a spur-of-the-moment trip to get measured for a few new suits at Gleves and Hawkes. I'm due back in the Lake Country by the weekend. You know, some estate matters."

"Oh, pity. Saturday, Zubin Meta is guest conducting the Symphony at the Barbican Center. Brahms, I believe."

"Perhaps next time," said Sir James's London mistress, Miss Pamela Duggins, who had been masquerading as Lady Clifford for the past decade at Claridge's on those occasions when Sir James was able to slip into town without Lady Clifford. When the real Lady Clifford joined him in London, Sir James insisted on a suite at the Grosvenor. That way each lady believed she had "her" place.

In exchange for a noncommittal, ad hoc relationship, Sir James treated Pamela quite well financially, which was quite easy to do since he maintained the family books and records. Miss Duggins's stipends were discreetly labeled "miscellaneous." In 25 years of marriage, it had never occurred to Lady Clifford to question the accuracy of the family's inherited wealth.

~

Lady Clifford dashed from the dock to the phone in the library.

"Claridge's Hotel, may I help you?" said the voice on the other end of the phone. "This is Lady Clifford. My husband, Sir James is a guest. Could you put me through?"

"But, Madame, that's not possible, Lady Clifford is already here."

"Whatever are you on about? Just put me through to Sir James's room. Do we need the manager?"

"Right away, Madame," said the confused clerk. "The phone rang twice. A sultry voice answered the phone. "Hello."

"Sorry, could you redirect me to the front desk. They connected me with the wrong room."

"No problem. Whom shall I tell them to connect you to?"

"Sir James Clifford."

"This is Sir James's suite."

"Then who, might I ask, are you?"

"Why should I tell you?"

"Because I am Lady Clifford. Where the hell is my husband? I have something very important to discuss."

Pamela told Sir James his wife was on the phone. "She knows about us!"

"Jesus Christ, what did you tell her?"

"Nothing."

"My dear," said Sir James, calmly trying to bluff his way through the predicament. "Pamela says you're distraught."

"Who is Pamela?"

"She's Solicitor Brighton's paralegal. They were finishing off some revisions in our trust agreement because of the recent changes in the tax codes. Remember we discussed this before I left?"

'Why don't I believe you, you son of a bitch? We found a piece of Elizabeth's dress in a cove. I think something ghastly happened to her."

"Stay calm," said Sir James, deeply concerned about his own self-preservation. "I'll arrange for a helicopter to take me back immediately. Have Tobin meet me at the pad in three hours."

"Good, hurry. In the meantime, we've already called the police."

"Who is we?"

"Tobin and I."

"And, how did you get into the cove?"

"Tobin drove the steamer?"

"Tobin?"

"For Christ's sake, if it wasn't for him finding the dress wrapped around the rudder, we would never have known."

"Does he drive?"

"Why am I explaining my actions to you? It's you who have the explaining to do. But that will wait till later."

Lady Clifford slammed the phone down.

~

"I must return to Glassmere. Something terrible appears to have happened."

Pamela, who had dressed for an evening on the town, was noticeably frustrated. "When The Lady beckons, little Jamesie goes running. Certainly don't want to disturb that pile of wealth, no matter what emotional carnage you leave in your wake. I'm just your little dark secret, your well-paid whore."

"I don't have time to argue now. Here's two thousand pounds for your trouble. I'll call."

A highly insulted Duggins tossed the money to the floor. "Get out, you shameful excuse for an aristocrat!"

~

"Inspector, this is Lady Clifford. I'm calling about my daughter Elizabeth."

"Let me guess, like I told that young lady who called. I bet she turned up in London."

"What young lady?"

"That young lady from Brighton who said Elizabeth was a lesby."

"Oh, that tramp."

"My sentiments precisely. But rest assured, My Lady, I put her and her wild accusations in their proper place."

"Inspector, I need your help. My new caretaker and butler, Michael Tobin, found a piece of Elizabeth's dress in a cove earlier today. I think something terrible has happened to her."

"Are you sure it was her dress?"

"Inspector, it was a flowered lavender summer dress I personally bought for her to wear in Brighton last summer."

"I'll send some of my men over to the house right away. Can you identify the cove? We'll start dredging the lake from the shore outward. I promise we'll do everything we can, but remember, it's a large, deep lake so the operation may take some time."

James arrived home to bright lights on the lake, police setting up remote watch stations, and trained dogs sniffing here, there and everywhere. "This place is like a circus," he protested. "What will the neighbors think?"

"Sir," said a surprised inspector, "this is your daughter we are talking about."

Night turned to morning. James sat in bed, rightly concerned about the outcome. Would the police find Elizabeth's remains? Did he leave any fingerprints on the body or the bag? Other than leave right then and there, he concluded he had but one option. To wait and hope for the best—that Elizabeth's body would not be found.

A day went by. No Elizabeth. The winds increased. A second day passed. Still no Elizabeth. On the third day, the seas became choppy. Sir James took to brandy, one then another, then another. Day turned into night. He looked out the window from his bedroom and saw the police carrying a bag up the dock. He and Lady Clifford went to the scene.

"I think we found her," said the inspector. "But out of respect for your family, we wanted you to be present when we opened the bag."

Lady Clifford held Sir James tight. His body was shaking like a leaf in a storm. To everyone's surprise but his, the bag contained the battered remains of William.

"Dear Jesus," said the inspector. "Let's get this mess out of here and down to the morgue. We'll return in the morning to continue the search for your daughter. But we need to get to the bottom of this grisly affair."

"Johnny," said the inspector, "when we get to the station, contact Scotland Yard, I think we need some help on this one."

~

The contents of the bag were gruesome. The results of the autopsy cataclysmic!

Sir James's fingerprints were all over William's clothing. DNA testing of hairs and skin in William's nails clearly indicated Sir James was the culprit.

Out of respect for the family, the inspector wanted to inform Lady Clifford of their findings before they arrested Sir James outright. They called the house. Fortunately, Tobin answered. "Yes, Inspector, I'll get Lady Clifford straight away."

Lady Clifford listened to what the police had to say. "Could there be a mistake?"

"Not possible. DNA and fingerprints are irreversible evidence."

"And what about Elizabeth?"

"We're quite certain the matters are related. We recovered a few hairs from your daughter's dress fragments. They're also a DNA match to Sir James. I'm fairly certain we have a double homicide. I'm so sorry."

"The smug bastard. I detest everything about him. How could he? How long before you get here?"

"It's a long ride around the lake in the dark. Figure about 45 minutes."

"What should I do in the meantime?"

"Just act as normal as you can under the circumstances. I would strongly suggest you don't stir the pot."

By the time Lady Clifford had finished the phone call, she was completely ashen.

"I'm in the library my dear; come join me," called Sir James, unaware of the developments.

Lady Clifford slowly walked into the library. James was drinking a brandy and smoking a cigar. "What a terrible turn of events," bluffed Sir James. "William was a good man. Why would somebody do that sort of thing?"

"I don't know," she said, eyes downward.

"Who was that on the phone?"

"Oh, that was the inspector. He said he thought he'd have some results of the autopsy in the next few days, something about the water may have damaged the remains beyond recognition. On the other hand, he thinks there may be some correlation between William's death and Elizabeth's disappearance."

"What makes them think that?"

"I don't know. Why don't you talk to them in the morning. Maybe they'll have some new information. Right now, I would like to discuss Pamela."

"Please, let me explain." Sir James went through his entire routine.

Lady Clifford knew he was merely piling lie upon lie, as she now knew him for what he really was. Strangely enough, despite what he had done, all the years counted for something. She decided to give him a clue of what lay ahead. "You know John Donne was right. No man operates independent of his surroundings. If you don't mind, I'm going to bed. It's been a terribly long and painful day," said Lady Clifford.

"I understand." Sir James understood completely. He knew the police were probably on the way. She didn't want to be there when he was taken away. They had put the pieces together. That's what the police do. There was no point in running, no point in hiding. He was not the fugitive type. And, it had been a good life, filled with all the accoutrements of the good life. He had really lost his soul only at the end. Maybe God would provide some mercy.

He scribbled a short note and then walked over to the hunting cabinet, removed his favorite antique gun, a Colt 45 Root Revolver circa 1860, filled the chambers of the gun, took one last swill of whiskey, placed the gun to his forehead and pulled the trigger. As he fell to the floor, the glass cabinet in front of him looked like a Jackson Pollack splattered crimson original.

Tobin came running to tell her the news. She merely sat in bed without movement. "I expected as much. The police shall be here within the hour. Just leave everything as it is."

"Sir James left this note near the cabinet." It was short and sweet. "There is little to say beyond I'm so, so sorry. I ask but one thing, throw my ashes off the White Cliffs. From dust I came, to dust I wish to return."

44

~~~

THE POLICE ARRIVED to a rather grisly scene.

"I guess he wanted to leave on his terms,' said the inspector. "Shall we remove the body?"

"Actually, if you could do your autopsy at the castle it would be easier on all of us. Sir James's last request was to have his ashes sprinkled across Dover from whence he came."

"I understand, Lady Clifford. Whatever you wish. We'll complete the autopsy tomorrow and then dredge the lake for another 48 hours before we give up.

Around noon that next day, another sack containing the gruesome remains of Elizabeth was found. After Lady Clifford shed another ocean of tears, she began to make proper final arrangements. William and Elizabeth were buried side by side at the castle in a dignified service attended by some 88 close friends and a caravan of media reporters and TV cameras.

As last prayers were said over Elizabeth's casket, a strong wind unexpectedly filled the air on what had been a perfectly calm, sunny day. Some 3,000 miles away, on a bench in Central Park, Mary wondered what had become of her first love, as the blustery New York breezes chilled her face. Suddenly, the winds became still, and the sun bathed Mary's face in golden warmth.

~

The evening after the funeral, Lady Clifford decided to bring some measure of finality to Elizabeth's tragically shortened life.

For her own sanity as a loving mother, she did not wish to turn her daughter's room into a shrine full of depressing memories. Rather she looked through Elizabeth's personal effects, selecting only those things she felt emotionally attached. The rest went to two of Elizabeth's favorite charities. One side of the room contained piles of dresses, casual wear, shoes and athletic gear. The other side, a collection of stuffed animals from childhood through her teen years.

"Michael, in the morning, send this stack to the Lake Boys Club, and then neatly arrange the animals on the shelves."

"I understand Madame."

Lady Clifford then sat down at Elizabeth's desk and again began to weep uncontrollably as she opened the top drawer. There sat an envelope addressed to Mary Jones in Brighton. Lady Clifford opened the envelope and began to read the two-page hand-written letter.

Dearest love,
I hope all finds you well at this writing. I've thought long and hard since Father showed you the door. I've come to certain conclusions. First, and foremost, I love you more than life itself. I am ready, willing and able to give up my family heritage and inheritance to

be by your side as your designated partner.
The laws have changed in England, so we can
be properly married and move where we wish.
However, my preference is to stay in London,
obtain my master's degree in psychology
whilst you further your career as a theatrical
agent, where I am confident you'll succeed.
I think we need to be realistic and assume my
Father will provide no support other than a
bushel full of anger. As for Mum, while her
heart would be supportive, I don't believe she
has the internal fortitude to confront the old
blowhard. I plan to tell the family of my plans
in a fortnight, rather than ruin their anniversary celebration, Saturday next.
When that is done, I will call to make arrangements to stay with you, no matter how
modest the accommodations. I'll find a part-
time job till I return to Oxford. I'm quite certain with my undergraduate grades and activities, I can qualify for a scholarship.
I hope the above meets with your satisfaction.
If not… too bad, I'm coming anyway! We are
going to have a wonderful life together—
society and Father be damned!
Your One True Love,
Elizabeth

The letter gave Lady Clifford insight into the depth of her
daughter's emotions that she suspected but more fully grasp-
ed. Besides honoring Sir James's request, she concluded she
had one additional obligation.

~

Two days later, with Sir James's ashes in tow, Lady
Clifford made the long trip from the Lake Country in the
north to the coasts of Dover in the south of England. As a

courtesy to friends and acquaintances, she also published a funeral notice in the London papers on the off chance that someone might be willing to make the two-hour drive from London to Dover to pay last respects. The funeral notice became a full-fledged story in the London papers. *The Sun*, in its typical tabloid fashion, couldn't resist the catchy headline… "The Curtain comes down on James." To the Lady's surprise, over 350 people made the journey, some out of love, some out of respect, some out of pity and some out of sheer curiosity.

Vicar Longenes, a longtime family friend, performed the soulful last rites. "This is a last remembrance with no comforting final thoughts, only difficult questions. What does one say about a friend one thought he knew? How does a basically decent man enlist in Satan's Army? Why should a lifetime of good deeds be put asunder? What makes a man take his own life, no matter what his wrath? We have not been given the authority to judge another's deeds. That job is reserved for our just Maker. On this day, in this place, we can only ask for some measure of eternal justice, perhaps touched by an olive branch. As we make the long journey home, let us try to think kindly of Sir James Clifford, the honorable Samaritan who lost his way."

~

After the crowds had left the hillside service, Lady Clifford stood stoically on Dover's highest white cliff. She took the urn filled with ashes and turned it over. A gust of wind carried the tiny gray particles out to sea. Standing proud with the misty salt air swirling, Lady Clifford removed a small volume of Matthew Arnold from her purse, and began to read aloud Sir James' favorite poem, *The White Cliffs Of Dover*:

> *The sea is calm tonight.*
> *The tide is full, the moon lies fair*
> *Upon the straits; on the French coast the light*

Gleams and is gone; the cliffs of England stand,
Glimmering and vast, out in the tranquil bay….

~

Ceremonies and goodbyes complete, there remained one last piece of business. Lady Clifford knew the town of Brighton was two hours southeast of Dover. She needed to visit Chloe Jones to tell her what had happened to Mary's beloved Elizabeth and to personally deliver Elizabeth's letter. When she knocked at the door of the cottage, Annabelle Lee and Chloe were having tea. "You don't know me, but my name is Lady Clifford. I'm Elizabeth's mother."

"Ahhh, Elizabeth, sweet Elizabeth. Come in."

"I'll get right to the point if you don't mind." (Pause) "I think we both know how the girls were very much in love. I thought it only fitting to stop by after the funeral and tell you the news personally, rather than let you read about it in some newspaper."

"The funeral?" said Chloe, assuming she was referring to some tragedy with Elizabeth.

"Elizabeth's father did not take to his daughter's relationship with another woman."

"What a pity?" said Chloe. "Straight people don't understand. They are not willing to accept reality as it is."

"I know that now," said Lady Clifford. "Anyway, he killed our daughter in cold blood over the situation."

"Dear Jesus almighty, may God rest her soul."

"It gets a little sketchy from here. He apparently involved our butler of many years. Then he bludgeoned the butler to death with a steel hatchet and disposed of him in the same lake."

"When I was going through Elizabeth's personal effects. I found this unmailed letter to Mary. I thought she might want it."

"I'm sure she'll treasure it. I'll ring her and tell her what we've got."

"The letter is actually how I found your address. Did you know there are 41 Joneses in Brighton?"

"Well, we are a very common lot," smiled Chloe, thinking the Lady a decent sort. "It was very gracious of you to come all the way from the Lake Country to tell the dreadful news and deliver the letter."

"Actually, I was down this way. My husband, who committed suicide before the police came for him, asked that his ashes be spread over the Cliffs of Dover, where he was born. It was his last request."

~ ~ ~

CHLOE'S CALL WAS UNEXPECTED.

"Mum. It's been a while. Have you been reading the press releases I've sent?"

"You mean Allison has sent, don't you?"

"Mum, I'm sorry. I've just been so busy."

"Mary, sit down."

"I'm sitting."

"Elizabeth's mother paid me a visit."

Mary began to gush. "Oh my God, finally. How is she? Where is she? I haven't heard."

"Lady Clifford had just come from Dover."

"Were they on holiday?"

"No..." Chloe paused, taking a deep breath. "She had just spread Sir James's ashes to the wind on the cliffs. Apparently that was his last wish."

"Last wish. How frightful. He wasn't that old. What was the cause of death?"

"Suicide."

"Suicide!"

"What I'm about to tell you is rather shocking. After you left Elizabeth in Ullswater, she and Sir James got into quite a row about her sexual preferences. He demanded she stop seeing you, that the affair was a complete embarrassment to the name Clifford."

"That miserable buggar!"

"She refused. He apparently bludgeoned her to death with an andiron, and stuffed her in a burlap bag with the help of William, the butler. They took the family's steamer out to the middle of the lake and threw her body overboard."

Mary's head was reeling, her heart pounded in anger as she clenched her fist.

"This is where it gets a bit sketchy," continued Chloe. Sir James must have been concerned that William would crack under pressure, so either that night or shortly thereafter, he took William out to the middle of the lake and beat him to death. This time with an axe or something equally gruesome. When Lady Anne confronted Sir James, he confessed, and then promptly retreated to his hunting room, gathered a pistol and took license."

"Why in the name of bloody Christ would Lady Anne fulfill that miserable bastard's last request?"

"I wondered the same thing. But that really was none of my concern. Apparently, the details are now all in the hands of the police and stories will be appearing in the London papers and international press tomorrow and on the Internet. I was about to call so you'd hear directly rather than be totally surprised by the published story. Somehow the police discovered that a Mary Jones was the lover who caused the chain of unfortunate events. According to the report, they are looking for her as we speak."

"Did anybody ask you where I am?"

"No, and I don't imagine they would. The story does not identify where you two met. There are a lot of Joneses in this world."

A crushing pain pressed against Mary's chest; her head became lightheaded, her surroundings distant. She was in the midst of a full-blown, acute panic attack. "Mum," mumbled Mary quasi-coherently, "be aware, in the States I'm known as Mary Jackson-Peale. It must be our secret. Understand? Promise?"

"As far as I know, there are only two people who know Mary Jones is Mary Jackson-Peale. I'm happy to leave it that way. By the way, when Lady Anne cleaned out Elizabeth's room, she found what appears to be half a picture of the two of you in her wallet from one of those photo machines. She left it for you."

"Mum, I'd love to have it. Could you send it to me?"

"Eliminating all traces, eh," smiled Chloe.

~~~

THE REMNANTS OF A DRESS washed up on the private beach of a mansion at the end of Pond Road in the exclusive enclave of Kings Point overlooking Long Island Sound, some 25 miles north of where she had jumped off the Brooklyn Bridge.

The city edition of the *New York Times* carried a brief report about an apparent suicide since no body was recovered. Two days later, more details were published. The tattered label established the dress was made in England. A few strands of hair were recovered. A DNA test, performed with the help of Scotland Yard, revealed the dress belonged to a Sarah Heller of London. She was wanted for the murder of London theatrical agency power-broker, James Belfrage.

~

Sarah's suicide was all-consuming.

Mary wandered around the office like a caged lion. No one dared try to cheer up the normally chipper Mary.

"Mary, I don't know what is going on, but your unpleasant demeanor is affecting office productivity," said Allison, matter-of-factly.

"It's Sarah Heller. She committed suicide," blurted Mary.

"Who's Sarah Heller?" asked Allison, totally unaware.

"An enormously helpful London business associate." Mary decided to provide Allison an abridged version. "We met when I was a trainee at Belfrage and Associates, London's largest theatrical agency. Sarah was the firm's administrative operator who handled all of noncreative activities. She taught me the ropes. Saved me lots of wasted effort. She was also Belfrage's girl. Somehow we became attracted to each other and had an affair while she was living with Belfrage. One evening, he came back early from a business trip and found us in his bed."

"In his bed!"

"I know, I know."

"What happened?"

"He fired both of us on the spot, kicked her out of his apartment and told me he'd make sure I never got another theatre job in London. Rather than fight it, I came to New York."

"What about Sarah?"

"I'm not really sure. She had a terminally ill mother, so she stayed, doing menial jobs. I can only surmise she must have taken revenge."

"There's still a piece missing. How did she wind up in New York?"

"I don't know. I guess she read about our success on the Internet. One evening she just appeared on my doorstep unannounced. She told me her mother passed, and she was ready to continue our business and personal relationship and that I owed her. I didn't know what to say, so I invited her to stay for a while until I figured out what in the bloody hell to do. The David thing was quite spontaneous."

"How was David involved?"

"Foolish me. The night after she arrived, I had a business dinner scheduled with David to discuss some changes to his latest script. I invited Sarah. For some unknown reason, right in the middle of dinner she became insanely jealous. She walked out in a huff, packed her bags and left. I never heard from her again until I saw the story in the paper."

"Have you tried to contact her next of kin?"

"I tried but the internet yellow pages listed 2,160 Hellers in England with 298 of them in London."

~

It was now midnight. Mary sat in the darkness of her apartment staring at the stars. Her brain began incessantly pounding from recent events: Allison and David's surprise move-in, Mama Dapolito's unhappiness plea, Elizabeth's murder and Sarah's suicide.. She felt abandoned; she was losing all things and all people she held close and dear.

Mary walked over to her bar, grabbed a 12-year-old bottle of Glenlivet, and poured herself a tumbler full. Then she opened the blue bottle of tiny "magic" pills she pilfered from Allison on the copter ride and shook and shook the contents till the remaining six pills sat in the palm of her hand. She stared for a moment, then tossed the entire batch into her mouth and washed them down with the Glenlivet. One part of her wanted the same calming effect as before, another part of her wanted something else, something darker.

No matter. The damage was done. The combination of pills, booze, and her mental anguish left her frighteningly breathless. Mary's heart began to pound erratically as severe muscle spasms gripped the front of her chest and down her arms. She believed she was in the throes of a heart attack. She maintained her faculties just long enough to call 911, and then she fainted straight away. Minutes later, the paramedics crashed open her door, administered oxygen and whisked her away on a stretcher to the emergency room at Lenox Hill Hospital.

After declaring a Code C, the doctors administered CPR. To their surprise, her vital signs returned to normal almost immediately. Three hours later after a battery of tests, Mary lay peacefully in ICU (Intensive Care Unit). A handsome young blonde haired resident named Mathew Carson entered the cubical as she regained consciousness.

"How bad is it, Doctor?"

"Miss Peale, there is nothing wrong with you physically. You had an acute panic attack. Your mind tricked you into thinking you had a heart attack. (Pause) Have you been under a lot of stress lately?"

"In a manner of speaking."

"I thought so."

"Where do we go from here?"

"You go home. Take these and get a good night's sleep. Then I would strongly suggest you make an appointment to visit someone you can talk to--a psychiatrist."

"Psychiatrist. No, no, I'll be fine."

Carson glared. "No you won't!"

Mary became alarmed by his biting determination.

"Where do I begin? I don't know any shrinks."

"I don't know anything about your background, other than when we were trying to identify you, we found a Theatre Actors Guild card in your wallet. So I assume you're in the entertainment field." He handed Mary a business card.

As Mary left the hospital, she looked at the business card. It discreetly read: Dr. Harriet Myers, 155 Park Avenue, 212-333-6666.

ACT 3

47

~~~

THE ATTRACTIVE, FASHIONABLE 51-year old Harriet Myers was a psychiatrist revered by the medical community for her academic credentials and professional accomplishments. She was magna cum laude at the elite Vassar College in New York State's picturesque Hudson Valley, where she also served as two-time president of the Drama Society, recreating and producing classic Broadway musicals. Meyers received her Master's and PhD degrees at Yale University School of Medicine in New Haven, Connecticut. After a two-year internship at Cornell Medical Center in Manhattan, she opened a private practice on Park Avenue in Manhattan.

After a few chance meetings with noted celebrities at the proper cocktail parties, she decided to devote part of her practice to the performing arts. The niche thrived beyond her wildest expectations. She was considered the city's leading psychiatrist among the creative community and had twice been voted one of New York's 100 most influential people by *New York Magazine* readers.

Myers' personal life was another matter. She married the love of her life, Jeremy Cronin, when they were starving medical interns at Yale. He swept her off her feet literally and figuratively, one cold winter evening, knocking into her during an ice skating session. After apologizing profusely, and accidentally knocking her over a second time, they agreed dinner would be less hazardous, sharing Kobe beef burgers and a bottle of Chimney Rock cabernet in front of a cozy fireplace at a local restaurant/piano bar. Six months later they were married. Both were consumed professionally, leaving little personal time to cultivate their relationship. Their ability to resolve familial issues also suffered. He wanted children. She did not. A year later they were divorced.

Cronin went on to become a noted transplant surgeon, married a nurse and had three children.

About ten years after Cronin, Myers fell in love with a wealthy married woman named Marion Allman, a pillar of New York Society through marriage. Like Mary's Elizabeth, Marion graduated to the love of her life. Marion's husband, Franklin, discovered their relationship and threatened to divorce her, tarnish her reputation forever and leave her penniless. The ladies had a most painful dilemma. Marion didn't want Myers to go, and yet she wouldn't divorce her husband, his enormous wealth and her position of privilege. Allman began to physically abuse her. When the pain became too much, she'd retreat to Myers' place for a few days, then dutifully return home and absorb yet another beating. During Allman's restive period, he sent Myers threatening and vindictive notes. She thought about going to the police but hestitated, recognizing the entire affair would have been scandalous grist for the tabloid rags. Reputations would have been destroyed, and her practice would have shut down. In the end, Marion jumped out the window of their 44th floor apartment, leaving not so much as a note.

~

Unlike many psychiatrists who maintained limited office space or shared common spaces with other professionals, Harriet believed comfort and privacy were critical to patient wellness.

The spacious, well-lit, three-room suite contained her office with the usual chairs and couches, a living room style lounge stocked with every imaginable patient refreshment from seven flavors of Tecceno herbal coffees to Voss designer water, and a library containing an extensive collection of the latest "light duty" bestsellers for those patients who wished to temporarily escape their issues. Even the walls projected understated elegance—lightly-grained, contemporary Honduran mahogany panels adorned with original art from established artists Peter Max and Marc Chagall, as well as the best of up and comers, artists such as watercolorists Ross Van Duesen and Errol Etienne.

~

Harriet's voice mail indicated one incoming call.

"Hi, my name is Mary Jackson-Peale. The doctors at Lenox Hill Hospital suggested I call. The best time to reach me is 12 noon to 5 p.m. on my mobile phone. The number is 917-648-6711."

Harriet never accepted calls directly or scheduled appointments without a brief, essentially one-way consultation with patients over the phone to professionally establish some parameters around the patient's issues. She refused to abrogate that responsibility to an administrative aid. If she felt she could help, she scheduled the appointment. If she couldn't, she'd usually provide another professional referral, unless she sensed a non-cooperative or belligerent attitude on the other end of the phone. She didn't want pain-in-the-ass clients, and she didn't want a reputation for referring such to her peers.

"Mary, this is Dr. Myers. You called."

"I understand you specialize in the entertainment industry. I'm a theatrical agent who moved from England about four years ago. I started my own agency and have been very successful. But I feel terrible. Like I'm undeserving of the notoriety."

"Why…"

"I don't know, maybe because the rest of my life is so bollixed up. I so dislike myself," said Mary, her voice quivering.

"How did you wind up in the emergency room at Lenox Hill?"

"I drank myself into oblivion and thought I was having a heart attack."

"Why don't you come in to see me? Maybe we can help resolve some of your issues," said Harriet calmly and reassuringly.

~

A reluctant, visibly harried Mary visited Harriet's office.

"And how are you today," asked Harriet warmly.

"Typically, I organize my day around my little problem," Mary smiled rather pathetically. "Sort of like reading a book by starting in the middle."

"What do you mean?" probed Meyers.

"I evaluate scripts and discuss returns with my investors in the morning, when concentration and attention remain in full bloom. By afternoon, I've usually fried. Fortunately, my assistant, Allison, is an ace when it comes to picking up the slack. That way, I can go hide somewhere, away from it all. Then there's the evenings…"

"What about the evenings?"

"Evenings are a jumble of networking affairs and taking clients and prospects to dinner and drinks. Everybody expects this offbeat, wild and crazy Brit. It's like being on stage…." Mary paused to take another deep breath, as her eyes rolled.

"It all sounds quite exciting and frenetic."

"Let me put it this way. I'm Mary Jackson-Peale. No theatrical agent, and I mean nobody, has had as many hits as I've had during the last three years. Playwrights and directors are literally knocking down my door for access. We are the standard by which all other Manhattan theatrical agencies are now measured."

"That's quite an accomplishment."

"I quite agree," said a now agitated Mary, her hand beginning to quiver as she recalled the pressures of her daily routine.

"Perhaps we should start at the beginning."

Mary took a deep breath.

~

"David Marks told me, I'm having anxiety attacks." He is one of my dearest friends. He was certain you would write me a prescription. David said whenever he starts a project he has the same symptoms. Last week, he let me try a few of those capsules in that little blue bottle."

"Perhaps we should determine the appropriate medication, if any, after we properly diagnose your condition."

"No, you don't understand," said an increasingly twitchy Mary. "I've got to refill Allison's bottle before I give it back."

"I thought you said it was David's? Why is that so important?"

"I don't want her to know I used them all. She'll think there is something wrong."

"How many capsules were there?"

"Don't know, I didn't count them, two, three, maybe four, five, six. What's it matter? We just need to get me on an even keel."

"Mary, there may be more to your discomfort…"

"I knew it…I shouldn't have come," blurted Mary angrily. "This whole psychiatrist thing. It's just an indecipherable ruse to extricate fees."

"If that's the way you really feel, perhaps you should leave?"

Mary slowly raised herself from the chair and headed for the door. Then, she abruptly stopped and turned. "Do you think I'm going crazy?"

"Mary, non-normative behavior typically includes some sort of biochemical imbalance. It has been established with reasonable certainty that many emotional disturbances are chemically induced amid the neurotransmitters of the brain, probably as the result of systemic stress. This for some unknown reason causes a depletion of the chemicals norepinephrine and serotonin and an increase of the hormone cortisol. With all this upheaval in the brain tissues, the alternate drenching and deprivation, the mind begins to feel aggrieved, stricken, and the thought process becomes muddied."

"I'm not crazy, then."

"Of course you're not," reassured Myers. She was almost certain Mary urgently required immediate pharmacological intervention combined and the kind of traditional psychiatric counseling that required time, patience and, most of all, the patient's agreement to ascertain the root problem or problems.

~

The cab back to the apartment was stuck in rush-hour traffic. Whatever cross street the cabbie tried—Lexington, Park or Madison—the result was always the same. Honking horns and snail-like movement. Enough was enough! Mary took a ten out of her pocketbook, stuck it in the drawer of the plexiglas partition and jumped out of the car, gasping for air.

Walking down the street, she dialed her cell phone and apologized to Dr. Myers for her belligerent, noncooperative behavior.

48

~~~

"WHERE DO WE START? I don't want to put my foot in my mouth again," said Mary, repentant but visibly jumpy.

"Mary, this isn't a test. You can start wherever you want…Although some patients find it's easiest to begin at the beginning.

"I guess in some ways this all starts with my father. I loathe the bastard!"

"And why is that?"

"After 15 years of marriage, he just got up and left one day, leaving Mum and me to fend for ourselves. Mum, almost as a matter of survival, began to take in men of the theatre, if you know what I mean."

Myers nodded stoically.

"What else could she do? We needed the money. You know men. They're always on the make for a good lay."

"I see," said Myers, privately recalling her own failed marriage.

"She wasn't a whore."

"And what did you do?"

"I didn't become a whore, if that's what you're asking."

"I was just asking what you did."

"You mean after breaking my cherry with Bobbie O'Toole, one of the kids that hung around Brighton. I figured he was older, more experienced. And I figured it was time. Hell, I was 15, and a lot of my friends had already done it."

"Can you recall how you found that first time?"

"Can I recall! The experience was dreadful. He was like a clumsy animal. Losing my virginity to him is not one of life's cherished memories."

"Then…"

"I followed Mum's lead. She fell in love with Annabelle Lee when they were both working at the theatre. In fact, they're still together. Twenty-two years. Christ, traditional marriages don't last that long. Their affair got me to thinking. Finally, at University, I got the nerve to invite Phoebe Trincas out for a drink. She was drop-dead gorgeous, and I was so nervous. Phoebe was everything Bobbie was not. Gentle, sensitive, loving, tender. And when it came to making love, she was light years more pleasing than macho man and all his hang-ups."

Myers smiled knowingly. She had been in a similar movie.

~

"Perhaps we should get back to the relationship between you, your mother and Annabelle Lee?"

"I'd rather talk about Elizabeth."

"Elizabeth?"

"She was the love of my life. We met while she was vacationing in my hometown of Brighton. It's a sea-side community in the South of England, not far from Dover. We planned to live in London after graduation. When I visited the family castle on school holiday, her holier-than-thou father, Sir James, discovered we were having an affair. He told me he detested lesbians. He summarily tossed me out of his house. It appears, sometime after that, he bludgeoned his beautiful daughter to death with a fireplace andiron…I ask you, what kind of sick father would do such a thing?"

"How perfectly dreadful!"

"There's actually more. Apparently James, concerned that his butler accomplice might crack under a police interrogation, murdered him also. Then he dumped both bodies in Lake Ullswater, down the road from his castle. So much for Wordsworth's tranquil, serene Lake Country!"

Mary's fists were clenched in fits of rage as her mood yo-yoed from angry to psychotic.

"The miserable hypocrite, may his ashes rot in hell."

"Mary, as difficult as it may be, try to stay calm. Justice will prevail."

"Apparently when he was found out, he shot himself. Then his wife honors his last request to have his ashes tossed off the cliffs at Dover. I would have taken the bastard's ashes, mixed them with my father's, urinated on them and flushed them down the toilet."

Time was up. "Mary, we've made substantial progress today. I know it was painful. My heart goes out to you."

Mary began to sob uncontrollably. "Can you help me?"

"Mary," said Myers scribbling on a prescription pad. "You may be helped on your journey by a newer anti-depressant called Effexor. But I must advise you, it's quite powerful. So please follow the dosage instructions religiously. Call me immediately if there are any tolerance issues."

Mary half-smiled. The session left her emotionally drained yet cathartically relieved. For the first time in weeks, she went home and slept through the night.

~

Mary quickly gave Myers greater cause for concern.

"I'm glad you agreed to meet twice a week," said Myers three days later. "You were talking about the tragedy surrounding Elizabeth's"…Again Mary was off to the races, blurting whatever popped into her mind.

"I must admit—post-Elizabeth—I've had some perfectly enjoyable sexual experiences with David."

"So you're relationship with Elizabeth wasn't monogamous?"

"Certainly, when we were together. But after months of searching in London, I was lonely and I had needs. Is that so terrible?" asked Mary seeking affirmation.

"I thought, after Annabelle Lee and Phoebe you had concluded...People just need to be happy with who they are...."

"Are you happy with who you are?"

"Why wouldn't I be? I have a fabulous career. I'm a Broadway brand. I've got money. I'm an important person."

"I'm not talking about that kind of happiness."

"I don't know. I just don't know. I'm exhausted. I can't do this anymore today."

Dr. Myers tried to comfort her. "Some women find it difficult to come to grips with their own behavior because they believe it's out of step with societal norms. All I can tell you is that the latest scientific evidence suggests homosexuality and bisexuality are not a mental illness. It's perfectly natural for people to be attracted to members of their own sex as well as others of the opposite sex. What is normal to you should be your norm."

"You don't know the half of it," glared Mary through her now welted, puffy eyes.

~~~

MARY'S DAY WAS FAR FROM OVER. The cell
phone ran as she headed south down Park Avenue. She
looked at the readout. "Mum, what a nice surprise. I could
use one about now."

"The last three months have not exactly been the best on
this side of the world either. I really didn't want to bother you
but I needed to talk to someone." Chloe started to cry.

"It's okay, Mum. I'm learning it's better to release one's
emotions rather than privately brood. The British stiff upper
lip is not necessarily the best way to maintain one's emotional
well being. Besides, I'm your daughter. Mum and daughters
share."

"Scotland Yard reopened the James Belfrage case with a
vengeance."

Mary froze in her tracks. "Why?"

"They found some new strands of another woman's hair
in the closet.

Mary's memory scanned Belfrage's apartment the evening she murdered him. Had she left some evidence behind? "I thought they had concluded Sarah Fender was the culprit. I mean didn't they find her red hair in his flat?"

"That's what I thought. I just don't understand all this talk about DNA," said Chloe. "The second set of strands were also red but longer."

"That doesn't surprise me; in the short time I stayed with him, women went through that flat like a revolving door. He had an obsession with red-haired birds."

"The problem is that they identified the second set of hairs as those of Annabelle Lee."

Mary's heart began to race. She tried to remain calm. Lucid. "But she spent eight years as Mrs. Belfrage, isn't it quite possible that..."

"I know where you are going. But that argument is fruitless. The building concierge recalled the figure in the raincoat that dashed out the lobby had a head of red curly hair tucked under his or her hat. They put poor Annabelle Lee in a lineup and the sod identified her hair, since he couldn't see her face."

"That's circumstantial nonsense."

"There's more. The Yard obtained a sworn statement from two investors who claimed Annabelle Lee and Belfrage had quite a row about the marriage settlement in front of them at a restaurant. Apparently, the bastard refused to offer even a meager monthly stipend.

"According to the judge, the prosecution had an open and shut case. The jury convicted Annabelle Lee of 2nd degree manslaughter, and sentenced her to 20 years in prison."

"Oh my God!"

Mary momentarily hesitated. She wanted to confess.

But Chloe kept talking. "But we are not giving up. If there's a God, justice will prevail in our appeal."

Mary wondered if she had been given a reprieve. We are trying to get on the court dockets as soon as possible."

"The appeal process could be costly. I have resources. I can help."

"Thanks, love, but I think we'll be fine in that department. The Bright-Hove Legal Aid Group has raised £10,000 from about 500 families to hire a private detective in London to search for missing clues. And our attorney has agreed to continue on the case until the real killer is brought to justice."

Chills ran up and down Mary's spine as she looked at herself in the mirror. "What happens if you lose the appeal?"

Chloe would not accept that possibility. "I remain steadfast, optimistic and resolute. I'd appreciate you do the same. Plus a few prayers to the Lord wouldn't hurt our cause."

Mary was suffocating in guilt. Her distorted, self-indulgent behavior had turned her mother's world upside down. Should she confess to the authorities? To her mother? She chose silence. And with it, by default, entered a deeper level of darkness.

"Mary, always remember, Mum loves you and misses you."

~

That evening, 27 floors above Manhattan, Sarah, Belfrage, Elizabeth, Sir James, Chloe, Annabelle Lee, Riley and Bobbie O'Toole paid a house visit. She mustered all the inner strength she had left to avoid going stark-raving mad on the spot. Mary cried until she collapsed from exhaustion and then swallowed an unconscionable dose of Effexor. The raven vanished.

Her sense of touch abandoned and her mind a blurred mass, she stumbled down in the elevator past the concierge and wandered onto First Avenue in the midst of blinding lights and beeping horns from oncoming cars. Her head spun and her eyes rolled as she fainted in the middle of the street, splitting her lip on impact and coming to rest in a crimson pool.

Traffic backed up almost immediately from 37th Street to 59th Street. "Somebody call 911," screamed a man who had jumped from his car to help the desperate, disoriented Mary crawling her way to the sidewalk.

A few minutes later, the paramedics whisked her toward the closest emergency room, New York Hospital. A semi-conscious Mary overheard the paramedics.

"Crazy broad. Who knows what her problem is. This is a city of kooks," said one.

"She must be coming around. She's trying to pull off the oxygen mask."

"I think she wants to say something."

"So take the damn mask off. Her vital signs are stable, and there doesn't seem to be any internal bleeding. Maybe she wants to place a pizza order." The paramedic slowly removed Mary's mask and placed his ear close to her mouth as she whispered, "Lenox Hill…Dr. Myers…Please…Lenox Hill…Dr. Myers…Please."

"Can you make out anything?"

"Yeah, she wants to go to Lenox Hill. She must be a patient there or have a doctor there. Dr. Myers."

"Johnny," said the senior paramedic to the driver over the intercom, "The lady wants Lenox Hill."

Minutes later, Mary was resting peacefully in the emergency room with a liquid valium drip in one arm and a series of electronic monitoring nodes attached to her body dispensing vital statistics on the green LED readout above her head.

"Who is she?" asked the nurse.

"Got me. We found her in the street, booze all over her breath and a stomach full of pills."

"This lady's wearing a $2,000 pair of Jimmy Choo ostrich shoes. She's no ordinary abuser," concluded the nurse.

About three hours later, Mary regained consciousness. She saw the nurse hovering about. "I'm so sorry. I didn't mean to cause such a commotion."

"Do you remember what happened?"

"Yes," said Mary her British accent showing, "I was such a silly sod; I pegged out then devoured those frightful pills and washed them down with the Livet. I've been so frustrated with my life lately that I've taken to increasing the dosage of my anti-depression medication and washing it down with Scotch rather than water."

"What do you do, Madame?"

"I'm a theatrical agent."

"Are you under a doctor's care?"

"Yes. Dr. Harriet Myers."

"Doctor Myers has been an attending physician at Lenox Hill for a number of years. She's one of the City's finest psychiatrists."

"Am I all right?"

"As you Brits say, you look a sight, but your vital signs appear to be perfectly normal."

"Can I go?"

"Since you had no identification, I have to leave that up to the doctor on duty."

Moments later, in walked a smiling, Dr. Mathew Carson. "Miss Peale, we can't keep meeting like this. You know the diagnosis. Tests negative. No physical impairments other than a few stitches to stop the bleeding in your upper lip. I also took the liberty of calling Dr. Myers. She's on her way over to sign the release forms."

Mary was embarrassed. "You must think I'm looney?"

"To be perfectly frank with you, Miss Peale, you have made an excellent start on your way to becoming a looney, as you term it. Normal people don't go around swallowing anti-depressant pills like candy, washing them down with Scotch and then go for a midnight stroll up the middle of First Avenue. What the hell is an attractive woman like you trying to do to herself?"

"There are millions of people in this town who would kill to have your record of success, your lifestyle, and quite candidly, your money."

~

"Mary," said Harriet sternly in the cab on the way back to her apartment, "Suppose I hadn't been in town? Where would you be right now? We need to get you intensified treatment before it's too late. You're confused, you're angry, you're depressed."

"They were all there!" screamed Mary. "They were all there. My life...my twisted, dirty, unholy life."

She was a heartbeat from a complete nervous breakdown. Myers held her tightly.

"Mary, it's time. Time to check into an institution where you can get treated full time. It may be the only way to exorcise your demons. A few sessions a week is not enough. I've been talking to my colleagues at Silver Hill in Connecticut. It's a lovely setting with a caring staff. Silver Hill is a world class facility. Their forte is the discreet resolution of the unique emotional problems of the entertainment industry," responded Myers ever so calmly.

"I'm not going to be committed to some mental institution loaded with loonies. I'm a successful business person. People depend on me. Let's try some other medications....something. Do you know what would happen to my career if word got out that I had been admitted to a ..."

"Mary," said Myers firmly, "we are entering Silver Hill, voluntarily or involuntarily. Do you understand?"

Mary's tearful, mascara soiled face stared blankly. "I thought you were supposed to be my friend. How can you give up on me?"

"I'm not giving up. I'm trying to make you well again."

"I need to make a call."

"To whom?"

"My Mum. I need my Mum. She understands."

"Tell you what. Sleep at my place. Make the call from there. In the morning, we'll drive to Connecticut."

50

~~~

"YOU'RE GOING TO STAY involved during my stay, aren't you?"

"Absolutely. I'll discuss those details with Dr. Stanislaw as soon as I return from my trip."

"Trip" responded a fragile, trembling Mary.

"Relax," said Harriet, clutching her hand. "It's merely a brief vacation planned a year ago."

"I'm scared."

"Mary, what you're feeling is quite natural—it's the fear of the unknown. Let me demystify the process.

"After admission and a complete physical exam, you'll have a few private consultations with the doctor assigned to work with you. He'll talk to you about medications, administer a few additional coordination tests, and then prescribe a pharmaceutical and nutritional regimen specifically for you. You'll also receive an orientation of the activities that will be available to you, such as art appreciation, creative problem

297

solving, as well as a variety of other amenities such as movies, books, DVD's etc. There's even a spa."

Dr. Myers made a right turn up a lovely, tree-lined driveway to a red-and-gray brick structure that looked like a French chateau.

"This is not at all what I expected," said Mary, as a porter in a white suit with white gloves began to remove her luggage from the trunk. The entrance hall was grandiose, with a two-story circular staircase and floral arrangements—mostly brilliant white, Casablanca lilies and long-stem, yellow roses. A handsome, middle-aged gentleman who looked like George Clooney extended his hand, "Welcome, you must be Miss Peale. I'm Dr. Stanislaw. Why don't we go into my office and fill out the paperwork? Then you'll meet Dr. Henry, who has been assigned to your case. He'll give you a tour of the facilities, show you your room, and begin to work out your daily schedule."

~

Mary said a tearful goodbye to Myers as young Dr. Henry arrived, white coat, open shirt collar, silky brown wavy hair, thick eyebrows and a soft gentle smile.

"You blokes look like something out of GQ rather than ER," teased Mary.

Mary's smile disappeared quickly as she was shown to her room. In contrast to the lobby, the patient halls were austere with desolate, green-enamel hallways, winding corridors with locked and wired doors. Mary's 10' by 12' room was spartan at best. Plain metal bed, metal table and chair, built-in dresser with four large drawers, plain white enamel walls, a narrow window to the outside world that was out of reach, and a steel front door with a wired 12 inch by 12 inch plexiglas window. The ceiling also contained a tiny camera monitor and a highly sensitive microphone. The only lighting was a ceiling light also encased in a steel cage. Mercifully, the room did contain a tamper-proof dimmer switch.

"I know it seems a bit extreme, but, trust me, in a few days, you'll be so involved with your treatments that this room and a good book will feel like your personal sanctuary," assured Dr. Henry.

Mary sat on the edge of the bed. A voice came over the speaker in her room. "Mary, are you ready to go?"

"I'm assuming with all the damn monitoring devices around here, you know the answer to that question."

A large attendant in a white coat opened the door. "Good afternoon, Madame, I'm Robert." They walked side by side past a few doors with forlorn-looking people with their faces pressed against the wired windows and a few people walking the halls in various emotional states, some with attendants, some unescorted.

"We certainly have a mix of residents, don't we?"

"You married?"

"Yes."

"Children?"

"Two."

"Bloody me, you've got an heir and a spare."

"Heir and a spare, huh? Gotta tell my wife that one. That a Brit colloquialism?"

Mary smiled. It felt good.

"Very chuffed to meet you. Means pleased to meet you."

"AHHH…. Mary, very chuffed to meet you, too."

~

"Mary," said Dr. Henry "I've reviewed all the tests and blood work and I've had extensive conversations with Dr. Myers and read her findings. But I'd like you to tell me what's been going on in your life that's led you to seek help at Silver Hill."

"Are we on the psychiatrist's time clock?"

"There are no clocks here. You can take as long as you want and say as little or as much as you feel comfortable about discussing right now," said the empathetic doctor.

Mary leaned back in her chair and raised her eyebrows. "There's so, so much baggage. Where do I even begin?"

For two hours Mary told him her entire life story—"The Insightful, Terribly Coherent *Reader's Digest* Version of The Life and Times of Mary Jackson-Peale."

"What would you like to discover during your stay?"

Mary responded without hesitation. "In my mind—fragile as it is—I need answers to three most fundamental questions: Who is Mary Jackson-Peale? Is she a good or bad person? Where does she travel after leaving the depths of this darkness?"

Mary's lucidity pleased Henry. He felt her mind could be rescued, or at least her disease quarantined, more quickly than originally envisioned. "Good. As we progress, we'll deal with the issues you've raised in detail. But first I think we need to agree on pharmaceutical protocol. The most suitable drugs to help us during our journey. From what we've discussed and what your recent history indicates, you have three related emotional issues: Your insomnia is creating serious sleep deprivation; you suffer from periodic, acute panic disorder, and your bouts of severe depression suggest a significant chemical imbalance. My guess is, nutritionally, your diet is also quite erratic."

"That painful summary sounds like Mary Jackson-Peale circa today."

"I want you to understand something. Over 90 percent of people affected by mental illness improve or recover if they get treated properly."

"What about the other 10 percent?" said Mary, thinking dark side.

"Mary, Silver Hill is one of the finest facilities of its kind in the world," said Dr. Henry passionately. "You are fortunate enough to be able to afford our services. You will get better."

Dr. Henry explained Mary's new drug regimen—Efforex, lithium and Alrazolam to control her depression, mood swings and anxiety. "These drugs will take time to work into your system for maximum effect. And, we may have to adjust dosages based upon the side effects. Not every drug works the same for everyone. Our goal is to use the drugs to calm you down while we begin a psychotherapy regimen that will include support groups. You'll also learn new ways of thinking, modifying behavior and learning relaxation techniques. I'm also a great believer in behavioral therapies to treat insomnia. I'm thinking the therapies we'll want to teach you are stimulus control, paradoxical intention and sleep restriction. We'll also create a nutritional regimen. Your meals will be heavy in turkey, chicken, milk and cheese, and beans since they all contain tryptophan, a chemical that converts to serotonin in the brain which promotes relaxation and sleepiness."

"Do I get tucked in with cookies and warm milk?"

"Yes."

"I was being facetious."

"I wasn't...the carbohydrates will boost your production of serotonin."

51

~~~

MARY FOUND THE FIRST TWO WEEKS of her
medical confinement most difficult. Her body was adjusting
to the new drug regimen and its disconcerting side effects,
while her mind had to accept that institutionalization limited
individual freedoms.

"Mary, I think our first job over the next few days is to
work at overcoming your insomnia, so I've organized acupuncture and an acupressure session as well as a deep tissue
massage and a foot massage. The acupuncture needles will
have a calming effect on your nervous system; the acupressure session will teach you techniques you can perform on
your own. The massages are designed to help you relax and
are great insomnia-busters in their own right."

"It sounds wonderful."

"Think of Silver Hill as a spa for your mind."

Four hours of treatments and a nice dish of penne ala
vodka left Mary in a delicious mood. She slept like a baby—
for the first time in months—despite the austere surround-

ings. The hospital offered Mary a flight from the anxiety and discord of home into an orderly and benign existence where one's only obligation was to get well.

"I thought it would be useful for you to attend a support group and meet some of the other patients. How does that sound?"

The way the doctor phrased the directive made Mary feel as though she was making the decisions. That she was in charge of her destiny, when, in fact, her regimen was carefully planned and programmed. That was one of the unique strengths of the Silver Hill way.

Robert escorted Mary to a rather pleasant lounge, far less medicinal than her room. There were four other patients sitting around a table with a group facilitator, an attractive woman in her mid-forties, Rosalina, who had two PhD's and was published in virtually every psychology journal in the US and abroad. Her area of specialty: suicidal tendencies of the psychotic mind. Three of the male patients were known film and stage personalities, the fourth, a woman sitting quietly in the corner, was unfamiliar.

"Ladies and Gentlemen," said the facilitator gently, "I'd like to explain the session process. You are free to speak whenever you wish, say whatever you feel. The rest of us should place no value judgments on each other, our statements or our lives. We are here to listen and support each other on our respective journeys. There is no right or wrong. Everything just is."

"Doctor," said one of the men, "as you were talking, I couldn't help but think of Robert Frost…In three words, I can summarize everything I've learned about life—It goes on."

"Very good. The way I like to start each session is to ask each of you to close your eyes. Begin taking deep breaths until the only thing you hear are those breaths. Then think about a word or a phrase that best describes you in this moment. When you open your eyes, we'll then share our word, and why we selected them. Providing your name or any personal details is optional."

The group closed their eyes. About 60 seconds later, the doctor said, "Okay, everybody open your eyes. And, if you don't mind, I'd like to begin."

"My word today is grateful but frustrated. I'm grateful because I have the opportunity to share this time with you but frustrated because I got stuck in traffic on the way here and didn't get a chance to read your files."

Mary's wit had returned after a good night's sleep. "My name is Mary. Mary is wondering if Rosalina always prepares at the last minute."

Rosalina found the comment humorous but disruptive. "So Mary, what then is your word."

Mary smiled devilishly. "Ax murderer." You could hear a pin drop. "I'm an ax murderer turned theatrical agent. It was good training for the business."

The sheepish woman in the corner broke her silence, "I know you. You are that Peale woman. I tried to get my play read by your organization, and I couldn't get to first base. That Allison bitch turned me away."

"Now Gloria, remember positive thoughts," said Rosalina, concerned a tempest was about to break out.

Mary surprised everybody with her calm, cool and collectedness. "Gloria, let me ask you something."

"What?" said Gloria rising from her chair.

The facilitator grabbed Mary's arm, hoping that Gloria's emotional peak might pass. A confident Mary ignored the request. "Gloria, did Allison give you our one-page synopsis form to complete?"

"Why, no."

"I'm so sorry. As you can appreciate, we receive so many scripts, I instituted a process so we can identify the potential properties we want to represent. I read every synopsis myself and then make a determination if we wish to read the entire script. That's when Allison calls the playwright."

"I didn't realize that."

"Be a deaaar...Let's all get ourselves well, then you call me straight away. Since we're friends, we'll just forgo the synopsis process, and I'll read your script. How does that sound?"

Gloria was pleased as were the other members of the support group and Rosalina. The remainder of the session went without incident, although after listening to everybody's tale of woe for almost two hours, Mary wondered what all this had to do with her.

Roy, a big, burly Swede who owned a successful construction company had beat his wife into submission because his ungrateful forty-year-old son, a fabulous successful criminal lawyer, hadn't talked to him in ten years. Arthur, a teacher, had tried to commit suicide after the doctors declared he needed two more stents, his 15 and 16th. The other two men had equally disturbing events that led to equally irrational decisions.

~

That first session convinced Mary she was in a better place than most of the other patients. She felt she was generally logical, somewhat lucid and had some control of her faculties. Besides...why would a conflicted bisexual who had murdered her boss and had left an innocent person—her mother's lover no less—to rot behind bars 3,000 miles away, share her innermost secrets with a bunch of obviously unstable loonies?

After dinner, Mary decided to read a little T.S. Elliot in her room. But her eyelids became heavy. The day had had its challenges. She tucked herself into bed with the expectation that her second night would even be more satisfying than the first.

Unfortunately, the unintended side effects of her new medications began to rage within her system 30 minutes after lights out. The room whirled, she gasped for air. It was as though someone had shut off the flow of oxygen to the room. The experience was unlike any she had experienced before. Her physical body felt an unfathomable distance away while her mind touched the nerves of her pain and agony. She looked up at the monitor and screamed for help. There was no response. The staff knew this was a distasteful part of the process. A bone-crushing pain enveloped her chest. She stumbled to the tiny wired window, pounding and screaming until she passed out. The duty doctor, quite familiar with the ritual he had just observed on the room's monitor, directed the orderlies to gently pick her up, place her in bed and cover her with a warm blanket. The next morning no one even alluded to the incident. To Mary's surprise, she vaguely remembered a mild disturbance, nothing more.

"I gather you stimulated some patient dialogue during Rosalina's little session yesterday," said Dr. Henry.

Mary was dismayed. She felt was being chastised. "I don't mind taking responsibility for my actions, but I don't even know Miss Adams."

Stanislaw quickly realized the "inner-Mary" and "the outer-Mary" were two completely different personalities. "Mary, relax. That was supposed to be a joke. Rosalina simply told me you got Gloria to smile."

"Is that a big deal?"

"Gloria has been our most difficult case for some time. She's actually tried to commit suicide twice. Fact is, you helped us achieve what we call a positive cognitive breakthrough. She's been like a different person the last 24 hours. Gloria has been with us almost six months. We've tried every FDA approved medication protocol that exists. Even the ECT treatments failed."

"What's ECT?"

"Electro-convulsive therapy."

"Is that a fancy term for shock treatments?"

"Yes, it's only administered on select candidates because it's clearly a drastic procedure."

"Jesus Christ Almighty!" An alarmed Mary warned the doctor in no uncertain terms, "Don't ever try that on me. Do you understand?" Mary was now motivated to get the hell out of there as soon as she possibly could.

In a matter of weeks, Mary's fantasies of self-destruction and aimless personal flagellation visibly dissipated. In staff meetings, she was discussed as a potential success model. A patient who had found a way to create a tranquil sanctuary from her inner storms.

~

It was also just a matter of weeks until other members of her support group began looking to Mary as a model of revision. They wanted to know her secret.

"I sense the group would like you to share," said Dr. Henry.

Mary felt twelve eyes staring. "As you all know, I've shared my personal pain, my successes and my excesses. Frankly, my ofttimes circuitous journey toward self-identify has been a somewhat unpleasant experience...Why am I here? What's my purpose? I'm not sure I'm that much closer to THE answers, but I no longer fear my exploration of the unknown...*I now understand you must love yourself before you can truly love another. Accepting yourself, and fully being what you are, will create the inner peace we all seek.*"

~

Three weeks later, the general conclusion was that Mary's storm had passed. She slept soundly every night and ate balanced meals.

Mary had made peace with her sexuality. She was a healthy, normal bisexual, not some unholy, aberrant dysfunctional. It was time to stop mourning the loss of Elizabeth. She would always retain a place in Mary's heart as a touching experience on life's journey. And there was closure with respect to Sir James. She was not the catalyst for the destruction of his only daughter and loyal, lifelong aide, William. He was the evil one, not she.

Her guilt as the sole cause of Sarah's jealous rage was also seen in perspective. She came to distinguish the difference between being a player in and an author of a morality play. While she should never have let David and Sarah physically toy with her that evening over dinner, it was hardly cause for a rational person to take one's life. That was in Sarah's court. The fact was that Sarah heroically shielded Mary from Scotland Yard in Belfrage's murder; however Mary was wrong to accept it.

The two remaining issues, her murder of Belfrage and the wrongful incarceration of Annabelle Lee were wrongs that needed to be righted. That emotional finality, while painful, provided a measure of solace. She could only ask god's forgiveness for allowing her rage and anger to take Belfrage's life; Annabelle Lee needed to be freed.

~

It was time for the final phase of detox.

"Robert, the fifth floor please," instructed Dr. Henry. As the elevator rose, Robert smiled. "I understand you've done well, real well. This is where I leave you. Goodbye and good luck."

Mary's new world was reminiscent of the lobby at the Ritz Carlton Hotel. Marble counters, glass and brass walls, fresh flowers galore, comfortable seating arrangements and decaf coffee and cappuccino machines brimming with flavor. She walked over to the reception counter. "Good morning, Miss Peale, here's the key to your suite. Hopefully you'll find everything satisfactory. If not, just ring. Oh, one other thing, just press Channel 4 on your television monitor for your daily activity and dining program."

Mary smiled. "This is Silver Hill?"

"This is Silver Hill, phase two."

"I gather I passed phase one?"

"With flying colors, I'm told...By the way, once you've had a chance to freshen up, you have a guest coming within the hour."

52

~~~

MARY COULDN'T BELIEVE HER EYES. Gone were the enamel paints, the wired doors, and the claustrophobia she had come to accept. Her room was a generously proportioned, traditionally furnished one-bedroom suite like one would find at the Carlyle in New York for $1,500 a night. The bathroom contained a selection of her favorite cosmetics, and the closet contained a complete wardrobe from her apartment. She showered, dressed and made herself up. She still had no clue about "the guest." But, since she hadn't talked to anybody in the outside world for almost six weeks, it mattered little, so long as it wasn't the Internal Revenue Service paying a friendly house call.

The phone rang. "Miss Peale, your guest has arrived. She will be waiting in the Garden Café. She said you'll recognize her. I guess it's kind of a surprise."

She walked into the Café and started to look around. There, sitting next to a large floral arrangement of Casablanca lilies, was Harriet Myers.

"Mary, you look fabulous. From what I gather, the place seems to have done wonders for you."

"I haven't felt this good in a long, long time."

Mary was full of questions. "Do you have any idea how my business is doing?"

"Allison figured you'd want to know that," said Harriet, handing Mary a thin, brown envelope. "She did a little summary report. She says things are going exceedingly well. I believe there is a check in there for some $200,000 which represents your share of the profits for the last six weeks."

Mary was surprised and pleased. "So, tell me all about your vacation."

"What vacation?"

"The one you planned last year."

"Forgive my fib. That was the best excuse I could think of to get you here. I don't have your creative mind."

"What a terrible thing to do."

"You're out of the darkness, that's all that matters. You have about two more weeks in the program. Mostly to review decompression techniques and begin the process of rebalancing your prescription protocol. And then I'd suggest you take a nice vacation for a month or so before you go back to the theatrical grind. Allison seems to have a good grip on everything, and you're not hurting financially."

"Do you mean a real vacation or a Harriet vacation?"

Harriet smiled. "I mean a real vacation. Go somewhere you've always wanted to go but have never been. Have some fun. You can always call me if you need to, and when you return, we can set up some kind of counseling schedule. But, I believe, the worst appears to be over."

~

Mary decided to follow Myers's advice.

First stop after her release from Silver Hill was a welcome-back party at the agency. To everyone's amazement, she promptly announced she was going to Italy for a month or so, Venice, Florence, Rome and Sorrento.

Allison pledged the staff would keep the flame burning brightly in her absence. "Just no computers, no blackberrys, no emails, no text messages, nothing."

"Maybe I should just retire," laughed Mary.

Allison took Mary aside privately. "There is one piece of unfinished business that seems to need your touch. An unknown playwright from England brazenly marched in here last week with a property he insisted you read personally. My first instinct was to toss the property. But he seemed so certain about…"

"What's the name of the play?"

"It's called *Belfrage*. Something about a murder set in England."

~

The following morning, a handsome man in his late twenties with a head of black curly hair walked into Mary's office.

He shook her hand, but didn't seem to recognize her. He was all business. "I know you're bloody busy, and Allie there told me you're on your way out of town today. I'll be short and to the point.

"Miss Peale, *Belfrage* is the story of a powerful British theatrical agent, an unpleasant, arrogant sod who's terribly successful. He hires a young administrative aide named Sarah. They have an affair. He dumps her for a young messenger boy. She poisons him in a mad frenzy by tricking him into having sex again. To escape the Yard, she bolts to the States. In the meantime Belfrage's ex-wife is accused of the murder, based on some old DNA evidence. She is convicted of second-degree murder and spends the rest of her life in jail."

"Is this based on a real event?"

"Yes and no. There was a lady up near where I live who actually got herself into a similar fix. I just built my story around that concept."

"The woman who spends her life in jail, does she have friends or family who try to appeal the decision?"

"As a matter of fact, there is. I just didn't know how to weave it into the story."

"And, what about what's her name, Sarah…What becomes of her?"

"Well, I haven't totally worked that out. Right now, I'm thinking she commits suicide, but my research suggests there was somebody else. It's all a bit sketchy, but I think there was another woman involved."

The play was clearly too close for comfort.

"Plays are living organisms," counseled Mary. "You can just leave pieces dangling. It feels like you're working too hard at being true to the facts. Don't let that get in the way of making a great play."

"I understand."

"I'll scan what you have under one condition. You don't pitch the property to anyone else. This town is filled with plagiarists

"Agreed."

Mary reached out to shake his hand. She wondered if she should say anything. "I couldn't help but notice your accent. Where in England are you from?"

"Brighton."

A shaken Mary remained calm. "You've got the makings of a good play, but it needs a lot of work. I'm going to Italy for a month."

"There'll be a polished work on your desk when you return," said the young man enthusiastically. "I'd do anything to get *Belfrage* on the New York stage."

"Just remember, creative excellence has its own time table," advised Mary.

53

~~~

FIRST STOP WAS VENICE

A chartered plane to a week of personal pampering at the 16th Century Villa d'Este on Lake Como, stopovers in Milan and Parma, dinner in Bologna at the Pasotti Family's landmark Serghei Restaurant on Via Piella. Final destination: the 15th Century boutique Hotel Casci on Via Cavour in Florence, the former home of world famous composer Gioacchino Rossini, two blocks from the Uffizi and David Galleries and the Ponte Vecchio.

Due to delays at JFK, Mary arrived in Venice closer to sunset than the scheduled noon hour. That first evening, thanks to a suggestion from the concierge, she walked a short distance from the hotel along the Grand Canal to Riva de Vin, an open-air wine bar and café next to the Rialto Bridge, favored by the locals. There she watched the gondolas and vaparetti crisscross the Canal's shimmering red-yellow waters with many of Venice's historical sites serving as a picturesque backdrop.

She came prepared to capture the moment with her time-delay digital camera and lightweight portable tripod. After running back and forth between the camera's timer and her selected locations, she was satisfied with her first collection of photographs. Mary then turned to the water's edge to absorb the romantic scene one last time, leaving her camera resting on the tripod less than 20 yards away. Seemingly, out of nowhere, a teenage boy popped up—perhaps fourteen or fifteen—snatched her gear and started to run across the square.

"Help, I've been robbed!" she screamed. "Somebody help. I've been robbed!"

"Not yet, Senorina," said a man with a leather backpack.

"*Lo assassinare tu bastardo,*" screamed the man, who ran like the wind, quickly closing the gap between himself and the boy.

Realizing he was about to be apprehended, the boy dropped the camera and tripod. Perspiration dripping down his olive brow, the man smiled and proudly handed Mary her camera equipment. "How you say, American tourist unfair target. Please be more careful. Sad to say."

"Thank you so much," said Mary to the man who looked like something out of an Italian fashion magazine. "But I'm not American, I'm British."

"Hey, same thing. You both very swallowable."

"Do you mean gullible?"

He shrugged his shoulders and smiled again. "Hey, same thing, gullible, swallowable, no?"

He was charming. Mary was smitten.

"May I buy you a cappuccino as a thank you?"

They sat and chatted for almost two hours, somehow overcoming their mini-language barriers. Mary learned his name was Gianni Spagnoli. He was born up North in Turin and worked as an assistant winemaker at his father's vineyard near the little hilltop town of Barbaresco in the Piedmont Region. Summer was his slow season as he waited for the young grapes to mature. "I like to see Italy each summer. Big country. Regions very different," he said with pride and passion.

"Gianni, my name is Mary. Mary Jackson-Peale. How do you say Mary in Italian," flirted Mary.

Gianni looked perplexed. "Mary is Marie."

"Last call," said the waiter. Mary looked at her watch. It was almost midnight. "If you don't mind, I've been traveling since quite early this morning. Would you mind walking me back to my hotel?"

"Si," said Gianni. "But let me carry your camera...Where you stay?"

"The Gritti Palace."

"Nothing but first-class for first-class."

At the front door of the hotel she asked, "Would you like to come in for a few minutes?"

"No," said Gianni. "Not dressed for Gritti" as he pointed to his tattered and worn jeans and sandals. He kissed her hand and started to walk away. She did not want him to disappear into the night...forever. "Gianni, could you have breakfast tomorrow? Maybe you can show me Venice...If you don't mind, that is."

His dark brown eyes peered deeply into her blue eyes. "No, I no mind. Pick you up at nine o'clock." Mary nodded, skipped down the hall to her room like a little school girl and quickly fell into a deep, uninterrupted sleep. The phone rang at 9 a.m. "This is Gianni. I'm in lobby."

~

She tossed on some jeans and a tee shirt and just a touch of makeup—mostly mascara to highlight her eyes and a little blush to give her cheeks some color.

They sat in the Café Floria at Piazza San Marco listening to an open-air orchestra, sipping lattes and munching on homemade almond biscottis. Mary learned more about Gianni and Venice.

Gianni's grandfather, Mario, a shoemaker in Turin, loved Venice. He and Gianni's grandmother, Philomena, used to take Gianni to Venice whenever time and money permitted. As a result, he knew the history of Venice and the cultural idiosyncrasies of Venetians.

Mary learned that Piazza San Marco was called "the drawing room of the world" by the architect Musset in the mid-1400, and had been the center of Venetian life for years and years.

"Originally, the square was in two pieces separated by the Canal Rio Batario. It was filled during the 12th Century but took hundreds of years and the contributions of Italy's most famous historical architects—Sansovino, Longhena, Scamozzi, Rizzo and Triani—to create its present form because the Venetians argued like—how you say—cats and dogs, about everything."

As Mary sat and listened, she crumbled a biscotti and fed it to the pigeons. "That's no good," said Gianni, holding her arm when he realized what she was doing.

Their table instantly became inundated by aggressive pigeons who stole every last crumb as she stood and tried to shoo them away. He watched her fight a losing battle. She feigned annoyance, pushed his chair to the ground, and bracketed his body between her legs, *"pigro Italiano."* (Lazy Italian).

He was surprised *"Parla Italiano?"*

"Poco!"

Gianni reached for the check as it arrived. Mary put her arm out and intercepted it. "I'll make you a deal. You show me Venice, and I'll buy the food."

"How long are you staying in Venice?"

"Another six days."

"That's a lot of food and wine."

"Don't you worry, Gianni. I'll get my money's worth!"

~

"Today is the Spagnoli Island tour. We begin by vaporetto to Murano for a little glass blowing, maybe some lunch, then on to the island of Burano, where you see some

Venetian residences not overrun by tourists. On way back, we stop at Torcello, a tiny 5th Century community with two very old Churches, Santa Fosca and Santa Maria Assunta. I show you lots of Byzantine mosaics."

As the vapo docked in Murano, Mary could see the charming streets lined with shops and sidewalk cafés. First stop was the pink stucco and green shutters of the Mazzega Glass Factory, where artisans had been making intricate Venetian glass artifacts and chandeliers since the 17th Century. After watching a glass-blower turn heated silicon into some of the most beautiful colors and shapes imaginable, Mary and Gianni went into the glass shop with rack after rack of spectacular functional works of art. Mary decided on a green and red flower vase for Allison's apartment and an unusual blue glass desk lamp for David's office. The bill including postage and insurance was 2,340 Euros, which Mary was prepared to put on her credit card.

Gianni stopped her from signing the charge slip. He glared at the merchant behind the counter, "*Quanto costa?*" The man repeated the amount written on the bill.

Gianni shook his head and started waving his hands in anger. "*Malto Costoso, malto costoso.*" Mary could see the veins protruding from Gianni's neck. She tried to restrain him. He and the shopkeeper became ensconced in a terrible shouting match. Everybody in the store was now listening to the two men. Mary wanted to hide under a table.

The merchant took back the credit slip, ripped it up and completed a new one. Gianni looked at the new total, smiled and nodded. "This one okay to sign." It was 1,420 Euros.

Minutes later, the couple sat at a casual canal side restaurant, Osteria Pescatore, eating a tender broiled calamari steak caught that morning by the local fisherman. "I appreciate what you just did, but I thought you were going to have a stroke."

"What stroke? replied a confused Gianni. "He give you tourist price. We have discussion Venetian style."

~

After their tour of the churches on Torcello, Mary realized virtually everything in Venice was at least 400 years old. She was looking forward to a sunset gondola ride. The vapo dropped them outside the Locanda Art Deco Hotel, where a half a dozen gondoliers beckoned her. Mary noticed a female gondolier at the end of the line sitting quietly in her boat, the "Pegasus." Mary took Gianni's hand and they climbed aboard her boat. As they pulled away from the docks, the male gondoliers could be heard cursing. Gianni shrugged as if to say, 'she made me do it.'

Gianni explained, gondoliers are an all-male craft, with jobs handed down from father to son, at least until their driver, Miss Alexandria Hai, broke the gender barrier about a year earlier. Roberto Luppi, president of the gondoliers association, said that Ms. Hai was incapable of handling the complicated duties of a 35-foot-long gondola. But Ms. Hai cleverly used the fact that she was a woman to whip up interest in the news media by accusing gondoliers of being racists and sexists. Eventually, the city was forced to grant her a license. "That's the Venetian way. It is almost impossible to introduce a new idea that doesn't take a century to pass in this city. Venice very fragile city. The flooding and tides have left many historical palazzos decrepit and uninhabitable. In time they fall into the sea. Was 200,000 in 1950, is now less than 70,000."

Alexandria's gondola turned into a smaller canal, the Rio de la Veste, to give her guests a closer view of the local neighborhoods. Suddenly, the boat came to an abrupt halt next to a small bridge. Hai waved to another gondolier to help her because she was stuck on a bed of algae. He stuck a single finger in the air and yelled in Italian, "Bitch, take care of your own problems."

Gianni took a knife out of his backpack, climbed out of the boat onto the rocks under the bridge. He started to hack at the bed of algae. Moments later the boat was freed. Mary and the other passengers gave Gianni a round of applause. He bowed in recognition of their gesture.

Mary thought, *Gianni seems too good to be true. Is there nothing he doesn't know or can't fix? Could I have stumbled into the man of my dreams 4,200 miles from Manhattan?*

~

"What a colorful sign on that street post" exclaimed Mary as the couple exited the gondola. "What does it say?"

Gianni pointed to the poster and translated the words, one at a time in English. "Signor...Goldoni Carlo...and the Comici Company... presents *La Mascherata*...Tonight at 9 p.m. ...Piazza San Marco."

"What is *La Mascherata*?"

"It is a 300 year-old Venetian tradition. The Pageant of the Grand Masks. The people masquerade as fantasias. Men become snakes and serpents, women become goddesses and princesses, little children become animals and birds. The masks are made by the people with paper, paste and paint. The winners receive a cash prize from Signor Carlo for the rights to their masks. He and his family are fourth-generation Venetian mask makers who then make commercial fantasia versions that are sold all over the world. In four hours, the square will be filled with participants and spectators."

"Would you take me?" asked Mary.

"I have no suits. The ceremony is to dress up."

"Let's go shopping." Mary dragged him down the narrow streets adjacent to the Gritti Palace, found a reasonably priced local clothier, had dressed him in a new sport jacket, shirt and shoes. The clothier handed the bill to Gianni. Mary tried to pay. "My treat." Gianni waved his hand. "In Italy, man pays. No gigolo!"

~

Despite numerous trips to Venice, Gianni had never been inside the Gritti Palace. He marveled at the opulence of the highly buffed white Carrerra marble floors, wall panels and countertops, the perfectly restored 17th Century ceiling murals. Paintings by Venetian masters Bellini, Giorgione, Tintoretto and Titian and the Murano Glass Gallery encircled the entire lobby.

Mary opened the double door to her suite called the Churchill, named after its most famous occupant. The oversized living room had two sitting areas, two working fireplaces and a generous balcony with a spectacular view of the Canal. Down the hall on the right was the den/library, the kitchen and dining room. On the left was the master bedroom, spa and steam cabinet.

"*Splendito. Molto splendito.*"

"Make yourself at home. I'll go change."

Gianni had one double Glenlivet, then another. He discovered a bookshelf laden with literary masterpieces. There was a leather-bound book of poetry by Christopher Marlowe, the English dramatist, poet, and translator of the Elizabethan Era. Gianni was feeling no pain as Mary re-entered the room in a low-cut, form-fitting leopard print evening dress. Her curly red hair was blown into sexy, frizzy strings. "Will this do for *La Mascherata*?"

"*Bella. Molto bella…* How you say, I could eat you all up." She walked over to him, slowly placed her arms around his waist and delivered a sensuous tender kiss and pressed her body against his. "Not now, maybe later," she whispered in the ear of the befuddled and aroused Gianni.

"What were you reading when I came in?"

"Your poet, Christopher Marlowe. He wrote how I feel."

> *What we behold is blind from our eyes.*
> *Where both deliberate, love slight:*
> *Who ever loved, that loved not at first sight?*

54

~~~

LA MASCHERATA WAS SPECTACULAR. Almost 270 locals paraded through the crowded square with candles in hand to highlight their delightful creations. By about 10:30, the judges had awarded the Grand Prize to a 17-year-old wearing a white swan's mask atop a white sequin gown. The crowd dispersed and flooded the nearby cafés. Gianni took Mary's hand and led her through the city's winding streets until they came upon a small neighborhood trattoria called Da Raffaela.

"Best shrimp fra diavolo in all Venice," announced Gianni. Two plates of fra diavolo and a bottle of wine later, the couple walked hand in hand to the Quadri Bar on the Piazza San Marco, not far from the Gritti Palace, where they drank espressos and talked until 4 a.m.

"I go home now," said Gianni.

"No, *we* go home now." It was now her turn to playfully pull Gianni by the hand back to her hotel. By the time they reached the front door, their passions were bubbling.

As they lay naked side by side, Gianni began to doze. Mary, recalling an unfulfilled agreement, shook him gently. "You no eat me all up like you promise," imitating his staccato English.

~

When they woke, Mary was exhausted, Gianni was invigorated.

"This afternoon," said an excited Gianni waving his hands and pointing from the balcony, "I take you to the Gallerie dell'Accademia in Dorsoduro, see the most important Venetian paintings. You see Tintoretto's 16th Century masterpieces, *Adam and Eve* and the *Death of Abel*, three of Bellini's *Madonna and Child, The Feast of the Gods*."

As he spoke, Mary thought culture, and the appreciation of antiquities was an integral part of Gianni's personality. It was not something he had learned just to impress.

"Then we *mange*…Then I have something special planned for the evening. Tonight we vapo to The Theatro Verde to see *Eine Nacht in Venedig Operetta* (*A Night in Venice*) by Johann Strauss."

The Theatro was nestled in the middle of a cypress grove on the island of San Giorgio Maggiore directly opposite St. Mark's Square. The light-hearted, dreamlike operetta, filled with waltzes and lilting melodies concluded after three and a half hours. The night air turned cool and breezy, and Gianni wrapped his arms around Mary as if to say all is right with the world. For the first time in a long while, she felt comfortable, safe and secure.

On the way back, Gianni chose to take a gondola rather than a water taxi. It was more in keeping with the evening's spirit of romance.

"How cold your little hand is," smiled Gianni as he held Mary's hand while they watched the moonbeams shimmer on the water. "I warm your heart with a song. You know opera songs are about the story. I sing to you from *La Bohème*. Have you seen?

"Is Christmas Eve on Left Bank Paris. Rodolfo is home writing. A stranger knocks at door. It is Mimi, his neighbor, who needs a match to light her candle. Mimi is not yet out the door, when she know she lose her key. They look for it, Rodolfo's hand touches hers. He sings *Che Gelida Manina—How Cold Your Little Hand Is.*"

Gianni kissed Mary's hand, pulled her close to him, and began to sing.

> *Che gelida manina! Se la lasci riscaldar.*
> *Cercar che giova? Al buio non si trova.*
> *(How cold your little hand is!*
> *Will you let me warm it for you? Why bother   looking?)*
> *Or che mi conoscete parlate voi.*
> *(And now that you have met me,*
> *I ask you please, Tell me, lady, who you are.)*

When Gianni finished, Mary looked deeply into his eyes. They embraced. Their lips touched slowly and gently. Enthralled passengers applauded. Mary stood and made Gianni take a bow.

They had cappuccinos at the Gritti lobby bar. Mary felt her heart racing. She assumed it was the emotion of the moment. "You have a wonderful stage voice," said Mary, thinking classic Broadway musicals like *Phantom of the Opera* and *South Pacific*.

"No stage. I sing opera just fun," replied Gianni thinking, *La Boheme* and *The Magic Flute*.

"Your voice can make lots of money in America."

"How you so sure?"

"Because that's my business. My job is to find shows and performers that people want to see and hear. I'm very good at what I do."

"That is why you stay at the Gritti Palace?"

"That is why I stay at the Gritti Palace."

"Where you go from Gianni and Venice?"

"I plan to spend a week in Lake Como, then a few days in Milan, Parma and Bologna, then head to Florence…What about you?"

"I have no arrangements," he shrugged. *Molto tempo* until the harvest."

Mary reached across the table and clutched Gianni's hand. "I've had a wonderful time. You make me feel so special. Come with me to Lake Como."

"But one condition. You visit Spagnoli family in the Piedmont Regione."

Mary hesitated. "But I have to be back in New York at the end of the month. My business needs me."

"Business, business, business… What about life? She more important…No?"

"Yes."

"Then we forget Milano and Bologna. I tell all about. I promise you no regrets."

Mary paused for a second and then called the Villa d'Este. "Senorina Peale, we'll take care of the changes in your itinerary," said the concierge, "and arrange an additional seat on your plane."

~

The next morning Mary entered the limo secured by the Gritti for their short ride to Marco Polo Airport. "Why car? The train station is just a short vaporetto ride," said Gianni, thinking the limousine was an extravagant tourist mistake.

"Because we're not going to the train station. I've arranged for a private plane."

~

Gianni couldn't believe his eyes when he realized the charter flight was Mary's personal seaplane resting on the canal next to the airport runway. "I never been," said Gianni nervously.

"A big strong man like you…You're not frightened, are you?" said Mary sensing his trepidation.

"If woman can do, Gianni can do." Mary thought Gianni's touch of sexism was a charming trait she could adjust to later in their relationship.

It was a sparkling clear day as the seaplane flew low enough to see the decks of the fabulous estates at Lenno, Albanvilla, Bellagio and Cernobbio. The hills, mountains and farms surrounding the massive lake were a breathtaking kaleidoscope of greens, blues and browns. The water so clear, you could almost see the bottom from their 3,000 metre cruising altitude. "I understand, the Clooney and Versace Estates are around here somewhere," said Mary to the pilot, who pointed to her right and then tilted the craft at a 60 degree angle about 700 feet above two magnificent pink and yellow estates resting at water's edge. The seaplane tilted westward toward a magnificent white stone structure sitting directly on Lake Como with its own dock, floating outdoor pool and acres of picturesque manicured grounds. It came to rest a few hundred metres from the massive, weathered wood dock. A luxurious, flat-bottom cabin cruiser pulled alongside the plane's landing pontoons that were gently bobbing in the waves.

"Welcome to Villa d'Este, Senorina Peale," said a white-gloved porter. Mary held Gianni's arm tightly as her wobbly, weak-kneed companion struggled to board the craft. He smiled. "I have seen a lot of Italy, but never like this."

"We are going to have a wonderful time here," said Mary, scanning the magnificent surroundings. Once settled in their suite, Mary called the hotel manager, Sergio Giancarlo. "Sergio, I know you've been asked this before, but I'd like to maintain my privacy during our visit. Can you make sure nobody gives out information about my presence?"

For the next several days, the couple toured the lake and the surrounding towns during the day, ate in the hotel's magnificent dining room at night, and frolicked in their king-size, down-covered bed until the wee hours of the morning. On the fourth night, somewhere between cocktails and appetizers, Robert DeNiro, sitting on the other side of the room, spotted Mary and Gianni.

"Mary, what a small world," said DeNiro with his trademark darting eyes and gruff but friendly manner. "Andy and I were just talking about you. Working on *Pigs* was a real pleasure. I forgot how much fun live theatre was. We were just sayin', when's Mary going to pitch her next one."

Gianni was overwhelmed. He was sitting right next to one of the stars of his all time favorite movies, *Godfather I and II*. At the same time, he didn't understand what Mary was doing working with pigs. From the short time they knew each other, he was certain she knew absolutely nothing about working on a farm!

"Who's the lucky guy?" questioned DeNiro.

"This is my friend, Gianni Spagnoli. He's from the Piedmont area."

"Hey, Gianni, I don't know what you do," said DeNiro, "but you're sitting with Miss Broadway. The lady everybody wants to do business with in New York. Know what I mean?"

Gianni was intimidated. To him, Mary was Mary, the woman he loved. He nodded silently for fear of saying the wrong thing....whatever that might be.

"Cat got your tongue," teased DeNiro, who then turned to Mary. "So what kind of friend is Gianni?"

"A very good one."

"Gianni could no longer restraint himself. "She woman I love."

"Good, that's very good," said DeNiro, bobbing his head and raising his upper lip. "Let me leave you two lovebirds alone."

"Did you mean that?" asked Mary. "What you said."

"Absolutely, completely, with my whole heart."

~ ~ ~

THE WEEK AT VILLA D'ESTE flew by. Mary and Gianni were in love and enjoying every moment together. It was now on to Piedmont.

"Fairy tale over. Now I show you Gianni's Italy," said Gianni as he packed their belongings into the rented car. "From here to my town of Barbaresco is about a three hour drive. Since it's only 10 o'clock, let's make detour to Parma. You meet Uncle Vincenzo, we have some lunch. Mama and Papa not expecting us till near five. We have plenty time."

The car sped south on Highway 415. Around Milano, the hillside turned a lush green and brown, dotted with cyprus and olive trees and tiny villages hundreds of years old with lyrical names such as Codogno, Vigévano and Salsomaggiore Terme. "Gianni, you were right. This is breathtaking!"

"No, this is beautiful…you are breathtaking."

She smiled, placed a *Phantom Of the Opera* disc into the car's player and scanned the selections until she reached Michael Crawford's spellbinding solo, *Music Of the Night*. "This is one of the American theatre's most memorable moments. I want you to listen. You can do this." The more Gianni listened, the more enthralled he became. *Could Mary be correct?* he wondered. Her confidence was comforting because he knew she would never deceive him. Suddenly, he brought the car to a screeching halt. "You make me believe so much, I pass Uncle Vincenzo."

They drove down a dusty dirt road not far from Asti. Suddenly, in front of them sat a modest, working farm. Mary heard the squeal of pigs coming from a large, wooden structure. "Nephew, welcome to Treiso!" said the tall, sturdy man with a deep olive complexion, large bushy eyebrows and a broad, honest smile. He hugged Gianni warmly and then walked over to Mary. "Not every day Gianni brings such loveliness to his old uncle."

She felt an instant kinship to Vincenzo. "You Spagnolis certainly know how to make a girl feel important." Vincenzo noticed Mary's accent. "But you no Americano like Gianni suggest. I fight in World War II, I know."

Mary smiled. "As I explained to your nephew, I'm British."

"No matter," said Vincenzo as he waved his hand and looked at his nephew. "All the same. Americano…British."

Mary shook her head… like nephew, like uncle.

~

A proud Vincenzo gave Mary a tour of his facilities. "We produce the products of Parma here. Parmagiano-Reggiano made from the milk of local cows fed on the valley's green pasture," said Vincenzo, pointing to the rolling hills. "We use the same process my family has used for almost seven centuries. We take two milkings; the mixture is then boiled and heated in the copper pots we own almost 250 years. Then we separate and mold, press and drain. Lots of imitations but to produce one round of real Parmagiano-Reggiano takes 500 liters of milk and nearly two years of work."

"Why would you spend that much time making one cheese?" asked Mary.

Vincenzo thought the question curious. "Because to make right, takes time and love of the land. God gave these gifts."

Mary was struck by the simplicity and honesty of the answer. She wondered if her life would ever be that orderly, that comfortable.

"So is with Proscuitto di Parma. We have special breeding and feedings of the pigs, gentle salt rubs and extra rinsing. Then comes long hanging-and-curing process in progressively warmer aging rooms. It takes almost 12 months to make ham perfect: pale pink color, sweet flavor and silky texture. Only then does piggy earn five-point ducal crown of Parma."

The tour completed, the three sat on the sunny patio with a huge platter of peppery rucola greens topped with flaky shavings of Vincenzo's Parmagiano-Reggiano and paper-thin curls of Prosciutto di Parma, accompanied of course, by a bottle of one of Gianni's newer varietals, a light red aromatic Mocagatta Barbaresco.

As the couple returned to their car for the last leg of their journey to the village of Barbaresco, Vincenzo came out of the barn with two large shopping bags. "Give to Francesca, send my love."

One bag contained a large wheel of cheese, the other a perfectly cured prosciutto....with the five-point crown of Parma.

~

A small sign on the right side of Route 231 said, "Barbaresco 18 kilometers." The gently sloping, winding road passed a number of the region's larger producers—Bruno Giacosa, Angelo Gaja, Alfred Prunotto and Pio Cesare—with fruit-filled vines of powdery grapes as far as the eye could see. The unplanted lands between the vineyards were a canvas of yellows and purples, reminiscent of Longfellow's beloved valley in England's North Lake Country.

"These vineyards are incredible,' said Mary.

"Be warned," commented Gianni, trying to manage expectations, "the Spagnoli's Mocagatta and such not as grand. But they have provided the Spagnolis with an honest living for almost 100 years."

Gianni's great-grandfather planted the first Nebbiolo grapes at the beginning of the 20th Century. Then his grandfather, Vito, bought adjoining acreage, discovered the soil was very acceptable to the grape, and planted more. Gianni's father, Antony, enhanced the soils to deliver a consistent aroma and flavor complexity from vintage to vintage.

"I will be the fourth generation Spagnoli to run the vineyard and make the wines. Many neighbors produce the heavier Barolo wines. I want our Barbarescos to be elegant, so I have been experimenting with the premium winemaking process. The more elegant we make the wines, the higher the price. I'm not the man to buy more acres and grow more. Probably have to spend more time here soon. Papa is getting on in years. Also, he has other responsibilities as the Mayor of Barbaresco. The town only has 670 people, but he also wants to run for post of Director Generale of the entire Langhe Region."

Gianni turned off the main highway and began to drive down a long, narrow, winding road with vines as far as one could see to the left and right. At the top of the hill was an 18th Century stone house covered with colorful, flowering vines. Gianni's mother Theresa and father Antony waved enthusiastically.

~

The origin of Gianni's good looks was obvious. Theresa and Antony were a strikingly well-groomed and handsome couple with well-tended complexions that made them appear years younger than their actual ages. They were the complete opposite of Uncle Vincenzo.

"Antony, why don't you and your son bring the bags up to Gianni's room, and then go have a glass of wine on the patio. Mary and I will finish making dinner and get to know each other a little better," said Theresa in perfect English.

"I know this sounds old-fashioned, but Gianni loves his mother's spaghetti and home-made marinara sauce. I hope you don't mind."

"Mrs. Spagnoli, that sounds delicious."

"Gianni also loves my spicy meatballs. Want to help prepare? The recipe is like everything in Italy, a third-generation tradition to which I've added a few embellishments." Theresa took a mountain of fresh ground beef out of the refrigerator. "This should make about eight meat balls. This is not America where they make meatball marbles!"

Mary chuckled. She wasn't going to get into that American-British thing again! "What do you want me to do?"

"Take the bread and break it into small pieces then soak them in the milk and add oregano and rosemary. While you're doing that, I'll cut the garlic, then we'll mix it all together and roll and brown the meatballs, put them in the sauce, and let them simmer for about an hour."

Mary nodded and began to break the crusted bread into pieces. "Smaller, dear." Theresa created a mini mountain of raw chopped garlic. "You must be a very special lady."

"Why do you say that, Mrs. Spagnoli?"

"Call me Mama."

Mary liked the sound of the salutation.

"Gianni only brought one other woman home in his whole life."

"Really. And what happened to her?"

"He married Marianna. They were so in love. Terrible tragedy. They went rock climbing in the Alps during the summer. She slipped and fell 3,000 feet to her death. Now, take this garlic and the oregano and rosemary and mix it in with the meat."

"What happened to Gianni?"

"At first he thought he bad luck and wouldn't leave the vineyard. Gradually, he began to travel again. But he dropped the opera. Good, you've done an excellent job of mixing everything together. Now it's time to roll the meatballs before you brown them in the skillet. Gianni and Antony like them large. Take this orange. Roll the meatballs till they are about that size."

"No problem Mama....What did you mean about the opera."

"Ahhh, the opera. Don't know if you've ever heard, but Gianni has a magnificent operatic voice. He studied for years. His goal was to eventually become a member of La Scala."

"What happened?"

"Marianna was his engine. She was a ballet dancer with the Maggio Danza Ballet Company in Florence. When she died, he retreated. Said somebody had to manage the vineyards because Antony was getting into politics." She handed Mary a large cast-iron frying pan, a bottle of homemade olive oil and a round stainless-steel splatter screen. "Heat the oil, put the meatballs in the pan and keep turning until they have a nice brown crust. Then they are ready to simmer in Mama's homemade sauce."

Mary began heating the pan.

"No, put oil first. Otherwise it will splatter. Marianna not cook much either. Gianni never attracted to girls like his Mama."

Mary began to drop the giant meatballs into the heated oil. The oil splattered over the side of the pan and caught fire. Mama grabbed a wet cloth and quickly smothered the flames. "You have to put the meatballs in gently. Don't just dump."

"Where did you learn all this?"

"Here, there and everywhere. Cooking is like having a family. It takes a while to learn all the little tricks." Mama raised her eyebrows. "So Mary Johnson Pierce," said Mama, butchering Mary's name, "what you do?"

"I'm a theatrical agent."

"What's that?"

"Do you ever go to live theatre?"

"Every year we go to the Easter pageant, *Christ's Passion* at San Secundus Church in Asti."

"Mama, imagine a city with 100 stages like San Secundus, with plays all year round. I find shows to put on the stages, performers to act in them and directors to organize the plays."

"Do you write the plays?"

"No."

"Do you sing or act in plays?"

"No."

"Do you make the plays?"

"No."

"So, you like a middle man like Giuseppe Verone."

"Who's Giuseppe Verone?"

"He tells us how many reggiano wheels customer wants. We make, he sells. We deliver. Giuseppe never uses his own money. He takes commission from us and stores." Mama looked in the cast-iron pan. "They're ready. Now gently place in saucepot." Mary carefully lowered the meatballs one by one into the thick red sauce.

"So, Mary, how many children you like?"

"Mama," responded Mary delicately, "I don't think so."

~

The foursome drank six different bottles of Gianni's wines that ranged from lightly tannin to fruity and aromatic, while Mama kept piling the garlicky meatballs on the table till they were all finished.

Mary was feeling no pain—she was drunk as a skunk! She struggled up the stairs, one step at a time, as Gianni guarded the rear in case she tilted backward. Once in their room, Mary collapsed on the bed, fully clothed. She awoke several times during the evening due to a case of acid reflux and a cough.

"I heard you coughing last night, child," said Mama at the breakfast table. "Do you want to visit our doctor?"

"I think just resting a few days in the sun will do me a world of good."

"How long do you like to stay?" asked Theresa.

"You want to get rid of me just because I almost burned the house down making meatballs?" joked Mary.

"I asked because next week Antony and I are married 50 years. I know you are a big deal in New York, but I would like for you and Gianni to be here... It would mean a lot."

~

Thanks to Dr. Myers, the caregivers at Silver Hill, and the Spagnolis, Mary recollections of her times with Elizabeth were now pleasant and distant memories from another life. Her mind, her heart and her soul were now in a better place. While she wasn't completely healed, she was confident she had gone beyond the state of slipping backward. As the fresh clean air filled her lungs that insight made her feel good about herself. And thanks to Gianni's love, she had regained her self-esteem.

~~~

Manhattan, about the same time…

MARY'S PROTRACTED SILENCE rattled her stable of needy, creative clients. Playwrights and directors alike were accustomed to her sensitive shoulder when the inevitable crisis–be it professional or personal—arose.

Allison sensed the problem might be terminal. She had run out of plausible excuses. She expressed her concerns to David, who told her "she was getting as dramatic as Mary."

Marianne Kaufman dropped the first bomb. "Allison, this is very difficult for me," she said on the phone. "I love you guys. But business is business. I need collaborative help, I need my work presented. Mary seems to have vaporized. Rumors are flying up and down Broadway—she's had a nervous breakdown and is in seclusion somewhere. Where the hell is she?"

"Somewhere in Italy."

"How can I reach her directly?"

"I really don't know. I'm sorry."

"And so am I. I am moving my representation to Blumgarden and Associates, effective immediately. I expect a prompt accounting and dispersal of any remaining royalty and fees from my properties."

Allison promptly called David. "I'll handle this. She's just suffering from a creative tantrum. I recognize the symptoms." But Marianne's mind was made up. David told her, "Without Mary, you'd still be a nobody."

"Bullshit, cream eventually rises to the top," retorted Marianne. "The fact is, if it wasn't Mary, somebody else would have cracked the code. She was just in the right place at the right time."

David was glad Mary was not there to hear. Kaufmann phoned fellow playwrights Manners, Ingram, and Oboto, and they phoned others they had recommended to Mary, who also became clients. By morning, Allison was deluged with cancelled representations and requests for checks to be returned. In less than a week, there were no more clients, and every last dollar had been drained from Mary's business and professional accounts.

Mary Jackson-Peale and Associates was finished.

57

~~~

Back in Italy....

THAT EVENING, GIANNI AND Mary walked hand in hand to a hill called Mount Dora, where they watched the twinkling lights of the ancient villages that stretched for miles in every direction.

Gianni opened his backpack and uncorked a bottle of the region's Asti Spumante sparkling wine. They toasted each other as he presented a gift wrapped in newspaper. "Happy Fourth-week Anniversary."

She opened the package to find a hand-picked bouquet of yellow, lavender and red wildflowers. Her body snuggled next to his. "You are the most romantic man in the world. These are the most beautiful flowers in the world. This is the most romantic place in the world. I have never been happier. I wish I could freeze this moment in time."

Gianni whispered softly into Mary's ear. "I love you with all my heart. Come live with me." They kissed tenderly.

"We'll see," she whispered, wondering what her life's priorities should be, what really mattered.

Around 2 a.m Mary woke with a rapid pulse and pains in her chest. She didn't want to alarm Gianni. After all, she had been through anxiety attacks many times. She checked her pulse. Normally it had been around 70 beats a minute—now it was at some 122 beats. She began to experience a shortness of breath. She opened the window to let the clear, night air fill her lungs. The more she tried to calm herself, the faster her pulse beat. Reluctantly, Mary shuffled through her belongings and took an Alprazolam capsule from her emergency kit. Usually, her pulse would soon begin to slow and her shortness of breath would dissipate. Tonight that was not to be the case. As she sat in the dark waiting for relief, she felt a crushing chest pain. She was certain she was having a heart attack. She had to wake Gianni.

"Gianni," she whispered softly as she tugged at his shoulder. "Gianni, wake up." He rolled over. She tugged harder. "I've got to get to the hospital right now. I think I'm having a heart attack. I've never experienced chest pain like this."

He carried Mary down the stairs. Mama Spagnoli heard the commotion and came running. "Mary's very sick. Maybe she's having a heart attack. I've got to get her to the hospital in Asti. Call Dr. Rienzi. Tell him to meet us at the emergency room in 20 minutes. Then call the hospital."

Dr. Rienzi and his cardiac team were standing at the door to the emergency room of Cardinal Massaia Hospital when Gianni arrived. Mary was wheeled on a stretcher into the ICU unit where they placed an oxygen mask over her face, started a Naproxen IV drip in her vein and began to monitor her vital signs.

After a series of tests, she was resting comfortably, heavily sedated. Dr. Rienzi entered the waiting room where Gianni was pacing up and down. "How is she?"

"Not so good. Mary has an acute case of Left Ventricular Hypertrophy, where the left pumping chamber of her heart has thickened beyond repair, maybe the result of very high blood pressure. Her blood tests also indicate large amounts of anti-anxiety and depression drugs in her bloodstream. It would appear she has had severe emotional problems for quite some time. How old is she?"

"Thirty something."

The doctor shook his head. "What a shame. There's not much we can do. Her heart and the surrounding muscles are just wearing out. She may have one or two years at best. Who knows?"

"Can't we do a transplant?"

"Her chance of survival is very low. She would be rejected as a transplant candidate."

"When can I see her?" Gianni asked, shaking.

"You can go in now for a few minutes. But she won't recognize or understand you for a while."

Gianni walked into the room. His lady love was resting with tubes in her arms and mouth. He touched her hand. She remained still. He kissed her on the cheek. "I see you in the morning." Then Gianni asked the nurse for a blanket, took a chair from the waiting room, and went to sleep by her side.

~

Gianni was not ready to tell Mary she was dying. He had something more important to discuss first!

"I want to marry you," proposed Gianni.

Mary stared wide-eyed from her hospital bed. "I'm not sure that's such a good idea." She had reached *her moment of truth*. Should she continue to spin her web of lies and half-truths, or should she take her chances and trust someone with the truth, the whole truth and nothing but the truth? "You don't understand. There is so much you don't know about me."

"Then tell me."

"On one condition...If you decide you don't want to marry me after I tell you everything, I will understand." Mary took a deep breath and spent the next hour explaining everything. "Your Mary has been a bad, bad girl. Over the years, I've had sex with many men and women. I like them both. I'm not ashamed. Then I fell in love with a beautiful woman in England. Instead of insisting she leave with me, I abandoned her to her father, who detested me. Her father murdered her and also the man who helped him dump his daughter's body deep into a lake.

"Then I moved to London. I got involved with a man, then another woman, Sarah, at work. My new boss, a famous theatrical agent named James Belfrage, found me with that woman in his house. He fired us both. I killed him. Scotland Yard blamed her. She lied to save me and then came to New York. By then I was with another man. In a jealous rage, she committed suicide. In a strange twist of fate, my Mum's lover, a woman who was once married to the man I murdered, got charged for the murder that was originally blamed on my female lover."

Gianni's eyes glazed as he tried to keep up with who was who.

"My mother's lover, a lady named Annabelle Lee, is now in prison for a murder she did not commit. I have been torn for some time. I had been wondering what to do about the Annabelle Lee situation, and then you came along. Recently, Scotland Yard called my office in New York looking for me. I don't know if they've put two and two together or what, but my office manager suggested I stay in seclusion."

"That's why you hide here with me?"

"No. I can hide anywhere. I chose to stay here because of you."

"What about your business?"

"I'm very successful. I have a long list of loyal clients. The business can survive nicely for a period without me."

"And what about the pills? The doctor tells me your blood tests showed your system was full of very powerful medications."

"As you can imagine, keeping all the lies straight has damaged my mind. I have fits of depression, anxiety attacks, and who knows what else. My psychological problems have become so intense, I receive regular psychiatric counseling and recently spent three months at a fancy looney bin, Silver Hill in America. Somewhere along the way, I also became an alcoholic.

"The hospital and my doctor said I had made good progress in battling my mental problems and that I should take myself on a trip far, far away from my past. Then I met you and here we are. The anxiety attack I had the other evening was the first since I left Silver Hill. I guess all the drinking and all the loving activity was more than I was ready for."

"According to the doctor you no have anxiety attack."

Tears welled in Gianni's eyes. He got up and walked over to the window. There he watched two doves chirping on the branch of a magnolia tree in full bloom as the sun streamed into the room. "First, you agree to marry me."

"You still want to marry me after everything I've told you?"

"Even more."

"I will marry you, even though I think you're crazier than I," smiled Mary reaching out her hand.

"You no crazy," said Gianni, "You just very sick. I guess all that has gone into your body and mind has worn down your heart. It will only pump for so much longer."

Mary stared in utter horror and disbelief. "How much longer?"

"A year, maybe two. They not sure."

"Then I have two marriage conditions."

"Ahhh, conditions already," smiled Gianni. "Just like a woman. Make a decision then make barriers." He looked into her eyes. "Anything you want. Anything."

"When I'm stronger, I would like to go to New York and get a second opinion on my situation, and I would like to make a videotape confession to send to Scotland Yard to free Annabelle Lee."

"When you want to do this?"

"After we're married, of course."

Mary and Gianni and Theresa and Antony decided to have a double ceremony. On Saturday, November 14th, the parents reaffirmed their marital vows, while the children became Mr. and Mrs. Gianni Spagnoli.

~

The ceremony took place in the 400-year-old Church of Giovanni Battista on tree-lined Via Ovello, precisely where Theresa and Antony had been married some 50 years prior. Many of Barbaresco's 670 residents attended the ceremony. Former Mayor Alberto Bianco was Antony's best man, then and now, while his wife Francesca was again the maid of honor.

As Theresa and Mary entered the carved mahogany double doors and started to walk slowly down the aisle hand in hand, Gianni, waiting at the altar with his father, began to sing a tender but powerful arrangement of *Ave Maria* accompanied by a single mandolin. Gianni's voice reverberated off the walls, stirring the souls of everyone in the little church. It was a shining moment that Mary would remember vividly for the rest of her short life. When it was her turn, she read a poem to the man who had taught her to dream again.

Theresa cried tears of joy. She knew her wonderful new daughter-in-law was happy at last with her son, clearly the love of her life. As Mary read her affirmations, Theresa squeezed Antony's hand and thought about the Spagnoli family treasures built into the fabric of this tiny hillside town. A good life, full of emotional richness, a love that had stood the test of time, a wonderful son to carry the Spagnoli name, an inner peace and tranquility not measured in dollars or material pleasures but in lasting friends who truly cared about them. Their journey to this place at this moment had been truly blessed.

~

"So where you children going to spend your honeymoon?" asked Theresa over dinner and a glass of wine. "As your Mama and Papa promise, Gianni, that is our wedding gift to you and your lovely bride."

Mary looked at Gianni. He knew it was his job to explain the situation. "Mama and Papa, this is very difficult to say, but Mary is very sick. We go to New York to see her doctor to get second opinion. Mary has a very weak heart. It doesn't pump so good because it's wearing out."

"How long?"

"A year, maybe two."

"*Dio omnipotente, dio omnipotente!*"

"Mama, no matter what happens, you have made me feel very loved. I'm very fortunate."

"When do you leave?"

"We've made reservations to leave from Milan on Thursday."

"That's just two days," said Mama. "Then we do everything together till you leave."

"Maybe not everything."

~

Leaving Theresa and Antony was hard for Gianni but even more heart-wrenching for the Mama and Mary. Mary's soul had found a real home. She had experienced peace, tranquility and a constancy that she couldn't find in London or New York. For Theresa, Mary was the daughter, blessed by God, whom she had always wanted. They had gotten to know each other so well in such a short time that there was no need to restate the obvious. Theresa knew she would never see Mary again.

Theresa and Mary hugged one last time before the car left for Milan. "Mary, take care. Mama loves you very much."

Moments later, the car disappeared down the country road.

~~~

IN NEW YORK, GIANNI and Mary sat in the office of the efficient Dr. DiRe, who had completed his examination and reviewed all of the medical records from Italy. "Mary, I wish I had better news. Unfortunately, I agree with the original diagnosis. Your heart is weakening every day. It's just a matter of time. I can give you some medication for the arrhythmia but in some ways that's only cosmetic. Your heart's pump will continue to deteriorate until...."

She had heard all this before. It was too depressing to listen to a replay. "Let's switch gears, if you don't mind. What can I do to maintain the quality of the time I have left?"

"Avoid any excessive exercise and stay away from any circumstances that create stress. When your body seems tired, don't fight it, just go relax."

~

It was a magnificent summer day as the couple sat in Chelsea Park. Gianni was listening to Luciano Pavarotti, Maria Oran and Giuseppe Taddei perform Puccini's *La*

Boheme on his IPOD. His eyes closed, head titling to the rhythm of the orchestra and lips mimicking the songs of Pavarotti and Taddei. At the other end of the bench sat Mary with a book of poems by her favorite poet, John Keats.

"Gianni, I've been thinking."

The earphones muffled her voice. "Gianni, I've been thinking. I think I still have enough influence in this town to get you an audition at the Metropolitan Opera House and the New York City Opera....You interested?"

"I have no commercial credentials."

"But you have a spectacular voice, you are very handsome, and you can act."

Gianni again hesitated. The whole idea sounded preposterous.

"If I can get you an audition, would you keep the date?"

Gianni figured he'd just humor Mary. After all, Dr. DiRe said no stress.

"You arrange the audition, I be there."

~

The next day Gianni stood on center stage at the Metropolitan Opera with artistic director James Levine sitting in the fifth row, listening to Gianni's audition.

Mary wanted to attend, but she was too weak. She and Gianni had chosen one of the opening pieces from *La Bohème*. He imagined he was Schaunard the musician and, having just gotten a job, was bringing food, firewood and drink to his starving friends, the painter Marcello and the poet Rodolfo. He sang brilliantly, filling the giant hall with sound. Even Levine had tears in his eyes. "That was masterful," said Levine. "You'll be hearing from us."

An elated Gianni bounced down the sidewalk from Lincoln Center to their apartment. Along the way, he passed an opera singer with a beautiful baritone voice standing on the street corner of 53rd Street and Fifth Avenue singing an aria from *Madame Butterfly* into a microphone as people rushed to and fro. He placed a dollar into the man's plate and vowed to himself he would never do the same.

"How do you think you did?" asked Mary.

"I think pretty good. Mr. Levine say, 'you'll hear from us.'"

Mary knew Levine personally. He was a straight shooter. "This is where you leave things with me. I'm the agent."

The call two days later was disappointing. Levine wanted to hire Gianni, but he did not have a green card. The Met couldn't circumvent immigration laws.

"That's final?" said a disappointed Gianni.

"It's my fault. I forgot all about the damn green card policy. Tomorrow we'll go down to the immigration department and fill out an application. Since you're married to a person who already has a green card and has filed preliminary citizenship papers, it shouldn't be too difficult."

~

Allison had no choice but to break the news. She told Mary all the clients had left during her absence, the office was forced to close, and she was dead broke.

Mary tried to keep a stiff upper lip, but Gianni knew their money was running low. He had exhausted his savings and had a strong suspicion Mary's tank was almost empty—just from little things such as making coffee at home rather than frequenting the local cafés. Quietly he scanned the newspapers looking for a job. After a lot of interviews, Gianni felt he hit the jackpot.

"Mary, I got a job."

"Without a green card?"

"This building on West 47th Street and 12th Avenue is desperate for a superintendent."

"No wonder they are desperate. That is a terrible neighborhood."

"Mary, time to forget pride. We need money. They pay me $100 a week; plus, we have free two-bedroom apartment with free gas and electricity."

"Gianni, I feel so guilty I took you away from your home in Barbaresco for what? This?"

"We are together; that's all that matters," said a smiling Gianni. When Gianni was not making life as comfortable as possible for Mary, he worked in the building taking care of tenants' needs and doing some inexpensive refurbishing and repainting. The landlord was delighted with his new superintendent's work ethic.

Mary grew weaker by the day.

~

Gianni was painting an upstairs hallway. "While you work, love, I'm going to go for a little walk."

"You need company," said a concerned Gianni from the top of the ladder.

"Don't worry. I'm feeling strong today."

"You not lie?"

"I would never lie to you. I'm through with lies. No more."

Mary went for a little more than a walk plus…She had actually booked production time with an old friend, Andrew Lustig, the owner of National Video Center on 42nd Street and 9th Avenue, where many of America's leading soap operas are shot on their sound stages each week.

"Andrew, thanks for helping me with my two little projects," said Mary.

"Anything for an old friend. I was beginning to wonder what the hell happened to you after all those audition tapes we used to do for your clients."

"Things changed."

"We should talk about it some time."

Mary was in no mood to get into that dialogue. "I've prepared a script I'd like to put down. It's a close-up with me sitting behind a desk. Very businesslike."

Andrew directed one of his stage crews to arrange a setup.

Mary then made a flawless confession for Scotland Yard. "Inspector Herbert, my name is Mary Jones from Brighton,

England. I'm also known as Mary Jackson-Peale in the United States. I want to confess to the murder of James Belfrage in London five years and three months ago. I will go into detail on this videotape about how and why I committed the offense, in order to clear a number of innocent people who have been dragged into this mess, notably Sarah Heller of London, who eventually committed suicide in Manhattan, and Annabelle Lee Sartre, currently serving an unjust 25-year prison sentence in Eastwood Park Prison in Wotton-Under-Edge."

Andrew listened as Mary recounted the entire story. He was flabbergasted but cool.

Without missing a beat, Mary said, "That's a wrap. Get ready for a second tape. This one's a little different, I need a relaxed setting like a living room with a wall filled with theatre posters."

Andrew again directed his crew to create a stage set. While they were working, Andrew and Mary checked the first tape for clarity.

"Are we ready on that second set?" asked Andrew over the control room speaker.

"Locked and loaded, Boss."

"Is this the other murder?" joked Andrew with some dark side humor.

Mary glared. "That was sick."

Andrew headed back to the control room. "Rolling. Whenever you're ready."

"Gianni, my love, now that I'm gone, I wanted to tell you how happy you've made me during the last stages of my life." Mary continued for some 15 minutes, talked about his tenderness, how he changed her life, how much she loved his family. Then she turned to her theatre friends. She told them how honored she was to be a part of their lives. How special they made her feel. And that however egocentric Mary Jackson-Peale replete with her leopard-skin dresses and martini glasses may have appeared, she always put the well-being of her clients ahead of all else.

"If I had one wish, I would hope that you would all find it in your hearts to say Mary Jackson-Peale made Broadway a little more fun, a little more interesting, a little more entertaining. If I had one final thought it would be this… 'Life should not be a journey to the grave with the intention of arriving safely in an attractive and well-preserved body, but rather to skid sideways, chocolate in one hand, martini in the other, body thoroughly used up, totally worn out and screaming, Woo hoo what a ride!'"

Andrew sat in the control booth with tears streaming down his eyes.

On her way home from the studio, Mary stopped at the post office and mailed the first tape to Scotland Yard.

~~~

IT WAS MARY'S 37TH BIRTHDAY. She knew her time was short. Life had been one heck of a ride, from the gates of heaven to the depths of hell and back, with unfathomable happenstances along the way.

On a bone-chilling, damp, drafty winter night at 437 East 47th Street in Manhattan, the wind whistled though the antiquated casement windows. Occasionally gasping for air, she lay peacefully in a pair of bright yellow, paisley pajamas, tucked between her monogrammed pink silk sheets trimmed with ivory lace. The bedroom's décor was vintage Mary Jackson-Peale, but the look and feel of the room recalled superstar Claudette Colbert's dressing room backstage at the Walter Kerr Theatre a few blocks west. At the base of the bed was a brown porcelain-tiled castiron fireplace. The walls were covered in navy and white fabric and theatrical memorabilia. On the wall to the left hung playbill covers and theatre posters trumpeting award-winning Mary Jackson-Peale productions.

The wall to the right had Thank Yous from many of Broadway's best and brightest directors—whom she had discovered, nurtured and represented through successes and failures. On a small table sat life-long friend, Edgar, a forest green, plastic seahorse with a big smile and a set of bright white teeth. Despite the superficial bravado, the room, not unlike Mary herself, seemed fragile.

~

"Gianni, daaarling," she purred softly with her raspy voice, "be a dear and put some moisturizer on my face."

Gianni nodded and thought to himself, *vain to the end.* A youthful facade masked a body ravaged by drug abuse, booze binges, a never-ending emotional roller coaster, dark bouts of depression and imaginary personal demons and insecurities.

As Gianni finished applying the cream, she took his hand, looked into his eyes and smiled. "Read me Willie. You know the one." Gianni walked to a small bookshelf, pulled down an antique leather-bound book embossed, W.B.Yeats. He began to read one of Mary's all-time favorite poems, *When You Are Old and Grey.*

When you are old and grey and full of sleep,
And nodding by the fire, take down this book,
And slowly read, and dream of the soft look
Your eyes had once, and of their shadows deep;
How many loved your moments of glad grace,
And loved your beauty with love false or true,
But one man loved the pilgrim soul in you,
And loved the sorrows of your changing face;
And bending down beside the glowing bars,
Murmur, a little sadly, how Love fled

And paced upon the mountains overhead
And hid his face amid a crowd of stars

As Gianni reached the end of the poem, Mary pointed to a plain brown envelope sitting on the side of her bed. "That is for you. Thank you, Gianni. You have made my life complete." Mary's eyes closed and her heart stopped beating. She was gone.

Gianni sat and held her hand quietly for what seemed like an eternity as he repeated over and over again. "Mary, Mary. Mary, Mary. Mary, Mary." A few hours later he watched the tape. The next day he had Mary cremated and put the urrn on a little table next to his bed.

~

As Gianni went through the last of Mary's belongings, he found her book of contacts. He remembered she had mentioned her friend Allison on numerous occasions. Gianni dialed her number. "This Allison?" My name's Gianni Spagnoli."

"Ahhh, Mary's husband. She's told me so much about you. When are David and I going to meet you?"

"I have some bad news. Mary died yesterday."

"Oh dear God, how?"

"Her heart just stop. All the pain, the medications, she just tired."

"What are the final arrangements? I want to help. She was my best friend."

"Arrangements? I no make any. Who would come? I don't know anybody."

"David and I would come. Also, Mary had lots of friends. I'm sure a few would like to pay last respects. And besides, Mary never missed a party. She so loved to laugh. We should send her out with a bang…And, don't forget the usual Monday closings and the fact that theatre people are night owls."

Gianni was confused. He didn't understand any of it—parties, closings, bangs, owls. "I no understand."

"Find a church you like, and let's have a service that celebrates her life, not mourns her death."

"Now I understand. In Italian we call it *commemorare decesso*."

~

That evening, Gianni checked his mailbox for the first time in days. It was full. Notes from tenants, a few bills, some theatrical junk mail, and a letter from the United States Department of State which read:

"Mr. Spagnoli, We are pleased to inform you that under the guidelines of section 203 of the Immigration and Nationality Act dated 1990, you have been awarded permanent green card status by the United States of America. This status entitles you to work and pay taxes as any United States Citizen and for you to apply for final citizenship five years from the date of the issuance of this card."

60

~~~

IT WAS 8 A.M., DAY 325 OF Annabelle's incarceration at Eastwood Park Prison for Women. She had 8,800 days remaining in her sentence. She was angry, bitter and despondent. A butch, oversized guard started clanking the bars of her cell. "Up and at 'em Sartre, the warden wants to see you!"

Everybody knew everybody's business in Cell Block 13. Being asked to pay the warden a visit was not a good thing. As Annabelle Lee walked down the corridor past the other inmates, wondering what she had done wrong, she was inundated with choice catcalls…"Fucked up, eh bitch!"

Warden Catherine Bolton was a foul- mouthed, tough-as-nails enforcement officer. "Sit down, Sartre, sit down. I have some good news for you."

She threw a brown envelope stamped Evidence-Scotland Yard on the desk in front of Annabelle Lee. "You're free to go. Somebody confessed to the Belfrage murder. It's all here on this tape. Watched it myself. Crazy fucking broad."

"You're joking," stuttered Annabelle Lee.

"I'm not known for telling jokes."

"Consider yourself lucky. Pack your bag, your clothes are waiting for you downstairs. Get the hell out of here!"

Annabelle Lee reached her hand out. Warden Bolton sneered and slapped the brown bag in her hand. "Take your souvenir tape. Two last things. The state wants you to have this." Bolton handed Annabelle Lee a thin business envelope. "It's a check for £9,750. Apparently the fat and happy House of Commons enacted some wrongful penalization code. You get £30 a day for wrongful internment. You're also supposed to contact this attorney when you get back to Brighton. Something about your other rights. The bus to the shore communities leaves in 30 minutes."

~

Annabelle Lee decided to surprise Chloe. Anticipation made the three-hour bus ride feel like ten. When the bus pulled into the Grand Junction Road Station, she grabbed her bag and headed straight for their cottage on Duke Lane. She put her key in the door, and jiggled the knob. The locks had been changed.

Chloe heard the noise from the kitchen and became frightened. She called the police then hid in a closet. Annabelle Lee walked around the cottage looking for some sign of life, an opened window, an open rear door, something. Suddenly the police drove up with sirens blaring and lights flashing. Annabelle Lee was in cuffs, screaming "You don't understand."

Chloe heard the sirens and came out of the closet, figuring she was now safe. "Oh, my God," she said. "Officers, I've made a terrible mistake. This is my partner. Those damn locks must have stuck."

Chloe assumed Annabelle had escaped. The last thing she wanted to do was raise any suspicions. "I know what you're thinking," smiled Annabelle Lee. "But that's not what happened. Somebody confessed to the sordid matter, and I was released. No strings attached." Chloe hugged and kissed the love of her life.

"I come bearing gifts," smiled Annabelle Lee, first pulling out the check for £9,750 and the videotape. "It's a check from the state. It's guilt money. Apparently, I was worth £30 a day. And my going-away present from the prison, a copy of the murderer's confession about James. I guess the bloke taped it."

~

That evening, the women made passionate love for the first time in almost a year. "You're good as ever," smiled Chloe.

"What say we watch the tape in bed?" said Annabelle Lee.

"What a positively, wicked thought."

61

~~~

MARY'S *COMMEMORARE DECESSO* WAS held at St. Malachy's Chapel at 239 W. 49th Street, a few blocks from where she and Gianni lived. Founded in 1902, it was a Manhattan historical treasure, known as The Actor's Chapel, because of numerous funerals held for deceased theatrical performers.

Gianni explained his situation to Pastor Peter. "Normally, we have a casket and viewing with a Funeral Mass during the morning, but because she was cremated, a brief ceremony with personal remembrances at your suggested hour will be fine."

"Prete grazie infinite."

Gianni went back home and composed a loving announcement headlined, "Till We Meet Again." Below the headline was a picture of the smiling couple, with the caption Mary Jackson-Peale, 1973 – 2010. That was followed by *Funeral Blues*, a poem Gianni had selected from the works of W.H. Auden.

Stop all the clocks, cut off the telephone,
Prevent the dog from barking with a juicy bone,
Silence the pianos and with muffled drum
Bring out the coffin, let the mourners come.
Let aeroplanes circle moaning overhead
Scribbling on the sky the message, She is Dead.
Put crepe bows round the white necks of the public doves,
Let the traffic policemen wear black cotton gloves.
She was my North, my South, my East and West,
My working week and my Sunday rest,
My noon, my midnight, my talk, my song;
I thought that love would last forever: I was wrong.
The stars are not wanted now; put out every one,
Pack up the moon and dismantle the sun,
Pour away the ocean and sweep up the woods;
For nothing now can ever come to any good.

At the end of the poem were particulars about time and location of the remembrance and Gianni's phone number. At Allison's insistence, he placed the notice in the *New York Times* and the *London Times*. But the morning of the service, it was clear, Allison was mistaken. Gianni had not received a single condolence.

~

Gianni arrived shortly before the final service was scheduled with selected memorabilia he knew were important to Mary. He leaned maps of Brighton and Barbaresco and Green Village, Mary's favorite places in the world, against a wrought-iron railing to the side of the altar. In front of the priest's pulpit he placed a large picture of Mary in her trademark leopard-skin dress holding a martini glass. The rest of the altar area was filled with theatrical posters from her many successes. Off to the side, sat a small stereo and a microphone.

He had just finished designing his modest set when Allison and David arrived. "I think we may be alone," said Gianni sadly. They hugged Gianni. After Pastor Peter completed a short service, Gianni stepped to the podium and picked up the microphone. He imagined a full church.

"I want to tell you about my Mary. She faced great physical and emotional pain. But we fall in love. I make her happy, she do same to me. She was love of my life. There never be another Mary. I knew that for certain that first night in Venice. I held her cold hand. I sing to her. My love touch her heart. She give back to me.

"But like all, she human. Make mistakes, but she never stop loving all the theatre. It was in her blood.

"Only proper to think *time to say goodbye*"

Gianni walked over to the stereo, turned on the simple mandolin melody and began to sing to the picture Mary.

> *Con te partirò*
> *(I'll go with you)*
> *su navi per mari*
> *(On ships across seas)*
> *che, io lo so,*
> *(Which, I know)*
> *no, no, non esistono più,*
> *(No, no, exist no longer)*
> *con te io li rivivrò.*
> *(with you I shall experience them again)*
> *Con te partirò.*
> *(I'll go with you)*
> *Io con te.*
> *(I with you)*
>   - F. Sartori, L. Quarantotto, F. Peterson

Gianni's clear voice resonated off the walls. David and Allison's eyes welled with tears. After the couple left, Gianni sat quietly in the first pew. He heard a slight shuffling of feet in the darkness. He turned to see two figures leave the church without a word.

~

As Gianni packed the last of Mary's posters for the trip to Italy, the phone rang. "Gianni, this is Luce Jason Thomas calling. Do you know who I am?"

"No," said Gianni.

"I own the Walter Kerr Theatre on Broadway. I am an old friend of Mary's. I've been out of the country for quite a while. I met my old friend, James Levine, in Paris. He told me about your fabulous voice. I think maybe I can help expedite the green card process. I've decided to put on a revival of *South Pacific*. I think you'd be the perfect lead. Over the years, Mary's made me and my associates a lot of money. I figured we could meet in person and talk contracts."

Give my regards to Broadway,
Remember me to Herald Square,
Tell all the gang at Forty-Second Street,
That I will soon be there;
Whisper of how I'm yearning
To mingle with the old time throng,
Give my regards to old Broadway,
And say that I'll be there e'er long.

REFERENCES

VISIBLE DARKNESS. A MEMOIR OF MADNESS. William Styron. Vintage Books, New York, NY. 1990.

PSYCHIATRIC MEDICATIONS: ANTI-DEPRESSANTS, ANTI-ANXIETY.
www.healthplace.com/site/psychiatric_medications.asp

A FIVE STEP PROGRAM FOR HEALTHY AGING.
James Whitaker, M.D. Health & Healing, Vol. 17, No. 3A.
Healthy Directions, Potomac, MD 2006.

AGING GRACEFULLY AND SLEEPING WELL.
www.sleepfoundation.org/site/site/c.hulXKlxF/b.2417371/
k.26ED/AgingGracefully-and-Sleeping-Well.htm.

GUIDE TO CUMBRIA.www.visitcumbria.com/towns.htm

JOSÉ FERRER. Web site
www.en.wikipedia.org/wiki/Jos%C3%AP-Ferrer

PIEDMONT WINE COUNTRY. [Regione Piedmont Official Web site]
www.regione.piemonte.it.lingue/english/pagine/infastructure
/infrast.htm

WONDERS OF VENICE. [Venetia Official Web site],
www.venetia.it/s-piaza-eng.htm

ON THE CANALS, A WOMAN PADDLES AGAINST
THE TIDE. [New York Times Web site],
www.nytimes.com/2007/05/14/worldeurope/14 venice.html
ENGLISH POETRY AND PROSE OF THE ROMANTIC
MOVEMENT. George B. Woods, Ed., Scott, Foresman and
Company, Chicago, IL 1960

PAST TONY WINNERS. American Theatre Wing's Official Tony Award Web site],www.tonyawards.com/en-us/nominees/show.html

PAST OBIE WINNERS. Village Voice Official Obie Award Web-site],villagevoice.com/obies/index.php?page=search&year

APPROVED TREATMENTS FOR DEPRESSION AND GENERALIZED ANXIETY DISORDER. [EFFEXOR XR Official Web site], www.effexorxr.com/?sk=4646

RESTAURANT REVIEWS. [New York Times Web site]. www.events.nytimes.com/mem/nyreview.html

SEVENTEENTH-CENTURY PROSE AND POETRY. R. Tristram Coffin and Alexander M. Witherspoon, ed. Harcourt Brace, New York, NY. 1959.

COMPLETE WORKS OF SHAKESPEARE. G.L. Kitteredge, ed. Ginn and Company, Boston, MA. 1955.

HOW TO GET OFF PSYCHIATRIC DRUGS SAFELY. [The Road Back Official Web site], www.theroadback.org/benzotaper.htm

IN FAVOUR OF A SYSTEM VISION OF LIAISON PSYCHIATRY. [The National Library of Medicine Official Web site], www.nebi.nlm.gov/entrez/query.fegi?itool=abstractplus&db=pubmed&cmd
GUIDELINES FOR PSYCHOTHERAPY WITH LESBIAN, GAY AND BISEXUAL CLIENTS. [American Psychology Association Official Web site], www.apa.org/pi/lgbc/guidelines.html

SEXUAL ORIENTATION, PARENTS AND CHILDREN. [American Psychology Association Official Web site], www.apa.org/pi/lgbc/guidelines.html

LESBIAN ISSUES. [State of Victoria, Australia Official Web site], www.betterhealth.vic.gov.au

OVERCOMING INSOMNIA AND SLEEP PROBLEMS. [Helpguide.org Official Web site], www.helpguide.org/life/insomnia_treatment.htm

HOME TO GLASSBLOWERS. [About.com Web site], www.about.com/of/mediterreancruises/ig/Murano—Italy/index.htm

BURANO, RESIDENTIAL FANTASY. [Danheller.com Web site]. *www.danheller.com/venice-burano.html*